COMMERCIAL
FISH DECOYS
IDENTIFICATION & VALUE GUIDE

COLLECTIBLE DECOYS
AND IMPLEMENTS
USED IN THE SPORT OF
ICE SPEAR FISHING

FRANK R. BARON

COLLECTOR BOOKS
A Division of Schroeder Publishing Co., Inc.

The current values in this book should be used only as a guide. They are not intended to set prices, which vary from one section of the country to another. Auction prices as well as dealer prices vary greatly and are affected by condition as well as demand. Neither the author nor the publisher assumes responsibility for any losses that might be incurred as a result of consulting this guide.

Cover design: Beth Summers
Book design: Joyce Cherry

Searching For A Publisher?

We are always looking for people knowledgeable within their fields. If you feel that there is a real need for a book on your collectible subject and have a large comprehensive collection, contact Collector Books.

COLLECTOR BOOKS
P.O. Box 3009
Paducah, Kentucky 42002-3009
www.collectorbooks.com

Copyright © 2002 by Frank R. Baron

Contents

Dedication

This book is dedicated to my Dad who taught me the joys of fishing which have lasted a lifetime. I would give all I have to go fishing with him just one more time.

Author and his dad Frank Baron Sr. (1906 – 1984) ice fishing at southeast Michigan's Kent Lake in 1943.

Acknowledgments

A special thanks to my wife Patricia, my everything, for her many hours of working with me.

A special thanks to historians, collectors, and friends Clyde Harbin Sr., Memphis, Tennessee; Bill Roberts, Birmingham, Alabama, and Dale Roberts, Three Rivers, Michigan, who shared much invaluable information to make the Heddon chapter so exciting.

A special thanks to Bud Stewart (AKA Ratman) of Alpena, Michigan, a revered Michigan fisherman, hunter, and trapper, for his generous input of his trapping knowledge.

A special thanks to Joe Fossey of Barrie, Ontario, Canada, for the sharing of his knowledge to make the Canadian chapter an important part of this book.

A special thanks to Marcel Salive of Potomac, Maryland, for the sharing of his knowledge of commercially made spears, so important to the related fishing equipment chapter.

A special thanks to Dudley Murphy of Springfield, Missouri, a creative and talented artist who styled and took the beautiful cover photo and so many other images in the documentation of fishing tackle history.

More special thanks to the NFLCC library and all of the NFLCC members who unselfishly shared valuable information and items for documentation in this book.

Jerry Adams
Roseville, MI
John Anderson
Hinsdale, IL
Russ Armstrong
Witmore Lake, MI
Phil Babe
West Branch MI
Tom Bachler
Port Huron, MI
Dan Basore
Warrenville, IL
John Beck
Houston, TX
Walt Blue
Portage, MI
Robert & Liz Bulkley
Evansville, IN
Lynn Bunker
Midland, MI
Gary Carbaugh
Englewood, CO
Arlan D. Carter
Fall Creek, WI
Jeffrey Chung
Lake Placid, NY
Kim Clay
Rochester, IN
Doug Davis
Williams Bay, WI
Harold Dickert
Muskegon, MI
Gary Drolshagen
Alanson, MI
Rick Edmisten
Studio City, CA
Steve Ellis
Van Nuys, CA
Dennis Emerson
New Paltz, NY
Don Ferguson
Lakeview, MI

Tom Fleeger
Summerville, PA
Jim Foote
Marco Island, FL
Hubert Goings Jr.
Birmingham, AL
Dick Goldsmith
Zanefield, OH
John Goplerud
Park Rapids, MN
Charlie Hart
Mt. Clemens, MI
K. David Hirschey
Plymouth, MN
Dan Holmes
Plainwell, MI
Dave A. Hoover
South Bend, IN
Art Kimball
Boulder Jct., WI
Kevel King
Warren, MI
Blaine Kimmel
Grand Rapids, MI
Bob Kirk
Beverton, Canada
Ron Michael Kotch
Akron, OH
Keith Kristjanson
Grand Forks, ND
Conrad Kudelko
Livonia, MI
Jay Leitch
Moorhead, MN
Jerry Lemons
Olla, LA
Rick Loucks
Ashley, IN
Rob Lucal
Interlochen, MI
Don Ludy
West Chicago, IL
Marvin Meitz
Utica, MI

Marcel Meloche
Riviere-Aux, Canada
John McCormick
Bear Lake, MN
Tim Mierzwa
Jackson, MI
Dick Nissley
Birmingham, MI
Dale Nowland
Plymouth, MI
Frank Pasiewicz
Spring Lake Park, MN
Robbie Pavey, Jr.
Evans, GA
B.J. Pawlaczyk
AuGres, MI
Don Peterson
Chicago, IL
Tony Pryzbylo
Royal Oak, MI
George Rader
Berlin, WI
Derald Radtke
Francestown, NH
Drew Reese
Reeds Spring, MO
John Rogers
Holton, MI
George Richie
Honor, MI
Jacquie Salive
Potomac, MD
John Savu
Warren, OH
Dan Scollins
Lincolndale, NY
Fritz Scott
Saline, MI
Tom Shumaker
Sturgis, MI
Bill Smith Sr.
San Antonio, TX

Harold E. Smith, MD
Boonville, IN
Riley Smith
Battle Creek, MI
Keith Snider
Metamora, MI
Dean Sova
Taylor, MI
Randy Spagnoli
Fairless Hills, PA
Joe Stagnetti
Manlius, NY
Carter Stenberg
Spicer, MN
Don Stone
Allegan, MI
Bill Stuart
Bartow, FL
Larry Sundall
Estherville, IA
Joe & Donna Tonelli
Spring Valley, IL
Nick Torella
Au Gres, MI
Jim Urban
Livonia, MI
Russ Van Houzen
Empire, MI
Rich Vucina
Monaca, PA
Karl T. White
Luther, OK
Dick Wilson
Kent, OH
Dennis Wolfe
Royal Oak, MI
Terry Wong
Phoenix, AZ
Clarence Zahn
Traverse City, MI
Darrell H. Zwick
Ludington, MI

About This Book

The purpose for the creation of this book is to permanently preserve the history of the commercial fish decoy manufacturers and provide antique sporting collectors with information on the value of these artifacts. Prices established by collectors, dealers, or pickers vary greatly and are affected by variables such as condition, color, size, rarity, desirability, and market competition. Neither the author nor publisher assumes responsibility for any losses that might be incurred as a result of consulting this book.

This book concerns itself with any and all commercially made fish decoys and their related items deemed "tools of the trade" that are used in spear fishing. Availability, rarity, or value had no influence on the selection of an item for this book. All known and unknown commercial decoys familiar to the author at the time of publication are included in this book. While researching the related tools of the trade, in most cases the author had many examples to choose from and then showcase.

Some decoys cannot be accurately valued because there is no documentation of a sale or trade transaction. Listed values in this book are based on the price an item has brought or is likely to bring at sale or trade in an average market. When there is no record of an item purchased or traded, the author has used his expertise and the opinion of other knowledgeable active collectors for a jury evaluation.

Whether you are a historian, collector, or a dealer in sporting collectibles needing a guide, I hope this book will give you more understanding and enjoyment of the beauty and history of this commercial art form.

Introduction

The lore of spear fishing has been passed on from the North American natives to the European immigrants to the New World, and now from father to son. Along with the physical decoys, the tools of the trade and the expertise, the so-called tricks of the trade, are also passed on from one generation to the next. I know that I am a proficient fisherman because my father taught me all he knew about the sport. I taught my son, and he is now teaching his son.

With the fish decoy achieving popularity as collectible American folk art and with only a small number of reference books available at this time, a little known facet of this collecting hobby and its related history has come to light. This book focuses on that facet, the collecting of commercial fish decoys and related commercially made spear fishing items, the tools used in both commercial fishing and the sport of spear fishing. Fish decoy-related items may be made anywhere in the world, but naturally the majority of items studied in the research for this book were documented in Michigan, Wisconsin, Minnesota, New York, and also in regions of Canada where ice spearing is most prevalent.

Most existing books have listed the fish decoy in three categories, vintage, commercial, and recent. The commercial category can be broken down into two parts, commercial factory and cottage factory. This book focuses on the commercial factory decoy. Hopefully, someone in the future will thoroughly research and document the cottage factory category.

The criteria that I used to determine what defines commercial factory fish decoys follow, not necessarily in order of importance. *Uniformity in size, shape, and color* of decoys was considered as it would be for any manufactured production item. Production items are always designed and revised on paper, a prototype is made and then field tested to perfection for function and marketing eye appeal, and then finally the item is produced. During the life of their production run, decoys are spot checked for *manufacturing variation* with gauging fixtures or with templates for tolerance control. *Color range variation* is periodically checked, and spot checks are also made for both function and quality. Another consideration was the *amount of machine labor versus hand labor.* For example, were the fins die cut either by a machine or a hand die or were they hand cut and hand filed to shape? Were painting masks used for expediency, *painting uniformity,* and increased production rate? Were the *ballast*

hole or holes routered or drilled consistently in size, spacing, and depth? Was the *design patented* or its *name copyrighted* to protect it from being plagiarized by the competition? Was the *finished product marketed on store counter display cards or packaged with identification* for ease of shipping, stocking, and marketing? Was the product *advertised with brochures* or in sporting sales catalogs or magazines? Many major companies did not include their line of ice fishing decoys in their catalog because the manufacturing and marketing of the ice decoy was a low-volume, break-even or a money-losing venture.

The majority of the examples of decoys shown in this book do not meet all of the above-mentioned qualifiers to be deemed a commercial decoy. Only the largest most affluent companies that could amortize the tooling and marketing against the many other items that they manufactured and marketed had no problem meeting all the above qualifiers. The smallest companies, the so-called cottage factories or alley shops, are best defined as basement, garage, or small shop operations, that manufactured only one or two decoys in a few different sizes and colors and could not meet all of the qualifiers. These small shop operations had to be selective about their investment money, so most made just a few decoys to subsidize their owners' main income. Most decoys that are deemed to be cottage factory meet only a few of the above-mentioned qualifiers and were produced in low volume. Pure folk art decoys can be basically defined as one-of-a-kind creations, meeting none of the qualifiers.

Some of this book's readers may not agree with my criteria for differentiating between commercial versus cottage factory decoys. Some were selected and others not selected that were borderline and were tough calls. The author used his forty-plus years of experience in the business world of design, engineering, manufacturing, and marketing of many different automotive components, plus his thirty-plus years of collecting and researching sporting collectibles to make his decisions.

The primary purpose of this book is to document both the major and minor manufacturers of commercial decoys and commercial ice fishing items. Size or life span of each company had no bearing on its selection. My motivation for writing this book, as a compulsive collector of fish decoys, was my concern that with the passing of time, the history, especially of the

smaller companies, will be lost forever. Already a surprising number of quality manufactured decoys (see Chapter 5, Commercial Decoys from Unknown Makers) cannot be identified. I have high hopes that some of these examples and possibly some of their related history will be identified by readers of this book, who are encouraged to write me regarding the makers of any of the fish decoys or related ice fishing items included in this writing. The history of the commercial decoys and related items will probably never be total-ly complete. Research will always be ongoing.

It is my fervent wish that this book will be a learning experience and a pleasure for all who read it and a frequently consulted reference source for both new and advanced collectors.

Frank R. Baron
35824 West Chicago
Livonia, Michigan 48150

Painting by Les Kouba of a fisherman's view of spear fishing in a dark house. Courtesy of American Wildlife Galleries, Minneapolis, Minnesota.

Chapter One

Spear Fishing

A prerequisite before studying the commercial fish decoy and its related tools of the trade is first to understand the purpose of both their design and function.

Spear fishing has been practiced year-round throughout the world from the beginning of mankind. Some of the earliest documentation is found in the drawings on cave walls made by the cavemen. Other early documentation has been found in Egypt in hieroglyphic form. In the early days of Greece, one of their most revered Gods was Neptune, the mythical god of the sea, who was always depicted holding the trident, a long, three-pronged fishing spear. Throughout North America, native artifacts such as spear points and fish decoys made from stone, bone, ivory, and wood have been discovered in winter freeze areas. Early Eskimo artifacts (Plate 1) have been found in the Arctic Circle.

The earliest documentation of a commercial fish decoying device that I have found was a patent dated 1865 by Mr. I.E. Quimbly, patent no. 51120 titled "Fish decoy lamp." It was a device lighted by candles that was used by fishermen at that time to lure fish to their nets. Two other early patents, dated 1899 and 1904, for fish decoying devices that employed lighting, were used to attract fish to the fisherman's hook and line (Plates 2 and 3). One of the earliest sophisticated commercially made fish spearing decoys with fish form was patented and manufactured by the Enterprise Manufacturing Company of Akron, Ohio, in 1892 (Plate 4). This company had been established in 1881 and later became the Pflueger Bait Company of Akron, Ohio, one of the most prolific innovators and manufacturers of quality fishing tackle. The company was in existence for 80 years, going out of business in 1972. See Plate 5 for a spear fishing illustration from an early 1892 Enterprise Manufacturing Company (Pflueger) catalog.

The Native Americans and Eskimos fished for food for their families and tribes, but surely must have enjoyed the challenge of the hunt. Today modern man fishes mainly for sport, defined as the challenge of the hunt, and the fish he catches are a bonus of food for his family or friends or in many cases are caught and released for the future challenge of others.

Some of the earliest documentation of North American natives spear fishing, before the coming of the white man, is recorded by the early explorers who come to the area now known as the Great Lakes region of the United States of America and Ontario, Canada.

Documented evidence recorded in 1815 indicates that Lake Simcoe Canadian natives ignited dry birchbark torches suspended on poles at the front of their canoes to attract fish to the light for night fishing and then speared them. After the winter freeze, natives were seen making small domelike houses from pine tree boughs that they covered with animal skins. These houses would then be placed over a hole cut in the ice at one of their favorite fishing spots to keep out the light. The fishermen then lay prone, using a floating or suspending weighted decoy and a pointed wooden or flint-tipped spear while they waited for their quarry. The light passing through the ice and snow surrounding the hole area outside of the dark cover would illuminate the hole area, equivalent to the light from a television set in a darkened room (Plate 6).

The most common method used by fishermen for swimming the fish decoy is by manipulating it with a jigging stick, using a tether line from the end of the jig stick to the back of the decoy. Many commercial decoys were designed with a curved wooden tail or a curved light-gauge metal tail. This curved tail made the decoy more dynamic by enabling it to swim in a circle.

Fishermen also sometimes use the method of twisting the tether line a couple of hundred times, then letting it unwind after being lowered into the water to its desired depth. With the resistance of the water, the line would unwind slowly, giving the decoy motion to attract predatory fish.

This early Native American idea of spearing beneath skins or the dome of pine tree boughs (Plate 7) later evolved to the white man's use of the dark house, often called a shanty or hut. Homemade portable shanties gave way to some degree to commercially made shanties. With the coming of the machine age and mass production of all the essentials for a better life, including sporting goods, commercially made dark houses from wood, metal,

canvas, and later fiberglass came to market. Most were purchased by fishermen who did not possess the expertise or desire to design and build one or just did not have the time. The modern-day spear fisherman usually sits in one of these small portable canvas or wooden shanties with a door as its only opening. Like the Native Americans before him, the fisherman cuts a hole into the ice and places the shanty over it. Snow and loose ice are usually packed around the base of the shanty to reduce or eliminate light leakage and cold air drafts. The spear fisherman is able to see deep into the water because of the darkness in his shanty and the daylight passing through the ice around it. The patient fisherman sits silently, staring downward through the hole awaiting an opportunity to spear his prey. The fish come to the decoy in their endless search for food and out of curiosity. Fish have been speared as deep as 25 feet by the use of a heavy throwing spear. Dark houses are not exclusively used for spear fishing. Many fishermen fishing with hook and line use a dark house because of the comfort the dark house offers, protection from both the wind and the cold. Another advantage is that the fisherman can see the fish and therefore fish for a particular species by his choice of bait and method.

It is a mistake to believe that the fish decoy has only been used for spear fishing through the ice in a dark house. Hilary Stewart's book on the fishing methods used by Northwest coastal Indians reports that coastal Indians spear fishing from canoes often used fish decoys to lure fish up from the depths to within striking distance. An old-timer from upstate New York told me of his method for using hook and line to catch fish on opening day of trout season on his favorite lake. He always suspended a trout decoy from the bow of his boat. The decoy became dynamic because of the wave action on his boat; this in turn drew the fish to his baited hook and line. In other cases both folk art and commercially made fish decoys and critter decoys have been found in tackle boxes of deceased fishermen from southern states who were known to had never traveled from their native area.

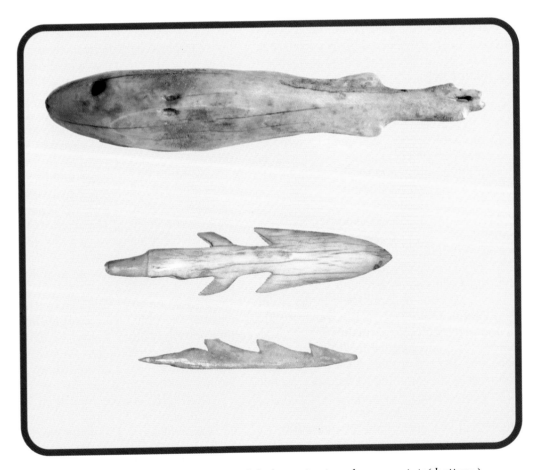

Plate 1. Ivory or bone Native American fish decoy (top) and spear points(bottom.)

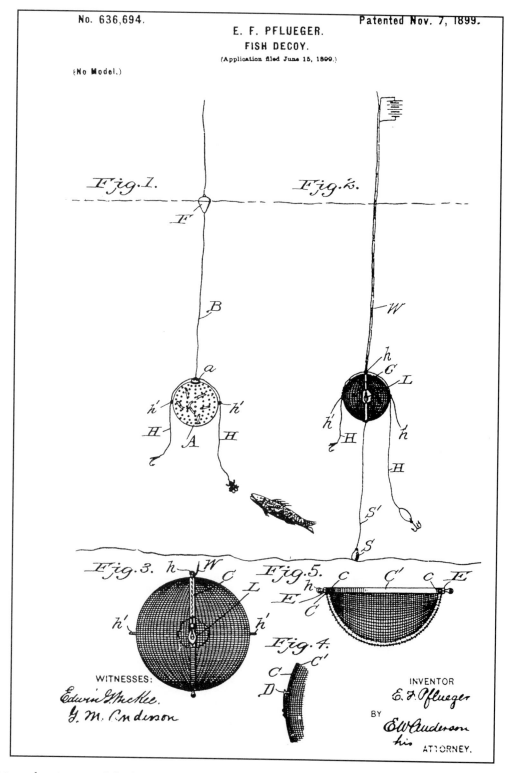

Plate 2. This early pre-1900 fish decoy was patented by Ernest F. Pflueger of Akron, Ohio, and assigned patent #636,694 on November 7, 1899. It was shown in the patent drawing as a spherical wire cage, hinged to open to hold minnows or other live bait, and also housed a lighting device. It had a number of attached fishing lines with hooks for either live or artificial baits. The patent also stated that it could be fished from a dock or boat. It was advertised in the Enterprise Manufacturing Company 1900 tackle catalog, which stated that it was supplied with both an anchor and cork float.

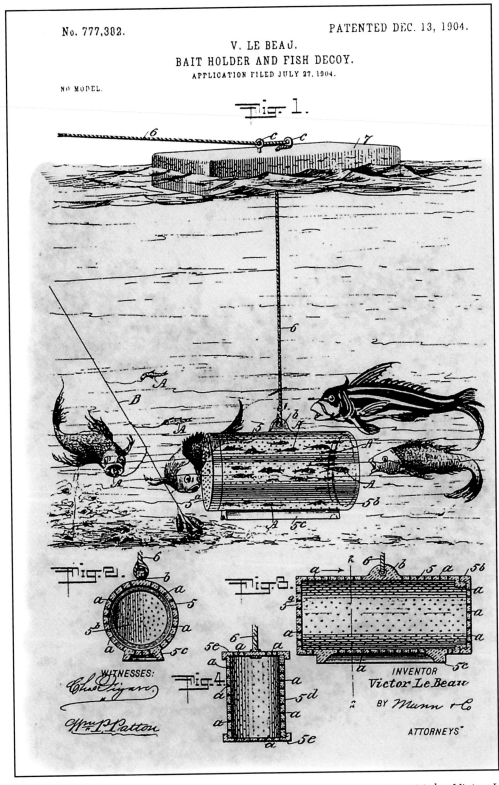

Plate 3. This early fish decoy was patented on December 13, 1904, patent #777,382 by Victor Lebeau of New Orleans, Louisiana. It was suggested to use transparent material, such as wire mesh or glass, to contain small fish to attract larger fish to baited hooks and lines. It was lowered to a desired depth through eye screws in a large wooden or cork float. This device called a bait holder and fish decoy is similar to Ernest Pflueger's earlier fish decoy, also using a lighting device and live bait to attract fish to nearby fishing lines. It was the forerunner of what some fishermen use today, using glass or wire mesh traps with bait fish as an attractor for the spear fisherman.

THE ENTERPRISE MANUFACTURING CO

The above scene represents Spearing Fish

through the ice using the life

like Decoy Minnow.

Plate 4. In this advertisement from an 1892 Enterprise Manufacturing Company tackle catalog, the sign in the fish spearing dark house reads, "The Enterprise Manufacturing Co. Akron, O. Largest Manufacturer of fish bait in U.S. with and without luminosity applied. 3½" & 7" soft rubber ice spearing minnow."

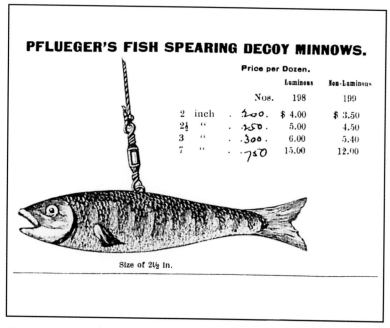

PFLUEGER'S FISH SPEARING DECOY MINNOWS.

Price per Dozen.

		Nos.	Luminous 198	Non-Luminous 199
2	inch	200.	$ 4.00	$ 3.50
2½	"	250.	5.00	4.50
3	"	300.	6.00	5.40
7	"	750	15.00	12.00

Size of 2½ in.

Plate 5. First catalog advertisement of a fish decoy by the Enterprise Manufacturing Company, 1892.

Plate 6. Painting by Les Kouba of a fisherman's view of spear fishing in a dark house. Courtesy of American Wildlife Galleries, Minneapolis, Minnesota.

Indians spear-fishing for pickerel at the mouth of the Fox River, Wisconsin.

Plate 7. Drawing by an early explorer of Native American spear fishing in the area now known as Green Bay, Wisconsin.

Chapter Two

Related Ice Spear Fishing Equipment

For readers to totally understand the sport of ice spear fishing, they must understand the importance and function of each of the many tools required in the sport of spear fishing.

Plate 8 shows two spear fishermen out on the winter ice of an unidentified frozen Michigan lake. This picture also reveals the necessary clothing and much of the equipment, the tools of the trade, helpful to have a successful spear fishing outing.

In this chapter discussing these tools of the trade, some items are obviously essential and others merely add to the enjoyment. This list of items will vary from fisherman to fisherman, but each would need warm clothing, an ice tester of some sort, a utensil to make a hole in the ice, a few decoys, a spear, and a gaff. A few hours of freezing on the ice quickly leads to the desire for some kind of shanty, and it won't be long before a heater is on the wish list. A fall or two on the ice leads to the purchase of ice creepers. As the amount of equipment increases, the need for a sled increases. The guy in the next shanty over has a larger amount of fish because he uses a tip up outside, and so it goes...

Plate 8. Two spear fishermen ready for a day of spearing on an unidentified Michigan lake.

Ice Fishing Clothing

Before technology brought us thermal boots, thermal underwear, hand warmers, electric socks, pocket warmers, and body belts powered by battery or chemical packs, ice fishermen of the early days were smart enough to layer their clothing to fight the cold. Probably no sport requires more stamina against the cold weather than ice fishing. Besides, higher winds are always more prevalent on the open ice. The fisherman must always be prepared to last the day out on the winter ice.

With the end of World War II, many Army and Navy surplus stores appeared. Cold weather boots and clothing had been developed by the government for both the Army fighting in the cold of Northern Europe and the Air Force flying at high altitude. This surplus clothing became available at a very reasonable cost. Fishermen and hunters were the first to buy these clothes for their cold weather sports. Here are men pictured wearing typical clothing used by ice fishermen for many years during the cold Midwestern and New England winters (Plate 8). The fisherman on the left is wearing World War II United States Air Force down-filled pants (circa 1943) and a Korean War United States Army winter field jacket (circa 1950). The fisherman on the right is wearing a Woolrich Co. woolen deer hunting suit (circa 1950).

Ice Creepers

Ice creepers are a device, either commercially made or homemade, for ice fishermen, trappers, and mountain climbers to wear on their boots to provide the sure footing so necessary for safety. For the ice fisherman, they are essential for pulling an ice shanty or a heavily loaded sled of ice fishing gear to the desired fishing spot. On slick or wet ice, creepers help to prevent dangerous falls. On windy days on wet or slick ice, I have seen ice fishermen crawl because they could not walk without creepers. Plates 9 and 10 show two different examples of ice creepers. The creepers in Plate 9 are made with a clamp-on design, and those in Plate 10 are a strap-on design. Notice the price for the Norlund's E-Z-FIT: 50 cents postpaid! Today we pay almost that much just to mail a letter.

Plate 9. Advertisement for a set of creepers from February 1913 Hunters, Trappers, Trader magazine.

Plate 10. Advertisement for creepers from Herter's mail order catalog, circa 1960s.

Ice Testers

An ice tester is a staff or walking stick used by the ice fisherman to test the safety of the ice and to avoid thin or rotten ice. It also functions like a cane as a support to prevent falling on slippery ice or snow. Since some of the best ice fishing occurs during first and last ice of the season, an ice tester is an important tool for the ice fisherman. Many ice fishermen use their ice chisel as an ice tester and support aid, as shown in Plate 11.

Plate 11. A spear fisherman checks the safety of the ice while towing his equipment to his shanty on a frozen Michigan lake.

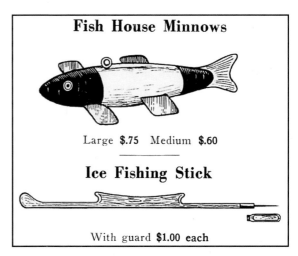

Plate 12. Advertisement for ice tester with guard from the Oscar Quam Company catalog, Minneapolis, Minnesota, circa 1940s.

Plate 13. Combination jig stick and ice tester, marked FLO-PAC BRUSHES Pat. Pend. It is 29" in overall length, circa 1950s.

Ice Awls/Ice Picks

An ice awl, also called an ice pick, is a safety device used by the ice fisherman as an aid to escape from the water back onto solid ice in case of accidentally falling through the ice while ice fishing Awls or picks are used especially during first ice, when ice was thin, or last ice, when ice is rotten. Usually some of the best winter fishing occurs during first and last ice. A pair of awls is usually worn around the neck under the fisherman's coat collar, but sometimes they are kept in a coat pocket.

I have been unable to find an advertisement showing commercially made ice picks, but I have found a number of sets that looked commercially made, possibly cottage factory. The set pictured in Plate 14 was made from file handles and spike nails. This set was found among ice fishing gear bought at a Michigan garage sale. The best illustration that I have seen for the use of ice awls comes from the 1942 edition of the Boy Scouts of America Handbook For Boys (Plate 15).

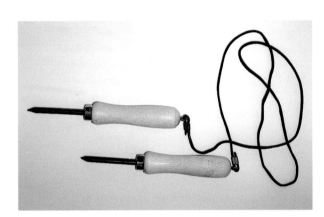

Plate 14. Commercially made ice awls, manufacturer unknown, circa 1950s.

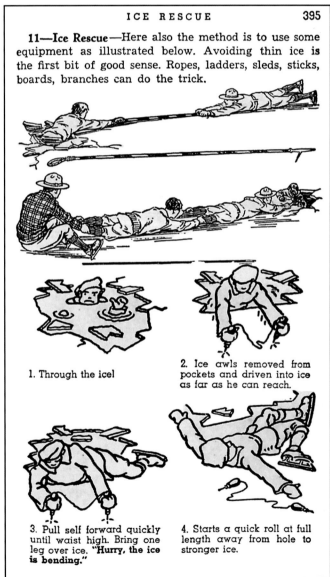

Plate 15. Illustration from the lifesaving chapter, Boy Scouts of America manual (1942 edition).

Sled/Snowmobile/Ice Taxi

An ice sled is an important and necessary tool for the ice spear fisherman. A large sled is required to transport the shanty and equipment daily or for the season (Plate 16). A smaller sled to just haul equipment can suffice when making trips to a permanent shanty location (Plate 17). Many times commercially made children's play sleds are used to haul shanties to and from fishing areas (Plate 18).

Many prime fishing areas, especially in larger bodies of water such as the Great Lakes, require the ice fishermen to travel many miles over rough ice and snowdrifts to their prime fishing areas. In the early days, stripped-down older cars and especially small trucks and World War II Army surplus trucks were modified. Chains were added to tires and some fishermen even replaced the front wheels with home-made metal skis to create what were called ice taxis (Plate 19). In many places, marinas and bait shops ran a shuttle service to the best fishing areas, bringing fishermen and equipment back and forth for a small fee.

Later in the 1950s and 1960s the first snowmobiles came to market and the ice fishermen quickly saw their great potential as ice fishing vehicles (Plate 20).

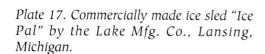

Plate 16. Ice shanty and spearing tools of the trade being pulled on ice sleds for a day of spearing.

Plate 17. Commercially made ice sled "Ice Pal" by the Lake Mfg. Co., Lansing, Michigan.

Plate 18. Commercially made child's play sled loaded and ready to go for a day of ice fishing.

Plate 19. A World War II Army jeep being used as an ice taxi, pulling a homemade sled taking ice fishermen and equipment to and from their fishing spots. Courtesy of Debbie Garrison Hubbard.

A snow sled will get you into hard-to-get-into fishing areas.

HERTER'S HUDSON BAY HUSKY MAGNUM POWER SNOW SLEDS

SPEED: up to 45 MPH.
MOTOR: 17.5 HP.
POWER TREAD: Steel and Rubber
TRACK: 15 inches wide
BODY: 4 ply Fiberglas
FRONT RUNNERS: Steel
WEIGHT: 320 lbs.
COLOR: Red and off-white
Crating charge $20.00 F.O.B. Waseca.

15-1028 Complete Shpg. wt. 420 lbs. **$589.00**

Plate 20. An advertisement for an early snowmobile, circa 1962.

Ice Chisel/Ice Saw/Ice Augers/Chain Saw

One of the more difficult tasks the ice spear fisherman faces before he can start enjoying his sport is cutting a hole in the ice before putting up his shanty. The ice chisel, often referred to as a spud, is an important tool used by fishermen to cut a fishing hole in the ice. The spud is a broad heavy chisel mounted on the end of a 5- to 6-foot-long handle. The spud was originally a tool used by cabin builders to debark logs and is more efficient than an axe for starting a hole in thick ice. Imagine trying to chop a hole in 3-foot ice! Sometimes the spud is used strictly to cut a starter hole (Plate 21). Next an ice saw is used, which is faster to use to cut the hole. In the days before refrigeration, ice saws were a common tool used in the winter for cutting ice, which was then kept in thick-walled ice houses through the spring, summer, and fall, so the ice saw was a natural tool for the ice spear fisherman to use to cut his fishing holes (Plates 22 and 23).

With the invention of the hand-operated ice auger and later the power ice auger and the chain saw, the hole-cutting task became much easier (Plates 24 and 25). Augers were also faster to use than the saw. Some of the drawbacks of these newer tools were that they were heavy and bulky to haul out onto the ice, and they were sometimes difficult to start in the winter cold (Plates 26 and 27).

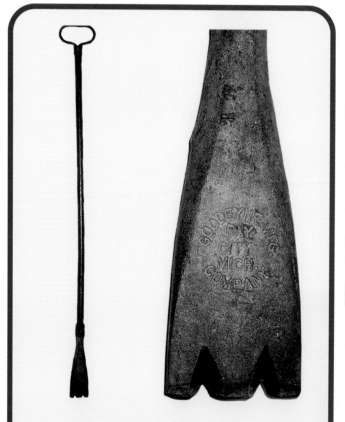

Plate 21. Commercially made ice chisel marked Goddeyne Mfg. Company, Bay City, Mich.

Plate 22. Ice spear fisherman with an early commercial ice saw.

Plate 23. Two examples of early commercially made saws used by ice fishermen.

HERTER'S SWEDISH AND NORWEGIAN ICE AUGERS

EACH AUGER INDIVIDUALLY HAND TESTED TO CUT ICE

Chiseling a hole through ice is hard slow work and the noise of the chiseling keeps fish from biting in the area for as much as several hours. Our Swedish "Snabb" and Norwegian "Mustad" have special offset hollow ground blades, completely painted against rust. Comfortable, tough, turning knob. Our ice auger allows you to cut a full 6", 7" or 8" hole through three feet of ice in 60 seconds. Many augers cut holes slightly undersize. It makes no noise and does not

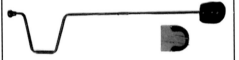

Snabb

scare away fish like a chisel does. It is made of the finest steel, solid shaft, two

Mustad

threaded 27" sections for easy storage in your car trunk, metal blade guard. Order one out and try it out. If it is not the handiest winter fishing tool that you have ever had and if it does not get you many more fish return within one month for a full refund plus transportation charges.

HERTER'S POWER ICE AUGER

Lightweight, 3 horsepower, 2 cycle ice auger complete. Cuts 8 inch diameter hole through 30 inches of ice

You and your family can now really enjoy winter fishing by taking the work out of cutting holes. This tool really makes the ice chisel and hand auger obsolete. Spiral flight clears the ice chips from the hole without lifting the auger out of the hole.

Starts immediately in all weather. Automatic centrifugal clutch engages only when the throttle is advanced. The throttle is adjustable for thumb operation for complete control.

Drills 7 inch hole through three feet of ice in 30 seconds.

Plate 25. Advertisement for power ice auger, circa 1950s.

Plate 24. Advertisement for manually operated ice auger, circa 1950s.

Plate 26. Spear fisherman using a chain saw to cut a fishing hole.

Plate 27. Spear fishermen pushing an ice block under the ice for stowage.

Ice Tongs

Ice tongs are a tool used by ice fishermen to remove large chunks of ice from the hole being cut for spear fishing. These large heavy chunks of ice are sometimes cut from ice two to three feet thick in the dead of winter and are very difficult to retrieve from the freshly cut hole. Surrounding ice becomes slippery from water being splashed from the hole being cut,

making the removal a dangerous task. Tongs make this tricky job possible.

Before the days of modern refrigeration, blocks of ice were delivered to millions of homes by an ice delivery man using ice tongs. Therefore, many commercially made tongs were and are still available for today's spear fisherman (Plate 28).

Plate 28. Wooden-handled ice tongs made by unknown commercial manufacturer, circa 1930s.

Ice Skimmer

After a fishing hole was cut into the ice and the larger chunks of ice were cleared, a skimmer was used by the ice fisherman to clear the smaller chips of ice (Plate 29). Also smaller holes outside the shanty used for tip-up fishing or jigging would freeze over during colder weather and need to be continually skimmed of ice.

Commercially made kitchen utensils such as deep fry baskets and vegetable strainers are also often used as ice skimmers (Plate 30).

Plate 29. Ice skimmer by unknown commercial manufacturer, circa 1950s.

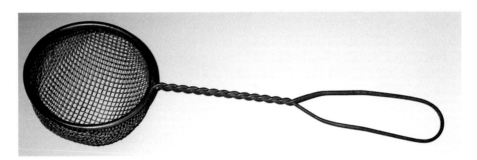

Plate 30. Kitchen food strainer used as skimmer, circa 1940s.

Ice Shanty

The ice shanty, sometimes called a dark house, ice shack, or fish house, is a small portable canvas or wooden structure with only a door (Plate 31). The shanty is placed over a large hole cut into the ice. Snow and loose ice are usually packed around the base of the shanty to keep light, wind, and cold out. The spear fisherman is able to see a great distance in the water because of the darkness in his shanty and the daylight passing through the ice. The spear fisherman sits silently, staring downward through the hole, awaiting an opportunity to spear his prey. Fish are usually speared near the surface but have been speared as deep as 25 feet by the use of a heavy throwing spear. Fish are sometimes also taken by hook and line from inside the shanty (Plate 32).

Most of the states allowing ice spear fishing require owner identification on ice shanties. These laws came into being in most states in the early 1940s (Plates 33, 34 and 35). These laws minimized the abandonment of shanties, which was sometime caused by severe winter wind storms or early spring thawing of ice. These abandoned shanties became a navigational hazard, whether they had sunk to the bottom or were floating mostly submerged. The Michigan regulation, for example, stated that the owner must remove any shanty before the ice became unsafe. Otherwise the shanty would be removed and stored or destroyed and the owner held liable for penalties. Thus this law prevented both fishing hazards and ecological eyesores.

Plate 31. Illustration of design and use of a typical ice shanty.

HERTER'S ICE FISHERMEN AND DUCK HUNTERS TENT

We make this up from a specially treated 4 ounce tent fabric. It has a special green color so it can be easily camouflaged for hunting or used as it comes. Has specially made tent poles so it can be erected in minutes, sewed in floor, positive high wind ice-anchorage feature. Tent size 5 foot by 5 foot with 19 inch hole in floor for ice fishing and 4½" hole flap covered in top for stove pipe vent. Tent is 5 feet high inside with a 18" by 42" flap covered door.

28-3000-F Shpg. wt. 12 lbs. ....Each **$11.93**

Plate 32. Advertisement of commercially made portable ice shanty.

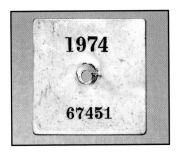

Plate 34. State of Wisconsin law requires a metal shanty identification tag with registration number to be affixed to the exterior of the shanty.

Plate 33. Spear fishermen on Lake St. Clair, Michigan, circa 1955. Note: Michigan law requires all ice fishing shanties marked with the owner's name and address.

**MICHIGAN
Fish Law
DIGEST
1952**

*Lake
Sturgeon*

Michigan Department of Conservation

MICHIGAN
1952 FISHING REGULATIONS
SYNOPSIS
All changes for 1952 are shown in bold face type.

EXPERIMENTAL FISHING REGULATIONS: Under authority of Sec. 3, Act 230, P.A. 1925, experimental fishing regulations have been established on certain waters. See local provisions, Lenawee and Newaygo counties on page 8.

GAME FISH: Designated as brook, brown and rainbow trout, mackinac or lake trout, landlocked salmon, grayling, black bass, bluegills, pumpkinseed or common sunfish, yellow perch, crappies or calico or strawberry bass, pike-perch (walleyed pike), northern pike and muskellunge. Illegal to buy or sell at any time, or to ship or transport outside state except as provided, or to possess same more than 60 days after season closes, except lake trout, perch, northern pike and pike-perch taken from Great Lakes under commercial fishing license or shipped in from without the state, or lake trout taken through the ice on Great Lakes waters, or trout propagated and sold under authority of Act 170, P. A. 1905. Persons possessing unexpired fishing license may transport or carry one day's legal catch of game fish but may ship only one day's legal catch under shipping permit issued with license. The catch of two or more persons may be combined in single package when shipping permit of each is attached.

HOOK AND LINE: Lawful to use for still fishing, ice fishing, casting or trolling two lines under immediate control, having a total of not more than four hooks on all lines baited with natural or artificial bait for fishing which shall be by fish taking bait or hook in mouth. Hook may be single, double or treble. Manufactured artificial bait counted as one hook. Unlawful to use on any trout stream except from June 1 to Labor Day, inclusive, a single hook of any kind more than $\frac{3}{8}$ inches between point of hook and shank, or any double or treble hook having diameter of more than $\frac{3}{4}$ inches. May use any number of hooks on one line for taking smelt.

Lawful to use in Lake St. Clair at any time one gang of not over 100 set hooks with cut bait for taking catfish, bullheads, suckers and noxious fish only. Name and address of owner must be attached to stake, float or buoy.

ICE SHANTIES, HOUSES AND SHELTERS: All structures and shelters placed or used on ice must be identified on outside with name and address of owner in letters of insoluble material not less than two inches high and must be removed before ice becomes unsafe. Otherwise same will be removed and stored or destroyed and costs assessed against owner in addition to other penalties.

ILLEGAL FISHING DEVICES: Unless otherwise provided, unlawful to use or possess on or along waters of this state spear or grab hook, snag hook, gaff hook, **bow and arrow,** artificial light of any kind, set or night lines, any kind of a net, firearm, or any explosive substance or combination of substances which have a tendency to kill or stupefy fish. Gaff hooks or landing nets may be used to assist in landing fish already caught by lawful device, except that gaff hooks may not be possessed or used on any trout stream. Possession or use of flashlight or lantern for removing fish from hook not considered illegal provided light is not used to attract or take fish. Artificial light may be used for taking white bass.

INLAND WATERS: Defined by law as all waters in state except Great Lakes, Detroit, St. Clair and St. Mary's Rivers and Lake St. Clair. Lakes or ponds created by a dam in stream subject to same laws as for stream unless excepted. Unlawful to fish in waters used by the state or Federal Government for propagation of fish except those designated by Director of Conservation as open to fishing.

INSECTS AND INSECT LARVAE: Unlawful to take or attempt to take from any trout stream except for personal use on such stream or under permit ($3.00) from Director of Conservation. Also see "Minnows and Wigglers" on pages 9 and 10.

LICENSES: Fishing licenses are available from agents in most communities of state.

RESIDENT FISHING LICENSE—Fee $1.50, expires Dec. 31. Required of all persons who have passed seventeenth birthday for fishing in inland waters, except persons fishing in waters wholly on enclosed lands on which permanently domiciled. Permits taking in season all species of fish except brook, brown and rainbow trout. License identification for wife issued without additional charge.

Plate 35. Notice paragraph four from the 1952 Michigan Fish Law Digest describing the state law for identification of ice shanties.

Ice Shanty Stove

Ice fishermen frequently had a small wood, oil, kerosene, or propane gas burning stove or heater to make the shanty comfortable out on the cold winter ice. The shanty stove had additional benefits in that it could also be used for heating coffee and soups and drying wet gloves or socks (Plate 36).

Plate 36. An advertisement for two different ice house stoves.

HERTER'S CANADIAN STOVES

They are easy to carry for long distances when necessary. They are used as follows:

For Fish Houses. If you use the wood model a very little wood will keep your house warm even in 40 below zero weather. If you use the oil model a quart of kerosene will last all day.

For Tents. These are the finest and most widely used tent stoves in the world. Used and recommended by such men as camping

Bottle Gas Model   Wood Model

editor of Sports Afield, Colonel Whelen. Widely used in Alaska. The wood model is the most popular for tents.

For Duck Blinds. The oil model will keep you warm all day with 20c worth of kerosene. Use canned heat in the wood model to avoid smoke.

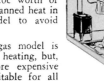

The bottle gas model is the ultimate in heating, but, is a little more expensive to operate. Suitable for all purposes listed.

This stove weighs 9 lbs. is 10" high by 10" wide by 10" deep. It is made from cold roll steel and plated in rustproof finish. It has a special propane valve for high or low volume heat that makes heating or cooking with it a pleasure. The stove pipe opening is for 3" standard pipe. There are no fuel burning odors using this stove.

The wood and kerosene stove measures 14" high, 8" wide and is 11" long. Weighs 7 lbs. Made of 18 gauge steel.

Wonderful stoves. Order out and try one. Return it if it is not just what you needed.

Fish Decoy

The fish decoy is the ultimate lure used by the spear fisherman. The fish decoy is defined as an attractor usually made from wood, but sometimes made of metal, rubber, or plastic, shaped in a fish form but sometimes in a critter form (Plate 37). Fish decoys can be painted to a particular species' pattern or be generically painted. Critters come in many forms; frogs are probably the most prevalent but there are also muskrat, beaver, turtle, mouse, and dragonfly. Decoys usually have a lead ballast to enable them to be suspended in the water near neutral buoyancy for sensitivity to be put into a swimming mode while being tethered to a jigging stick. Fish decoys are sometimes merely suspended in the water without any dynamic motion to simply be an attractor.

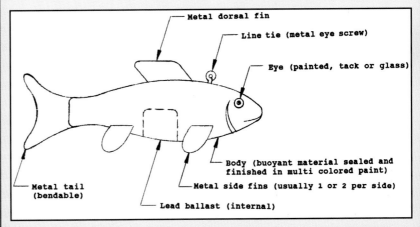

Plate 37. Nomenclature of the parts of a typical commercial fish decoy.

Jigging Lures

Jig fishing lures are often used as attractors by ice spear fishermen. Live bait, chicken skins, colored yarn, rubber and plastic worms and minnows are often added to enhance and make the jig more dynamic. The most typical jigging lures are metal, with a natural or bright plated finish. Many also have a solid or multicolored painted finish. Jigs can be single or gang hooked. These types of jigging lures are used year round by fishermen, including ice spear fishermen (Plate 38). The most typical jigging lures preferred by the ice spear fishermen are fish shaped with

a conventional fish decoy type line tie and have detachable hooks (Plate 39). Some jig fishing lures are dual function with separate line ties and are used by fishermen year round as casting or trolling lures in a non-ice-fishing situation, utilizing the frontal line tie. When these same lures are used by the spear fisherman, they are usually swum in a relatively horizontal position using the conventional type dorsal fin line tie, but they are sometimes jigged from the frontal line tie to create a crippled action swimming mode (Plate 40).

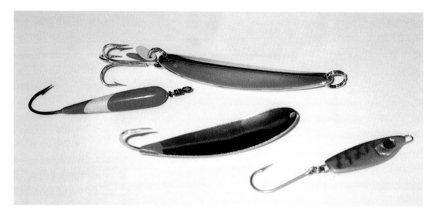

Plate 38. A group of the most common jig fishing lures. Top: Bay De Noc Lure Company "Swedish Pimple." Bottom left: unknown maker Bottom center: unknown maker. Bottom right: Luhr-Jensen & Sons, Inc. Crippled Herring.

Plate 39. A group of jig fishing lures designed for a horizontal swim mode. Note that these lures only have the dorsal fin line tie, and hooks that are detachable for ice spear fishing when desirable. Top and center: Heddon Company "Sonar." Bottom right: Creek Chub Bait Company Wiggle-jig. Bottom left: Burke Company Pulsar.

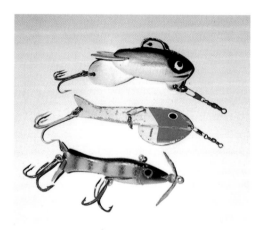

Plate 40. A group of dual-function jig fishing lures. These lures have two line tie positions, one at the nose and another at the dorsal fin. Hooks are detachable for ice spear fishing when desirable. Top: K. Sletten Water Bug. Center: Unknown maker. Bottom: Bud Stewart Tackle Company Jerk Bait for Jerks.

Cheater Hooks

Cheater hooks are typical commercially made fishing hooks, singles or doubles, but usually trebles, that are attached to a fish decoy for the purpose of better holding a fish that has attacked and then snagged the fish decoy (Plate 41). Because the fish is fighting to free himself from the hooks, the spear fisherman has more time to spear his prey.

Cheater hooks are found on both homemade and commercially made fish and critter decoys. The commercial examples that I have seen give the fisherman the option of fishing the decoy with or without the cheater hooks. The commercial decoys had this option because decoys rigged with hooks were illegal in certain states, and this option gave the manufacturers the freedom to market their product in all states allowing spear fishing.

Plate 41. Pike decoy by the Bear Creek Bait Company, Kaleva, Michigan, with two sets of factory-installed cheater hooks.

Decoy Boxes

Every ice fisherman needed a box to store his ice fishing decoys. Probably some of the decoys were thrown into the regular tackle box along with lures, hooks, lines, and so on. Other fishermen used metal cigar boxes, cut plug tobacco boxes, and lunch boxes (Plate 42). Some even made their own boxes, painting them with leftover porch or house paint, and used leftover screen door hardware for hinges and latches. I have never found any reference for a commercially-made fish decoy storage box.

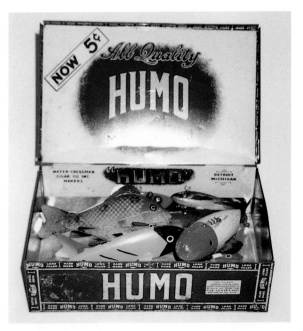

Plate 42. Metal cigar box used to carry and store fish decoys.

Sizing Decoy

A sizing fish decoy is a dual-function attractor that is used not only to lure the fish to the spear fisherman but also to aid in determining the legal size of the fish. All the examples that I have seen were sturgeon coaxer decoys about 42 inches in length, the legal size that sturgeon fish could be taken in Michigan for many years (Plate 43). No commercial sizing decoy examples have been found at this time.

The legal size limit for this species was 42 inches because sturgeon do not first spawn until they are at least 15 to 20 years of age, and then they spawn only every 3 to 5 years. Sturgeon can live to be 100 years old. The near-extinction of this species resulted in a closed or short sturgeon spear fishing season in all states that still allow ice spear fishing (Plate 44). The states that still allow ice spear fishing are Alaska, Michigan, Minnesota, Montana, South Dakota, Vermont, and Wisconsin.

Plate 43. The author with his carved working 42-inch sturgeon attractor sizing decoy.

Plate 44. This 85-pound sturgeon set the Michigan state record in 1957. This fish was speared by Steve Uhouse (pictured on the right holding the spear) on Black Lake in northern Michigan on Feb. 15, 1957. This fish was six feet long.

Live Decoys

Live decoys are the choice attractor for many ice spear fishermen. Each state law varies on the species of fish that may be used as a live decoy. The most common species used are suckers, perch, shiners, and chubs. The fisherman sometimes makes his choice on the basis of the abundance of species seen in the lake or river where he is fishing or by what is found in the stomachs of recently speared fish. Live decoys are fished as small as one inch and as large as 15 inches.

There is an old saying among fisherman, "The bigger the bait, the bigger the fish caught."

Most live decoys are fished with a decoy pin (Plate 45.) These barbless safety pin-type wire forms are put through the back of the fish just forward of the dorsal fin (Plate 46.) The live decoy is then free to swim around the spear fisherman's hole to be a dynamic attractor.

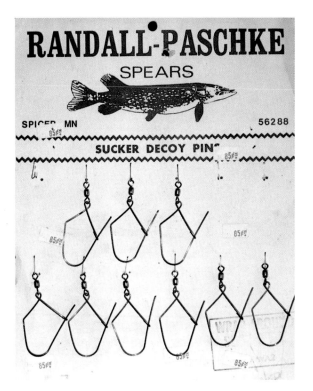

Plate 45. Two different style live decoy pins by the Randall-Paschke Company of Spicer, Minnesota.

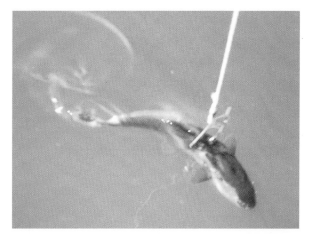

Plate 46. Live Creek Chub minnow on a decoy pin.

Ice Shanty Reel

A shanty reel is a device used to raise and lower a fish decoy to specific depth below the ice. Reels are hung from the ceiling inside the shanty. I have found several versions of homemade shanty reels but have only seen two references of commercial design. The first by the Bear Creek Bait Company is a simple design of two different size reels on a single axle shaft. It was marketed with 10 feet of heavy twine on the smallest reel to raise and lower the weighted fish decoy attached to the tether line on the larger reel. The fisherman then tied the twine to the reel assembly when the decoy was at its proper depth (Plate 47).

The second design, marked "Decoy Reel" Hopkins Minn.Pat.Pend, is also of a simple design of a single wooden dowel on a single axle shaft. The dowel and axle shaft is loaded with a compressed coil spring to keep tension on the assembly for raising and lowering the decoy (Plate 48).

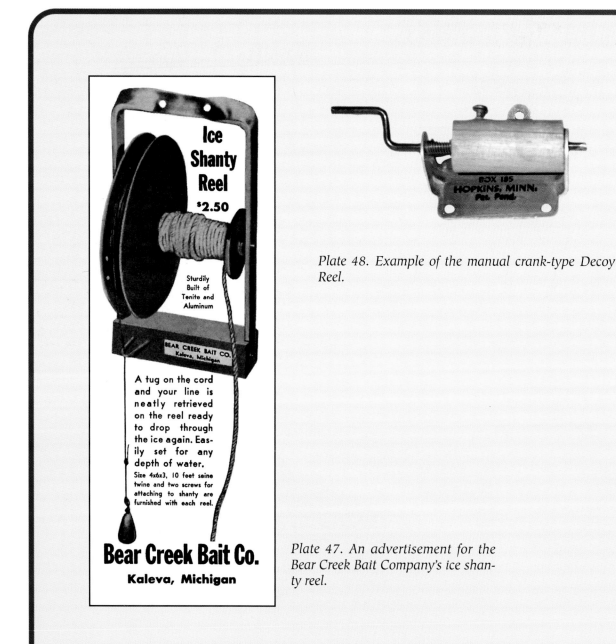

Plate 48. Example of the manual crank-type Decoy Reel.

Plate 47. An advertisement for the Bear Creek Bait Company's ice shanty reel.

Jigging Stick

Most decoys are designed to swim either clockwise or counterclockwise when jigged with an up-and-down movement. This is commonly done with a tool called a jigging stick. A jigging stick is a short stick with a line attached to a decoy. Most commercially made jig sticks are 12 to 18 inches in length, but a few larger examples have been found (Plates 49 and 50).

Plate 49. Spear fisherman with jigging stick working his fish decoy. Note the loop from the handle around the fisherman's wrist. This is a safety feature to prevent loss of the jigging stick to a large fish.

Plate 50. Three examples of commercially-made jigging sticks. Top and middle are by Bay De Noc Lure Company, Gladstone, Michigan. Bottom jig stick is marked Saga, Hermansville, Michigan.

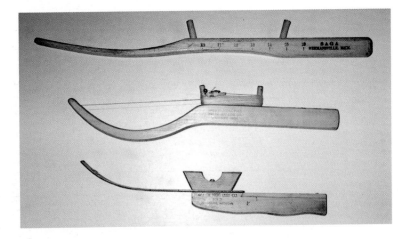

Ice Rods/Tip-Ups

An ice rod was sometimes used by the ice spear fisherman with hook and live bait, either inside or outside of his dark house (Plate 51). Tip-ups were used exclusively outside the dark house to give the spear fisherman an added opportunity to catch fish. Most were designed with a visual signaling devise that allowed the spear fisherman to be spear fishing inside his dark house and hook and line fishing with a tip-up outside with a periodic check for action (Plate 52). This way he could stay warm in his shanty but have double the fish action.

HERTER'S WINTER FISHING RODS

These rods are excellent for all winter fishing through the ice. Whether using live bait, jigs or artificial baits these rods will improve your fishing pleasure and get better results.

Model 1

Model 1 has a solid fiberglas tip which is a necessity when using jigs, grubs, worms, etc. This rod is excellent for fishing out of a boat for pan fish. Comes with 45 feet or more 10 lb. monofilament line, pear float and hook.

Model 2

Model 2 is a strong hardwood stick with clear lacquer finish. Comes with 65 feet of 10 lb. monofilament line, pear float and hook.

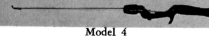

Model 3

Model 3 has a solid fiberglas tip with a monofilament reel permanently attached to the hard wood handle. The reel has drag adjustment for applying tension to the line.

Model 4

Model 4 has a solid fiberglas tip. The handle is unbreakable plastic, is off set for use with casting reels or closed face spinning or spin-cast reels.

Model 5

Model 5 has a 9″ stiff solid glass tip. An off set handle with cork foregrip and reargrip. This model was designed for lake trout, musky and northern pike fishing through the ice.

Be sure to try these rods. Return within one month for a refund plus transportation charges if not the best winter fishing rod you have ever used. Each has a place to wind the line and hold the hook. Shpg. wt. 1 lb.

Plate 51. Advertisement for different designs of ice or winter fishing rods.

HERTER'S NON-FREEZE TIP-UP

This tip-up is guaranteed to be the easiest of all to trip and will not freeze up as others do. It has two way action and comes with a non-rusting reel. All wooden parts are waterproofed to last the average ice fisherman a lifetime. Overall height 20 inches. Order out one of these and use for a season, if not the best you have ever used return for a full refund. NOT LEGAL IN MINNESOTA.

No.	Each	Shpg. Wt.	Per 3
AQ5Q4G	$.79	1 lb.	$2.25

Plate 52. Advertisement of tip-up with illustration of function.

Fish Attractors

Plate 53. Bud Stewart's "Triple Trouble" fish decoy.

Some of the unique items and methods sometimes used by the spear fishermen to attract fish were quite whimsical. Here are a few of my favorites.

Fish Charm (Plate 56) came in a 20-ounce tin can with a line tie soldered to the top, which housed a removable hole punch tool. The can contained alluring aromatic ingredients to attract all fish, so the advertisement on the can claimed. Directions on the can were to punch a number of holes into the can with the provided tool and then lower it into the water to a desired depth with a line attached to the line tie.

The Fish Caller was a colorful ballasted tin can with a built-in noisemaker to attract the spear fishermen's prey (Plate 54).

Besides the conventional method of swimming the fish decoy by manipulating it with a jigging stick, fishermen also use the method of twisting the line attached to the fish decoy a couple hundred times and then letting it unwind after it was lowered into the water. With the resistance of the water, the line unwound very slowly, giving the fish a swimming effect. Another effective method was for the fisherman to tie his decoy tether line to one blade of an egg beater and slowly crank it, swimming the decoy in a circle at any desired swimming speed. The most unusual method that I have heard was to tie a small fish decoy to a large chub minnow or sucker and let the live fish tow the fish decoy as it swam around on its tethered line. Spear fishermen fishing on flowing rivers designed unique straight-tailed fish decoys that swam with enough movement to attract fish as they bucked the current of the river. Another popular idea was for the fisherman to lower a jar of live minnows through the shanty hole as an added attractor before he started swimming his live or wooden decoy (Plate 55).

Some of these creative ideas in fish decoy design of a fish decoy surely must have worked, for examples seem to be found over and over again. Here are some that I have documented over the years. One is a floater fish decoy that has no ballast. A tether line from the belly to a weight on the bottom of the lake keeps the decoy at the desired depth in the corner of the shanty hole, away from the swimming decoy. One or more of these were often used as added attractors.

Another great idea was to swim two, three, or even a half dozen small decoys together, simulating a school of minnows (Plate 53). Some fishermen painted silhouettes of smaller fish on the sides of their larger decoys, also simulating minnows. Still another great idea was to mount a small mirror on each side of a decoy, the idea being that the fish would see his reflection in the mirror and become more aggressive because of the perceived competition. Some fishermen made two-headed and three-headed decoys, simulating more prey. Still other fishermen created decoys that were eating another fish, frog, or critter to excite their quarry. An open-mouth decoy was recently found in northern Michigan, made with a pin passing through the open mouth. The pin was used to impale a live struggling minnow, just as you would put a live minnow on a hook.

Critters of all kind have been carved as decoys after being found in the stomachs of larger fish. Some examples are frogs, songbirds, mice, muskrats, ducks, and snakes. Some other decoys were carved and swum to simulate a cripple, wounded, or dying fish or critter. Flashers have also been used as an added attractor on the tail and fin areas. Sometimes spinners were used in a hollow body cavity to make the decoy more dynamic. Some fisherman carved three-and four-jointed fish or else jointed fish with a spiraled rear body section to make it tumble when it swam. Multicolored glitter was often sprinkled on a new decoy while the paint was still wet for an added attractor.

It has been scientifically proven that fish come to the lure not only for the potential to feed but out of curiosity. That is why fish have been speared when fishermen used such oddities as car keys, shoehorn, bottle opener, and, most intriguing of all, false teeth as an attractor. These weird decoys were probably "invented" on the spot when the fisherman inadvertently forgot to bring his ice decoys to the shanty.

HERTER'S WORLD FAMOUS FISH CALLER

Patents Pending

Unconditionally Guaranteed to Call Fish or Your Money Back.

With The Cost of Fishing Trips What They Are, Why Take a Chance on Spoiling Them for A Mere $2.47?

Nothing More to Buy. No Batteries to Go Dead. No Springs to Break.

Take This Fish Caller to a Hatchery and Prove to Yourself That it Will Call Fish. The Only Fish Caller Used and Proven by Commercial Fishermen.

A Necessity for Still Fishing, Spearing Through the Ice, or for Shooting Fish with a Bow and Arrow. Better Than Chumming When Trolling.

We have carefully studied the calling of fish for generations, both here and throughout the world. We proved, at an early date, that fish make noises and communicate in a manner that is clear to them. During World War II, submarine listening devices recorded the so-called "talking" of fish. We tried, for years, to produce sounds that would be attractive to fish and we have finally succeeded — completely!

It is a scientific fact that sound travels a great distance underwater. Sometimes when you are in swimming, hold your head underwater for a moment while you strike two rocks together. You will be amazed at the intensity of the noise. However, this will cause a harsh, abrupt sound, which will frighten fish. We definitely established, early in the tests, that harsh or guttural sounds are useless for fish callers. Soon after this discovery, we learned that high pitched, or whining buzzing sounds are very displeasing to them, also.

By working within the ranges between these two types of sounds, we devised our fish caller and tuned it so that it will call fish from

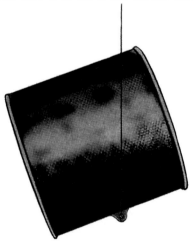

amazing distances. No other fish caller on the market has duplicated this sound accurately and our tests have proven that it is the only sound which is attractive to fish.

We learned, too, that it is impossible to call a fish from a strata of water where he is comfortable, into a layer of water where he might be ill at ease. For example, you cannot call a cold water species that is lying in deep water and entice him to enter a warmer level of water nearer the surface. Therefore, we designed our fish caller to work equally well in all depths. By using our Water Temperature and Depth Gauge, you can now set the Herter Fish Caller at the proper level. Do not be misled by claims of fish callers to the

effect that they will call fish anywhere. This claim cannot be substantiated! However, by using our Fish Caller at the proper depth, with the aid of the Water Temperature and Depth Gauge, you will catch fish when other anglers are trying to figure out how to use inferior calls.

Herter's World Famous Fish Caller needs no batteries which always run down when you want them most. It contains no springs which will break. It is a simple mechanism and absolutely waterproof for an indefinite period. To use it, simply lower your Herter Water Temperature Gauge into the water until you locate the proper fishing depth. Then lower the Herter Fish Caller to that depth and move it up and down slightly. Fish will

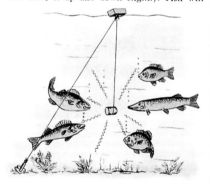

immediately enter the area out of curiosity. By attaching your Fish Caller to a buoy, the action of the waves will work the call automatically. For trolling purposes, simply buoy the Fish Caller as described above, and troll around the buoy, or back and forth close to it.

Our Famous Fish Caller works on all game and rough species found in most lakes and rivers. Among the fish most attracted by it are muskies, northern pike, walleyed pike, crappies, bluegills, bass, lake trout, land-locked salmon, brook trout, rainbow trout, carp, catfish, and bullheads.

We at Herter's give all of our products a tough field test, and our Fish Caller was given one of the most prolonged of all tests, since we were experimenting in a field little understood by man. We know, now, that you take no chances in buying a Herter Fish Caller. To prove this, order out one of these today and give it a three months' trial. If it does not help you catch more fish than you have ever taken before, return it for a full refund.

Plate 54. Advertisement for Herter's "Fish Caller."

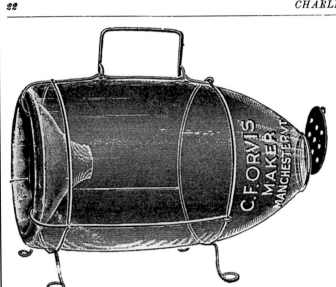

Plate 55. Advertisement for minnow trap sometimes used with live minnows as an attractor.

Plate 56. The "Fish Charm" utilizing scent may have been years ahead of its time, circa 1950s.

Ice Fishing Spears
by Marcel L. Salive

The harsh environment extending from the Arctic region down to the Great Lakes required the first inhabitants of that area to develop tools and skills to get food during the coldest days of the year when the land was covered in deep snow and the lakes and streams were frozen over with thick ice. Stocks of food laid up for the winter needed to be supplemented with fresh catches to extend the food supply and provide needed protein. Those peoples depending on the sea, lakes, and streams for fish as a significant portion of their diet learned methods for fishing through the ice. No doubt these northern people adapted methods used in the early spring to spear spawning fish to fishing through the ice in the winter.

The basic difference between spearing game and fish is that game can be followed until they succumb to their wounds, whereas fish must be caught immediately and placed where they cannot escape only to die in some unreachable or unfindable place under the ice. Thus fishing spears have barbs or some method devised to securely hold a speared fish so that the fish cannot pull away and escape the fisherman. We see fishing spears with points designed to penetrate the fish's scaly armor, barbs to keep the fish from slipping off the tines, multiple tines used either to get smaller fish or to stab more tines into a big fish. Spears have been tied to the fisherman or his shanty to keep them from being dragged off by a big prize. Some spears have long handles so that the fisherman has a longer reach or so that he can hold his prey against the bottom until it has given up its frantic effort to escape.

Every fisherman has an idea of how best to design a fishing spear for his particular prey and location. As a result, a major part of the charm of spear collecting is the wondrous variety of fishing spears ingeniously designed, made in all possible ways by craftsmen using the skills of their particular trade and developed to catch prey ranging from 300-pound sturgeon to muskies, walleyes, perch, and even the fish commonly called eels. An ice fisherman preparing to venture out onto a frozen lake needs to spend as much or more time considering the selection of his spear as he does his decoys, shanty, and other equipment.

Big spears with large sturdy tines are needed to take big fish, slightly smaller fish require smaller spears with lighter tines spaced to the width of their body, and eels because of their snakelike appearance and winter habits and habitat call for a different approach. How the spear was used, thrusting, dropping or throwing, can be seen in its design.

In areas such as Saginaw Bay, Michigan, where winter ice fishing was practiced commercially, especially fine spears were designed and made by the finest craftsmen. As industry turned to factory-organized mass production, the individual skill of the blacksmith was replaced by the use of jigs and dies and there was a change in the design of spears from tapered, forged spear tines to what can be best described as bent wire tines with welds used to hold tines rather than the wedge or key used in the old pierced forged boss. Cost of production came down, but the grace and beauty of the old handmade spears gave way to more utilitarian designs driven by ease of production and cost-saving considerations. Some of these early commercially made ice fishing and frog spears can be seen in the 1895 Montgomery Wards catalog #56, p. 481; Sears and Roebuck catalogs from this period offered a similar line of spears.

Several fishing lure and decoy companies adopted these commercial spear making methods to produce line of spears. Some of the better known names are Randall, Pflueger, Neely, Buel, and Goodeyne. Recent examples of commercially made spears have brand names like Surkatch and Ideal and have bent wire tines spotwelded to a rolled sheet metal socket. Examples of the commonly seen spear types are shown in Plates 57, 58, 59, and 61 along with some interesting oddballs like the unsuccessful bomb-shaped dropping spear with its cast iron body developed and sold for a short while in the late 1940s (Plate 60).

New England farmers found ice fishing for eels as useful a way to spend the frozen winter months as the Saginaw Bay area farmers did in pursuit of pike and walleyes. Winter was an excellent time to catch and ship perishable game to the major towns and cities. Most Midwestern ice fishermen are not acquainted with the common eel that was a turn-of-the-century favorite with Northeastern U.S. fishermen whose antique spears are an eagerly sought collectible. Eel spears come in several seemingly unrelated shapes.

The complex life cycle of freshwater eels found in coastal streams of North America and Europe affected the development of the eel spear's functional shape and beautiful form. Eels are bottom feeders and love the mud. During winter, groups of eels ball up in the mud at the bottom of freshwater ponds. The skinny, snakelike eel with its strange life cycle and different seasonal behavior was a real challenge for the spear maker and led to a wide variety of spear designs. Different shapes were developed to cope with the different habitats and sizes of the eel at each stage of its life cycle and during seasonal cycles. Eel spears are called "gigs" in some areas, "gleaves" in England, and the multipurpose eel/fish spear used on Long Island, New York, is called a "rag" spear.

Eel spears are basically of two types: one type

impales the eel on a sharp-pointed tine and the other catches the eel between the prongs and holds it by pinching the eel's body and snagging its skin so it can't slide out. The latter is the method of choice by the winter eel fisherman.

The different approaches resulted in three easily recognizable spear types that can be compared with flowers. The European mud spears have toothed blades looking like tulips. The winter spears have hooks at the ends of the tines and look like thistles. Summer spears that look like papyrus blossoms have barbless tines to impale the eel (Plate 62).

Thistle-shaped (winter) eel spears are used through the ice and have a fan-shaped array of from 2 to 16 tines with the tip of the tine bent into a U-shape with the sharp tip pointing back between the tines. The center of the thistle is a flat, dull-edged blade extending beyond the hooked tines to protect the soft iron tines from rocks in the muddy bottom. The eel slides up between the tines, the tines pinch the body, and the reversed point keeps the eels from sliding out. More tines indicate the fisherman's optimism about how many of the balled-up eels he could snag before they scattered. Winter eel spears are sometimes misidentified as perch spears because of the close spacing of the tines, but it should be noted that the winter spear's tines are not likely to hold the scaled short-tapered perch body as effectively as they hold the long tough hide body of an eel.

The Long Island "rag" spear uses closely spaced pointed straight tines to spear fish like skates or flounder. Each tine has many cut barbs to hold an eel between them as does the saw-tooth-bladed tulip-shaped mud spear. Rag spears are not particularly good looking because elegance has been sacrificed to make the spear dual purpose.

Like the Midwestern fish spear, the eel spear went through a design transition as the blacksmith was replaced by the industrial manufacturer; finely wrought iron work was replaced by considerations of ease of manufacture and cost cutting, like use of wire for tines and welding. Old, blacksmith-forged eel spears ceased to be made by the Fordham family, and general purpose rag spears made by companies like Pflueger were produced. Examples of some of these eel spears are shown in Plate 64.

Examining the spearhead gives clues as to what kind of fish or eel was sought, how the spear was made, its original use, and a little bit about its age. In a few cases spears have a maker's mark; in other cases the spear's maker may be recognized or known based on workmanship and design details. Early blacksmiths made many ice fishing spears reflecting the regional needs and preferences of their customers. Too many failed to mark their spears and are failing to get the recognition they deserve.

Serious spear collectors soon develop an appreciation for the wonderful work of the skilled craftsmen who made these spears. Quality of design, design details, quality of workmanship, and above all, condition are as important in evaluating spears as when evaluating furniture, jewelry or fish decoys. Look for damage and repairs. Regional characteristics can be identified. Attention to these details will help collectors to evaluate and appreciate the really fine spears. In our society, the modern spear is discarded when worn out or damaged, whereas the old spears were taken back to the blacksmith for repair. The knowledgeable fisherman looks for the old smith-made spear, treasures one when he finds it, and delights in its use when he takes it back out onto the ice.

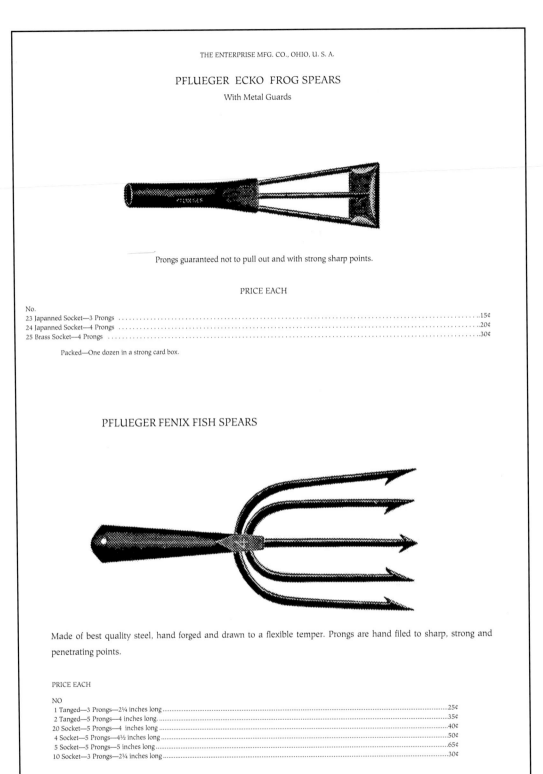

THE ENTERPRISE MFG. CO., OHIO, U. S. A.

PFLUEGER ECKO FROG SPEARS

With Metal Guards

Prongs guaranteed not to pull out and with strong sharp points.

PRICE EACH

No.
23 Japanned Socket—3 Prongs ....15¢
24 Japanned Socket—4 Prongs ....20¢
25 Brass Socket—4 Prongs ....30¢

Packed—One dozen in a strong card box.

PFLUEGER FENIX FISH SPEARS

Made of best quality steel, hand forged and drawn to a flexible temper. Prongs are hand filed to sharp, strong and penetrating points.

PRICE EACH

NO
1 Tanged—3 Prongs—2¼ inches long ....25¢
2 Tanged—5 Prongs—4 inches long ....35¢
20 Socket—5 Prongs—4 inches long ....40¢
4 Socket—5 Prongs—4½ inches long ....50¢
5 Socket—5 Prongs—5 inches long ....65¢
10 Socket—3 Prongs—2¼ inches long ....30¢

Packed—One dozen in a strong card box.

See Page 4 for our Unlimited Guarantee on PFLUEGER BULL DOG Brand Goods.

Plate 57. The Pflueger Ecko frog spear with its detachable metal point guard, and Pflueger's Fenix fish spear. Note the prices, 15¢ to 65¢.

Plate 58. Two examples of Shurkatch Company Fishing Spears. The large example measures 8" long (including handle socket), the smaller measures 6¾" long. Note the use of chisel cut barbs on wire tines spot welded to the socket.

Plate 59. An example of 5" long fish and frog spear by Ideal Products Inc. of Sykesville, Pennsylvania.

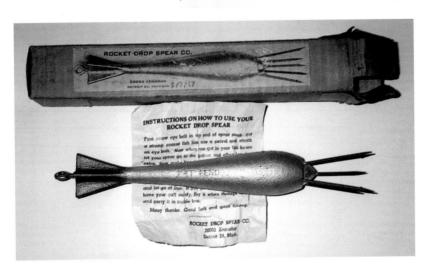

Plate 60. This is an example of the Rocket Drop Spear and one of the advertisements run in sportsmen's magazines to entice ice fishermen to buy this slightly less than successful spear. It came out shortly after the end of WWII and embodies the shape of a mortar or bazooka round and has allusions to the new high tech science of the time, rockets. Note that the R. D. Spear was sold out of Detroit and that examples still turn up in garage and estate sales in Michigan. The tines are especially sharp and, because they are made of hard steel, have a tendency to break.

Deluxe
BALANCED SPEARS

Rope goes inside handle making a nice smooth connection that will not splash or deflect flight of spear.

5 TINE
Width _____ 5⅜"
Tine Length _____ 7⅝"
¼" Hi Carbon Steel
5/16" Center Tine
Length of Head _____ 20"
Overall Length _____ 60"
2½-Lb. Weighted Head
1 1/16 Tubular Handle
R895   List $8.95   *65402

5 TINE
Width _____ 5⅜"
Tine Length _____ 7⅝"
¼" Hi Carbon Steel
5/16" Center Tine
With ½" Solid Handle
Weight 2½" Lbs. (Approx.)
S595   List $5.95   *43602

STANDARD SPEARS

7 TINE
Width _____ 7⅛"
Tine Length _____ 7⅝"
¼" Hi Carbon Steel
5/16" Center Tine
Length of Head _____ 22"
Overall Length _____ 60"
2½-Lb. Weighted Head
1 1/16 Tubular Handle
R1195   List $11.95   *87204

7 TINE
Width _____ 7⅛"
Length of Tine _____ 7⅝"
¼" Hi Carbon Steel
5/16" Center Tine
With ½" Solid Handle
Weight 3 Lbs. (Approx.)
S795   List $7.95   *54803

Randall
DECOYS & FISH SPEARS
WILLMAR, MINNESOTA

All Spears shown are breakdown models.

Plate 61. *Breakdown spear models offered by Randall, the fish decoy maker located in Willmar, Minnesota. The Randall ad offers the sportsman choices as to number of tines (width of the head), solid or tubular handle, and a weighted head.*

Thistle-shaped summer eel spear.

Rag type fish and eel spear.

Tulip-shaped European mud type eel spear.

Plate 62. Classic example of the thistle-shaped winter eel spear used on mill ponds along the Northeast coast compared to papyrus blossom-shaped summer and general purpose rag spears, and also the European mud spear. The winter and summer eel spears and the rag spear are typical of those made by the Massachusetts Fordham family of blacksmiths in the nineteenth and early twentieth centuries.

Papyrus blossom-shaped winter eel spear.

Plate 63. Winter eel spear, left, and sucker spear, right, are shown with a rare eel creel. Creel cover is in foreground.

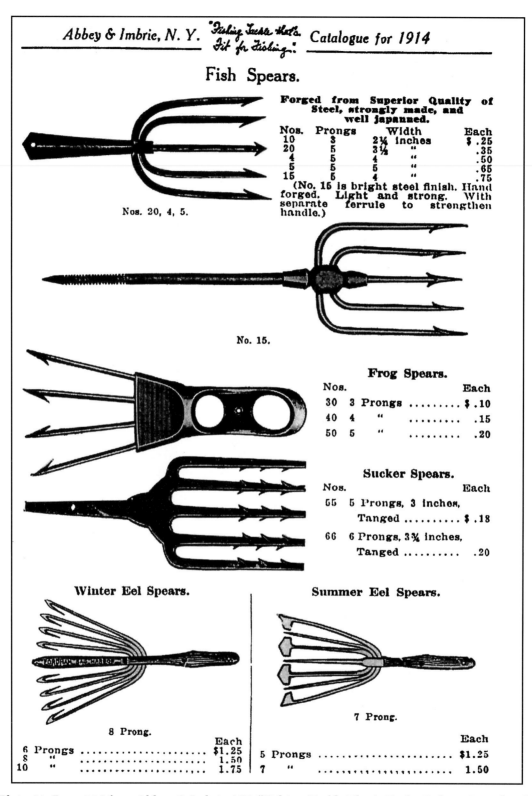

Abbey & Imbrie, N. Y. "Fishing Tackle That's Fit for Fishing." *Catalogue for 1914*

Fish Spears.

Forged from Superior Quality of Steel, strongly made, and well japanned.

Nos.	Prongs	Width	Each
10	3	2¼ inches	$ .25
20	5	3½ "	.35
4	5	4 "	.50
5	5	5 "	.65
15	5	4 "	.75

(No. 15 is bright steel finish. Hand forged. Light and strong. With separate ferrule to strengthen handle.)

Nos. 20, 4, 5.

No. 15.

Frog Spears.

Nos.		Each
30	3 Prongs	$ .10
40	4 "	.15
50	5 "	.20

Sucker Spears.

Nos.		Each
55	5 Prongs, 3 inches, Tanged	$ .18
66	6 Prongs, 3¾ inches, Tanged	.20

Winter Eel Spears.

8 Prong.

	Each
6 Prongs	$1.25
8 "	1.50
10 "	1.75

Summer Eel Spears.

7 Prong.

	Each
5 Prongs	$1.25
7 "	1.50

Plate 64. Page 206 from Abbey & Imbrie, NY, "Fishing Tackle That's Fit for Fishing," catalog for 1914. Note the variety of spearheads offered, including winter and summer eel spears. The protective tongue on the winter eel spear is marked FORDHAM, Sag Harbor. The sucker spear shown has the multiple barbs needed to make it a general purpose spear of the type that became known as the rag spear.

Fish Gaff/Fish Grabber

A fish gaff is a handled hook tool used by the fisherman to hold or lift a speared fish out of the water onto the ice or into the shanty (Plate 65). Some gaffs were mechanical spring-loaded devices called fish grabbers (Plate 66). Notice the 1915 price of $1.50 for the Harding lion gaff. Today these are considered collectibles and have sold for as high as $405, the price for a Vom Hofe flying gaff made in Amityville, New York.

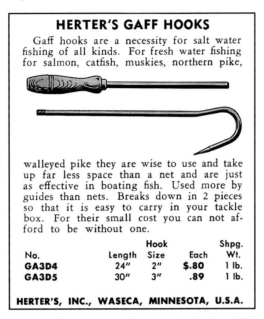

HERTER'S GAFF HOOKS

Gaff hooks are a necessity for salt water fishing of all kinds. For fresh water fishing for salmon, catfish, muskies, northern pike, walleyed pike they are wise to use and take up far less space than a net and are just as effective in boating fish. Used more by guides than nets. Breaks down in 2 pieces so that it is easy to carry in your tackle box. For their small cost you can not afford to be without one.

No.	Length	Hook Size	Each	Shpg. Wt.
GA3D4	24″	2″	$.80	1 lb.
GA3D5	30″	3″	.89	1 lb.

HERTER'S, INC., WASECA, MINNESOTA, U.S.A.

Plate 65. Advertisement for a typical fish gaff hook.

The Lion Gaff

The Only Combination Fish Gig and Gaff Hook on the Market—The center acts as a stop when opening and closing the Gaff; also as a trigger for springing the Gaff, and by coming in contact with the object sought for, closes the jaws automatically and with lightning rapidity. So a fish can be as readily caught lying close to the bottom as well as close to the surface. Our method of construction prevents teeth in jaws from becoming dull, and will not cut or abuse the fish and frogs so badly as the common gig, but will cling to its prey with a lion grasp. The Gaff is provided with a socket to which a handle may be fit very easily. In most cases a common broom handle can be used. No. 1 measures 8½ in. between points of jaws when open, suitable for gigging large fish and to be used as a gaff, and No. 2 measures 5½ in., suitable for gigging eels, small fish and frogs. No. 1, blue finish, **each, $1.50**; No. 2, nickel plated, **each, $1.50.** Given for Three new subscribers.

A. R. HARDING PUB. CO., Columbus, Ohio

M. J. RYAN   E. MUNCY

SNAPPERS AND TURTLES
We sell the Leading Hotels and Restaurants.
Can always get highest prices.

M. J. RYAN & CO.
Front and Spruce Sts., Philadelphia, Pa.
Established 1886
REFERENCES: Dun's and Bradstreet's Comm. Agencies; Fourth St. National Bank, Philadelphia; any Commission House, Philadelphia or New York.

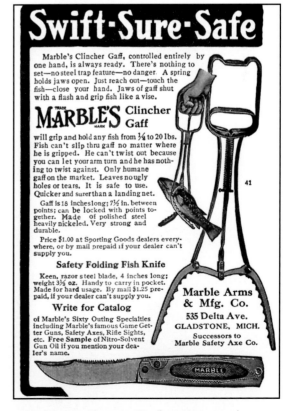

Swift-Sure-Safe

Marble's Clincher Gaff, controlled entirely by one hand, is always ready. There's nothing to set—no steel trap feature—no danger. A spring holds jaws open. Just reach out—touch the fish—close your hand. Jaws of gaff shut with a flash and grip fish like a vise.

MARBLE'S Clincher Gaff

will grip and hold any fish from ⅛ to 20 lbs. Fish can't slip thru gaff no matter where he is gripped. He can't twist out because you can let your arm turn and he has nothing to twist against. Only humane gaff on the market. Leaves no ugly holes or tears. It is safe to use. Quicker and surer than a landing net. Gaff is 18 inches long; 7½ in. between points; can be locked with points together. Made of polished steel heavily nickeled. Very strong and durable.

Price $1.00 at Sporting Goods dealers everywhere, or by mail prepaid if your dealer can't supply you.

Safety Folding Fish Knife

Keen, razor steel blade, 4 inches long; weight 3½ oz. Handy to carry in pocket. Made for hard usage. By mail $1.25 prepaid, if your dealer can't supply you.

Write for Catalog

of Marble's Sixty Outing Specialties including Marble's famous Game Getter Guns, Safety Axes, Rifle Sights, etc. Free Sample of Nitro-Solvent Gun Oil if you mention your dealer's name.

Marble Arms & Mfg. Co.
535 Delta Ave.
GLADSTONE, MICH.
Successors to
Marble Safety Axe Co.

Plate 66. Two advertisements for fish grabbers from 1915 Hunter, Trapper, Trader magazine.

Ice Fishing Carnivals

Ice fishing carnivals are wintertime get-togethers of ice fishing enthusiasts and usually feature parades, snowmobile races, and fishing contests. These carnivals are usually sponsored by a small town Chamber of Commerce, Lion's Club, or sportsman club. They promote good tourism and good fellowship and help pass the long Midwestern winters (Plate 67). Souvenir dated badges were sold to help defray the cost of these fun-filled events (Plate 68).

Plate 67. The winning fish in the 1956 annual Lion's Club New Baltimore, Michigan ice carnival held on Anchor Bay, Lake St. Clair, Michigan.

Plate 68. Some examples of ice fishing carnival badges.

Collectors Club

The National Fishing Lure Collectors Club, which was established in 1976, also serves to promote the sport of ice spear fishing with its efforts to gather information on both commercially made and folk-art ice fishing lures and decoys for its extensive library. The sale of related ice spear fishing badges and cloth patches helps defray the cost of supporting their historical library and goals (Plate 69).

Plate 69. Examples of National Fishing Lure Collectors Club badges and patches.

Chapter Three

Commercial Fish Decoys

Historical documentation of the manufacturing of commercial fish decoys was the primary motivation for the creation of this book. With the passage of time, this history becomes more clouded and it could be lost forever. Fish decoys are a relatively new and exciting collectible. They are collected for their beauty in both form and paint finishes. Information about each decoy manufacturer is important to most collectors, but not a high priority to others. This is reflected in the desirability and high prices of some of the yet-unidentified examples shown in this chapter. Many collectors of ice fishing decoys have never spear fished, but the mystique of this unique regional method of fishing and the rarity of some of the fish decoys make them a prized collectble.

In this chapter the author does not attempt to place the following examples in chronological order or order of increasing or decreasing cost, age, or desirability but rather to list them alphabetically for ease of a working reference. Hopefully the listed examples of both known and unknown makers will allow the reader a more thorough understanding and will lead to more enjoyment in viewing, studying, and understanding why people collect these scarce and unique fish lures.

Dick Baker Fish Decoys

Dick Baker was born on April 6, 1928, in Detroit, Michigan (Plate 70). His family moved to Fairhaven on the north shore of Lake St. Clair when Dick was 12 years old. While helping his father who established a small boat livery and winter shanty rental, Dick recalls meeting his dad's friend, the legendary spear fisherman and fish decoy maker Issac "Ike" Goulette. He admired Ike's fishing and waterfowl hunting abilities and in turn became a very proficient fisherman and waterfowl hunter himself. Dick married a local girl, Jo Anne Warner, in 1950. They had four sons, Dick, Mick, Rick, and Randy, all now also excellent fishermen and hunters.

After 32 years as a skilled tool maker, Dick retired in 1991. Shortly after retirement he implemented his idea for an all-metal ice spear fishing decoy, a natural for a toolmaker. He converted his home garage in Algonac, Michigan, into his manufacturing facility. His idea for an all-metal fish-spearing decoy came while he was repainting his stock of wooden spear fishing decoys. These decoys had lost paint and deteriorated with years of use. The metal decoy that he designed comes in only one size, 7" long, and most resemble a perch.

Dick designed and built four separate dies, one for blanking the body, one for the four holes required, and two for the blanking of the two different size side fins. The eyes were molded of lead in two halves and pressed together at final assembly. Dick and his friend "Spike" Krutze paint the fish decoys. Of the 10 different paint patterns the most popular among spear fishermen are perch, bass, herring, and the red and white (Plate 71).

His unique metal decoy was marketed by both large and small local tackle shops. The popularity of the decoy soon led to demand outweighing supply. Dick estimates that about 300 decoys have been made to date. Fulfilling the demand led him to realize that he was back working an eight-hour day instead of leading a retirement life, hunting and fishing whenever he wanted.

So in 1998 he brought in his sons as partners and expanded the business, which is still in operation today.

Dick continues to be an active, proficient ice spear fisherman and waterfowl hunter on the lake he loves in his backyard, Lake St. Clair.

Plate 70. Dick Baker with his colorful perch (left) and bass (right) decoys.

Plate 71. A group of Baker decoys showing six different paint patterns.

Bar Lake Fishing Tackle Company

Two partners, Everette Peterson and Sorne Hansen, established the Bar Lake Fishing Tackle Company of Manistee, Michigan, probably in 1938. Bar Lake is a small lake a few miles north of Manistee in the northwestern part of Michigan's Lower Peninsula near Lake Michigan.

Their chief product was the Bar Lake fish-spearing decoy named "Kingfish." The wood used for the decoys came from old pine porch railing. The bodies were turned on a lathe, had wooden tails, and were 7" long. Five drilled body belly holes were filled with poured lead for ballast and then filed and sanded flush to the convex shape of the belly. The bodies were airbrush painted in three different scale finishes. All paint patterns were the same except for the colors. All paint finishes had perch type vertical bars on the sides and a yellow underbelly with red at the chin and gill areas. All had two-color flat painted eyes. The four light-gauge tin-plated side fins were all die cut of the same size and shape and were left unpainted. As one of the final operations, they were then pressed into slits in the body. The line tie was a simple single eye screw (Plate 72).

The Bar Lake Tackle Company had an early design problem with the single line tie location. Many early decoys were returned because of poor swimming attitude. This led to a revised design with multiple line tie holes. These holes gave the fisherman the ability to tune the decoy by moving the single provided eye screw.

The Bar Lake Fishing Tackle Company was only in business for a few years, making slightly less than 3,000 decoys. All decoys were sold in boxes that had been glued together in their shop with a preprinted label applied (Plate 73). The Kingfish decoys sold for $1.50 to $2.00 in the late 1930s and early 1940s.

It is rumored that the Bar Lake Fishing Tackle Company also made a 3¼" sucker-shaped casting/trolling fishing lure with a Creek Chub Bait Company-type diving lip. The examples found are referred to by collectors as "The Bar Lake Sucker," but this has not yet been substantiated.

The Kingfish fish-spearing decoys seem to be rarer than the production numbers would indicate. Their sleek form and beautiful, colorful scale patterns plus scarcity of examples make these decoys very desirable among collectors.

Plate 72. The three different Kingfish paint finishes. Top: Dark green scale finish, middle: olive green scale finish, bottom: yellow scale finish.

Plate 73. The beautiful Kingfish yellow scale paint finish fish decoy with box.

Bear Creek Bait Company

The Bear Creek Bait Company was founded in 1946, in Kaleva, Michigan, a small town in the northwestern section of the Lower Peninsula of Michigan. The founders of Bear Creek Bait Company were Walter Wiitala, his brother, Elmer Wiitala, and a friend, Leo Manilla. At the time of the founding of new company, Walter Wiitala worked for the Makinen Tackle Company, a tackle manufacturer also located in Kaleva, Michigan. Walter Wiitala bought out his brother's share of the tackle business in 1948, and in 1950 he bought out Leo Manilla's share and became the sole owner of Bear Creek Bait Company (Plate 74).

The company produced fishing lures, ice decoys, tip-ups, sailfish plaques, and a unique item called the ice shanty reel (Plates 75, 76, and 77). The only fishing lures produced by the Bear Creek Bait Company were the Tweedler, Sucker Minnow, and Coho-King (Plate 78).

The first ice spearing decoys produced by the Bear Creek Bait Company were made of wood. The bodies were rough shaped by the Woltz Woodworking Company located in Grand Rapids, Michigan, and shipped to the Bear Creek Plant in Kaleva for finish shaping, painting, and hardware installation. The wooden ice decoys of the Bear Creek Bait Company were 7" in length and were available in pike form with a pike scale finish or sucker form with gray or gold scale finish. Only a few prototype trout decoys were ever produced. This beautiful decoy with its unique form and finish was never marketed (Plate 79).

In 1948 the Bear Creek Bait Company purchased the molds for making plastic ice decoys from the bankrupt Makinen Tackle Company. Approximately 10,000 of these finely detailed decoys were produced from 1948 through 1950 (Plates 80, 81, and 82). The change from wood to plastic for the ice spearing decoys was necessary because of cost savings and competition, mainly from the Randall Decoy Company of Willmar, Minnesota, but also from local competition generated by Bob's Fly Tying Shop located in nearby Ludington, Michigan.

The last spearing decoys of Bear Creek Bait

Company were designed to be hollow, with the unique idea of filling the decoy body with water through holes molded into the body. Thus water would sink the decoy, saving the cost of expensive ballast (Plate 83). Through the life of the company, Bear Creek Bait Company decoys were available in eight different models, seven different lengths, and a variety of colors.

The design evolution of the Bear Creek Bait Company ice spearing decoys went through four phases. For Type I, these decoys were solid wood, with die-cut screw attached unpainted metal side fins, with lead poured into drilled holes in belly area. The eyes were carved and spray painted black. The line tie was a simple eye screw. The decoys were 7" long, with both pike and sucker body forms. Two spray-painted finishes were available on the sucker model, and one spray-painted finish on the pike model. They were marketed in a two-piece cardboard box marked Ice King (1946 – 1948) (Plate 79).

For Type II, this decoy was hollow plastic with unpainted metal die-cut, screw-attached side fins, and an integral lead ballast. Dorsal and anal fins, gills, mouth, and eyes were integrally molded. Eyes were two-color spray painted. The line tie was a simple eye screw. This 6½" long pike model was available in a variety of spray-painted finishes. It was the only model available with factory-installed cheater hooks. It was marketed in a two-piece cardboard box marked Ice King Spearing Decoy (1948 – 1950) (Plate 80).

Type III, hollow plastic decoys, had integral lead ballast and integrally molded plastic fins, line tie, gills, mouth, and eyes. Eyes were two-color spray painted. A 6" long pike model and a 4¾" and 6" sucker model in a variety of spray-painted finishes were available (1951 – 1983). Also a hollow plastic 5" long sucker with a variety of spray-painted finishes was available. They were marketed in a two-piece cardboard box marked Ice King Spearing Decoy (1960 – 1983) (Plate 82).

For Type IV, these hollow plastic decoys had

Plate 74. Walter Wiitala, one of the founders and the final owner of the Bear Creek Bait Company, with his catch of the day.

51

unpainted metal die-cut screw-attached side fins, and water ballast filling the decoy through holes in the body. Dorsal and anal fins, gill, mouth, and eyes were integrally molded. An 8" perch, 9" sucker, and 10" pike were available in a variety of spray-painted finishes. Eyes were two-color spray painted. The line tie was a simple eye screw. They were marketed in a two-piece cardboard box marked Ice King Spearing Decoy (1960 – 1983) (Plate 83).

The Bear Creek Bait Company went out of business in 1983, and the molds for their decoys were sold to the K & E Tackle Company of Hastings, Michigan. The K & E Tackle Company's history is documented in this chapter on pages 111 – 115, and the company is still successfully marketing the ice decoys throughout the northern states where ice spear fishing is still legal.

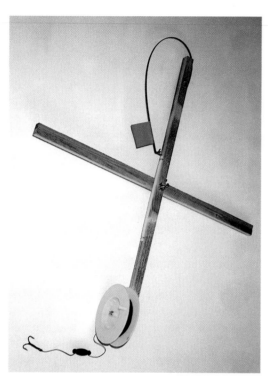

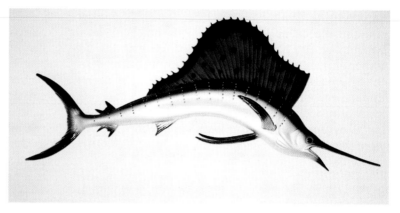

Plate 76. A 16" long solid plastic decorative jumping sailfish plaque, first made by Bear Creek Bait Company for an insurance company to distribute at a Florida convention, circa 1960s.

Plate 75. A Bear Creek Bait Company ice fishing tip-up made of wood, metal, and plastic. Circa 1961 – 1983.

Plate 77. A 4" x 6" x 3" Bear Creek Bait Company, ice shanty reel made of plastic and aluminum, circa 1956 – 1960.

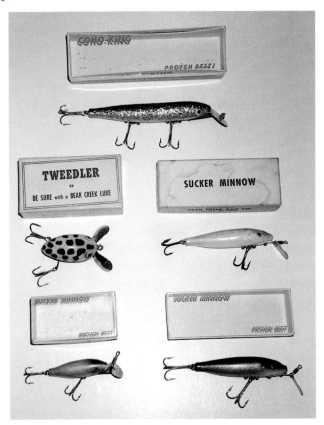

Plate 78. The only fishing lures produced by the Bear Creek Bait Company.

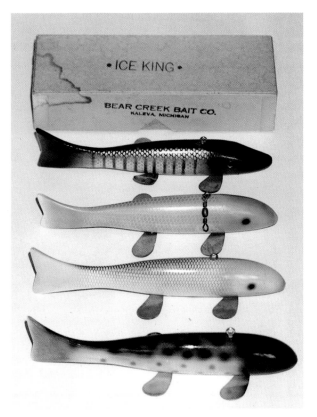

Plate 79. Type I wooden decoys were marketed under the name Ice King and sold in the same box. Top: Pike form in Pike finish. Middle: Sucker form in both orange and gray scale. Bottom: Rare trout form with trout paint.

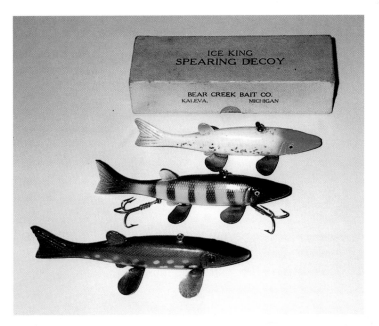

Plate 80. Type II decoys, each with a different finish. Note: The middle decoy has factory installed cheater hooks. Type II decoys were the only type decoy available with the cheater hook option.

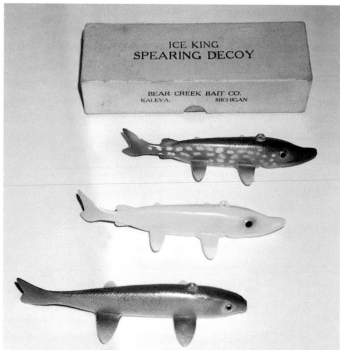

Plate 82. Three plastic Type III sucker decoys, 4¾"

Plate 81. Three plastic Type III decoys, 6" size.

Plate 83. Type IV fish decoys. Top: Pike form and finish. Middle: Sucker form and finish. Bottom: Perch form and finish.

Lawrence Bethel Decoys

The tradition of one of the most famous families of spear fishermen and fish decoy makers in Minnesota is carried on today by Lawrence Bethel (1930 – present) of Lake George, Minnesota, who marketed fish decoys commercially under the name "Bethel's Wooden Spear Decoys" from 1980 through 1990 (Plate 84). Lawrence began making and marketing fish decoys commercially until after the death of his uncle Cyril in 1980, for he did not wish to be in competition with Cyril, a well-known fish guide and fish decoy maker. Lawrence Bethel is an avid spear fisherman, which makes him a natural for designing and making great swimming quality fish-spearing decoys.

The fish decoys marketed commercially under the name Bethel's Wooden Spear Decoy came in three sizes, 6", 9", and 11" long. They were made of basswood in a sleek, generic fish form (Plate 85). The side, dorsal, and anal fins and tails were hand cut with a template from light-gauge metal. The fins were pressed into slits cut into the body, and the tail was nail attached. Lead ballast was poured into an oval-shaped cavity in the frontal belly area. The ballast also functioned to anchor the front side fins. Line ties were two to three U-shaped wires pressed into drilled holes in the frontal back area. Lawrence's wife Maggie hand-painted most of the paint finishes. The perch and trout

style paint patterns and the white body with red head were the most popular sellers. One-color and two-color eyes were flat painted and accented with flat painted eyebrows. The gills and nostrils were also flat painted. All fins, tail, and line ties were painted at the same time as the body.

Lawrence Bethel decoys made since 1983 have a "B" stamped into the wood in the mid-belly area. Packaging for Lawrence Bethel commercially marketed decoys from 1980 through 1990 was a plastic bag with a paper label marked "Bethel's Wooden Spear Decoy, 3rd Generation Decoy Maker, Made in USA" (Plate 86).

In 1990 Lawrence and Maggie Bethel moved to Eglin, Oregon, but still continued to market their decoy through the Carlson Sports International Company located in Sauk Rapids, Minnesota. In 1997 when Maggie Bethel passed away, Lawrence moved back home to Minnesota. Lawrence is still an active, prolific fish decoy maker, taking orders and selling his decoys at sporting collectible shows and by mail order. Special-order working fish-spearing decoys, especially critters such as frogs, crawdads, loons, or beavers, are in demand and can still be special-ordered (Plate 87).

Plate 84. Lawrence Bethel and his wife Maggie, makers of the commercial "Bethel's Wooden Spear Decoys."

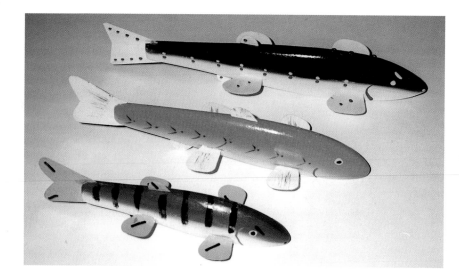

Plate 85. Three beautiful, pristine condition commercial fish decoys by Lawrence Bethel. Top: 11" long, middle: 9" long, bottom: 6" long.

Plate 86. An example of Lawrence Bethel's packaging for commercial sales from 1980 through 1990.

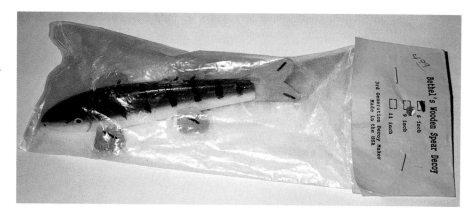

Plate 87. Two examples of special-order working fish-spearing critter decoys. Top: Realistic 9½" long swimming loon decoy. Bottom: Neat 10" long swimming baby beaver decoy.

Blackhawk Enterprises

The Blackhawk (AKA) Vibra-Coy combination fishing lure and fish decoy was first manufactured and marketed by Blackhawk Enterprises in 1951 by Theo "Ted" Himmelwright (1920 – present) of Edgerton, Wisconsin (Plate 88). Ted gives credit for the initial idea of the Blackhawk decoy and lure to George S. Bachay, a sportswriter for the Janesville, Wisconsin, newspaper, *The Gazette*. Because the lore of ice spear fishing in North America was passed from the Native Americans to the white man, Ted decided to name his company and decoy/lure after a Native American tribe that he admired, the Blackhawk (Plate 89). A dental technician by profession, Ted's knowledge of working with many different plastic compositions and water-resistant bonding materials was instrumental in enabling him to develop this hollow plastic, cleverly designed combination lure and fish decoy.

The Blackhawk had two unique features not seen before. The first was rolling or sliding lead or steel ballasts, functional both for submerging the decoy and acting as a noise maker to attract fish. This moving ballast also served to give the decoy a more dynamic swim pattern (Plate 90). The second feature was the capability of bending the plastic tail to a desired shape using the heat generated by holding the decoy in one's hand for a few minutes. With this bent tail, the Blackhawk became a circle-swimming fish-spearing decoy. This warming process could be repeated to straighten the tail to use the fish as a conventional lure, fishing it on a drop line from a boat or dock.

The plastic body of the combination decoy lure was made in two halves by a process called injection molding. The two body sections were made by the Evans Zire Plastics Company in Waunakee, Wisconsin, and shipped to Ted. Each body half had two matching bulkheads which, when bonded together, divided the finished body into three separate water-tight compartments. These hollow compartments served to establish the buoyancy of the decoy when the proper ballast was added to each compartment (Plate 90). The front compartment contained two small rectangular lead weights. The rear compartment contained one larger rectangular lead weight, and the center compartment contained two nickel-plated steel balls functional for ballast, dynamics of swimming, and noise-making attraction. Ted stated that it took a great deal of experimentation with his ballast design to perfect the perfect swimming attitude and desired dynamics and buoyancy. This decoy lure was molded in chub minnow form in only one size, 6½" long. The mouth, eyes, dorsal fin, line tie, and cheater hook tie were integrally molded into the body. The earliest models had a nickel-plated eye screw line tie. The two body halves were bonded together, waterproofing the hollow decoy. Once again, Ted's knowledge of waterproof cements used in dentistry made the choice of a bonding agent easy.

The decoy was then spray painted two colors. Examples have been found in three different paint color finishes, brown back with white belly, black back with a white belly, and red back with a white belly (Plate 89). Eyes were hand painted with either a red or white dot. A removable double hook was added to each lure before being packaged. This hook was designed to be removable to allow ice spear fishermen to use the hookless decoy where it was required by fishing laws. The decoys were marketed in a two-piece cardboard box with a picture on the box top with a brochure included, giving directions of how to fish this versatile combination fish-spearing decoy and conventional fish lure (Plates 89 and 91).

The Blackhawk was manufactured for approximately two years, and during this time about a thousand of these quality versatile combination decoy lures were produced.

Plate 88. Theo "Ted" Himmelwright (1920 – present).

Plate 89. Three examples of Black-hawk decoy lures with a marketing box.

Plate 90. A cut-away view of the Blackhawk decoy lure showing the three hollow compartments with ballast.

Have You ever used a FISH DECOY?

Here's a new way for you to catch more fish and bigger fish. You'll increase your chances of landing a really big lunker every time you go out when you use the "Vibra-Coy."

There's no great secret or mystery surrounding the "Vibra-Coy;" nor is it a novelty in any sense of the word. It's a real fish decoy that sells for only $2.00.

For centuries, Indians have used crude decoys to lure fish to their spears. Old timers have successfully carved decoys from wood for fishing from boats or through the ice. In both cases, the results are the same. More fish for the pan!

In the February 28 issue of SPORTS ILLUSTRATED, read the story on ice fishing—see why the fish decoy is such a great asset to the fisheman.

Now, for the first time, every fisherman can have a decoy . . . the "Vibra-Coy." Manufactured and tested under all conditions, it is modeed after a live chub minnow out of colored durable plastic. It has no hooks. You work it on a drop line or short pole. When in action, it darts, swirls and sends out sound signals that attract the fish. You use a live minnow or any type of live bait (depending on the type of fish you are after) and regular tackle near the "Vibra-Coy." When your fish is attracted in by the action of the "Vibra-Coy," you're ready for him.

Use it from a dock, boat, through the ice, or anywhere—the results are the same—You'll catch more fish—bigger fish— and ALL TYPES OF GAME FISH are attracted by its action.

Send $2.00 now for your "Vibra-Coy." Send check or money order. Sorry, no C. O.D.'s.

BLACKHAWK ENTERPRISES
P. O. Box 188, Edgerton, Wisconsin

Available with hooks in States where "Jigging" is a legal sport.

Plate 91. The advertising brochure from the box for the Blackhawk decoy lure.

Bob's Fly Tying Shop

Very little is known about Bob's Fly Tying Shop, a small manufacturer of fly fishing and spinning tackle and fish-spearing decoys. Bob's Fly Tying Shop was located in Ludington, Michigan, in the west central part of Michigan's Lower Peninsula on Lake Michigan. It is believed that this business existed for only a few years, sometime during the 1950s.

Bob's Fly Tying Shop's wooden-bodied fish decoys have been found in two sizes, 7½" and 8" long. The 7½" size has been found in eight different paint finishes (Plate 92). I have seen only two examples of the 8" long size, which has a different body form, but the same paint pattern as the 7½" decoy. Both body forms are flat bellied and flat sided, but the head shapes are different (Plate 93). All side fins were die cut from light-gauge metal with the front side fins a different shape from the rear side fins. The side fins were pressed into slits cut into the wooden body. The front side fins were anchored into position by the lead ballast, and the rear side fins were nail attached. The tail and dorsal fins were die cut from light-gauge sheet metal and pressed into slits in the back and body tail area and were also nail attached. A small hole was drilled into the rear of the tail. This enabled the decoy to be hung during the painting operation, and it could also be used for adding colored cloth or yarn as an added attractor. Three to six holes were drilled into the dorsal fin for tether line attachment. Ballast was lead poured into two overlapping drilled holes, creating an hourglass shape in the frontal belly area.

Decoys came in eight different, beautiful scale paint finishes. Each decoy was marked with a spray-painted number from No. 1 through No. 8 on the belly (Plate 94). The fine body side scale finishes were multicolored, usually accented with the tail or back color. All side fins, dorsal fins, and tail were painted during the body painting operation. The gills were spray painted flat black. The eyes were two-color hand painted with an accent of black spray painted around them. Most examples found were stamped, MFD. BY BOBS FLY TYING SHOP, LUDINGTON, MICH. (Plate 94).

Plate 92. Four beautiful examples of Bob's Fly Tying Shop's 7½" long fish-spearing decoys.

Plate 93. A body form comparison of Bob's Fly Tying Shop's scarce 8" long fish-spearing decoy to his 7½" long fish-spearing decoy.

Plate 94. A belly view of the identification stamp and color model number stamp on a Bob's Fly Tying Shop fish-spearing decoy. Identification stamp reads MFD. BY BOBS FLY TYING SHOP LUDINGTON, MICH.

Bonafide Manufacturing Company

Hiram H. Passage of Plymouth, Michigan, invented this early versatile casting, trolling, and fish decoy lure, the Bonafide Minnow. It was assigned Patent No. 841,429 on January 15, 1907 (Plate 95). The body of the lure was made of die-cast aluminum in two halves. There were two different models, a three-hook model, 3¼" long, and a five-hook model, 3¾" long. The final assembly contained a front and rear propeller spinner on the five-hook model, but only a front propeller spinner at the front of the three-hook model. Both models contained a hollow cavity to house either buoyant cork material for suspending the lure or a metal ball used in place of the cork for sinking the lure. The metal ball also functioned as a noise-making attractor.

The hooks were designed to be removable when using this minnow-shaped lure as a fish decoy by spear fishermen. A hole was cast or drilled into the integral dorsal fin to allow the spear fisherman to attach his tether line. This was designed on both models, but a few examples of the three-hook model have been found without the dorsal fin hole. A single slotted brass flathead screw at the approximate center body held the two body halves together (Plate 96).

Finish was natural aluminum scale finish, with red painted gills and black painted eyes (Plate 97).

It is hard for me, a retired automotive mechanical engineer, to believe that the technology existed almost a hundred years ago to make these quality aluminum die castings and also to assemble them with the accurate fit and finish seen in the final assembly of all the components of the Bonafide Minnow lure.

The 1907 patent of the Bonafide Minnow states within a portion of its text, "When fishing through the ice for purpose of decoying the fish to bring them within reach of a spear or when fishing with a dropline...." This patent statement substantiates that ice spear fishing was readily being practiced in the early 1900s.

The Bonafide Manufacturing Company also made frog and fish-spearing spears. They came in eight different sizes and were marketed by the dozen, packaged in a tan box with an end label (Plate 98). The finding of this box of 12 unused frog spears, mint in their original box, gives hope to lure collectors that the Bonafide Minnow lure may someday be found in a similar marketing box.

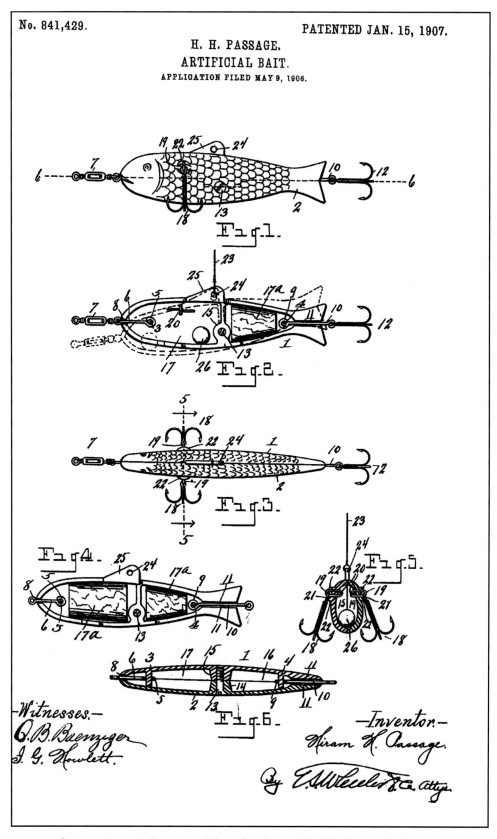

No. 841,429.

PATENTED JAN. 15, 1907.

H. H. PASSAGE.
ARTIFICIAL BAIT.
APPLICATION FILED MAY 9, 1906.

Fig.1.

Fig.2.

Fig.3.

Fig.4.

Fig.5.

Fig.6.

Witnesses.—
O. B. Baenziger
I. G. Howlett.

—Inventor.—
Hiram H. Passage.

By E. M. Wheeler & Co. Attys.

Plate 95. Patent drawing of the 3-hook model of the Bonafide Minnow.

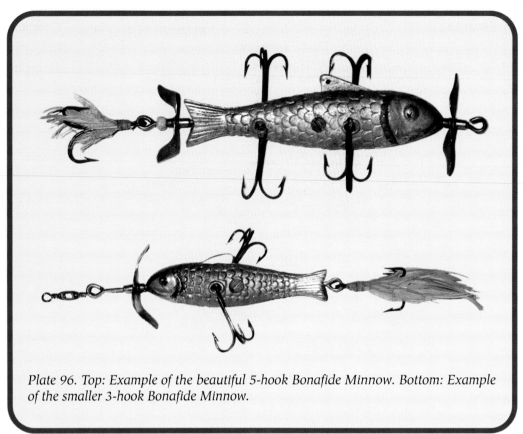

Plate 96. Top: Example of the beautiful 5-hook Bonafide Minnow. Bottom: Example of the smaller 3-hook Bonafide Minnow.

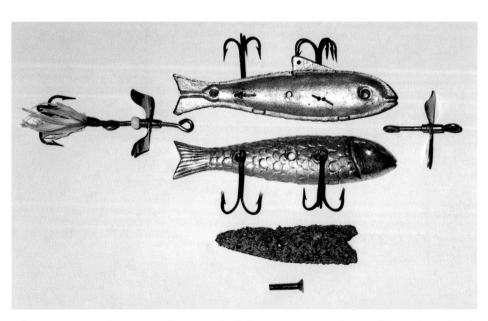

Plate 97. A revealing view showing of all the components that make up the 5-hook Bonafide Minnow. Notice the cork used for buoyancy in this example.

Plate 98. An example of one of 12 new Bonafide Manufacturing Company frog spears with metal sheaths found in this original marketing box.

Boone Bait Company, Inc.

The Boone Bait Company, located in Winter Park, Florida, was founded by Donald F. Boone in 1951 and incorporated on November 1, 1953. Donald Boone was the first president, and Joseph S. Showalter, an equal partner, was the first vice-president of the Boone Bait Company. About 1957 Don Boone and Joe Showalter had a disagreement over company policy, and Boone sold his share of the company named for him. Within a few weeks Don Boone organized a new company named "Don Baits" in nearby Goldenrod, Florida.

The Boone Bait Company grew and flourished, even manufacturing products for long-existing major tackle manufacturing companies like Heddon, South Bend, and Lindy Little Joe. In 1977 the Boone Bait Company made a major decision to focus entirely on salt-water products. The company is still flourishing today, marketing their products worldwide.

It was in the 1957 Boone Bait Company catalog that an ice spear fishing decoy was introduced, called the "Saucy Dancer" (Plate 99). It came in one size only, 6" long, including the long nylon tail (Plate 100).

The head was a molded solid lead fish-head-shaped jig. The tail was light-colored nylon hair, string wrapped to the base of the head. The line tie was a looped wire molded into the top of the head. There were six different finishes, four spray-painted finishes, and two plated finishes. The string wrapping of the nylon tail hair was overpainted on the painted models and unpainted on the plated models. Eyes were two-color hand painted on the painted models, but no eyes were on the plated models.

The Saucy Dancer was marketed on a sales card, and the catalog price was 85 cents (Plate 101). The Saucy Dancer decoy was also modified and marketed as a jig fishing lure by having a single 6/0 hook added to the rear of the head. This jigging lure was named the "King" (Plate 102).

Most people are very surprised to hear of an ice spear fishing decoy having been manufactured in central Florida. This is a testimonial to the versatility and aggressiveness of this southern company seeking growth in the 1950s.

SAUCY DANCER

Hookless Spearing Decoy

Designed specifically for use as a spearing decoy, the SAUCY DANCER combines every powerful attractant to bring the big ones to you. The colors are bright and alluring. Most models incorporate a 'come-hither' bewitched eye. All are tied with a long, dancing nylon tail that undulates invitingly in the water. When you work one of these decoys be ready with your spear.

Weighs 1 oz. Packed 1 dozen to an attractive display card.

Price $.85 each

Number	Color
K-10	Chrome head, red tail
K-11	Gold head, red tail
K-12	Black & yellow striped head, yellow tail
K-13	Yellow and red head, yellow tail
K-14	White and red head, white tail
K-15	Red head, white tail

Boone Bait Co., Inc.   Winter Park, Florida

Plate 99. A 1957 Boone Bait Company catalog advertisement introducing the Saucy Dancer ice spearing decoy.

Plate 100. An example of a Boone Bait Company Saucy Dancer decoy in the beautiful black and yellow striped head paint finish with a yellow tail. Note: This photograph simulates how the Saucy Dancer looks to the fish.

Plate 101. The marketing card of 12 beautiful Boone Bait Company Saucy Dancer decoys.

Plate 102. A 1958 Boone Bait Company catalog advertisement showing the King jig fishing lure and Saucy Dancer fish-spearing decoy.

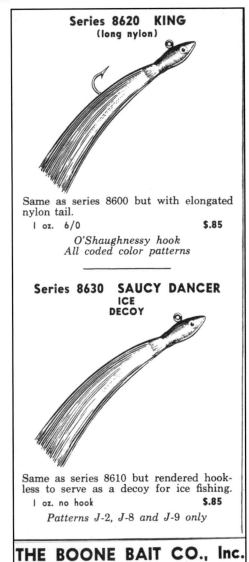

Series 8620 KING
(long nylon)

Same as series 8600 but with elongated nylon tail.
| oz. 6/0   **$.85**

O'Shaughnessy hook
All coded color patterns

Series 8630 SAUCY DANCER
ICE
DECOY

Same as series 8610 but rendered hookless to serve as a decoy for ice fishing.
| oz. no hook   **$.85**
Patterns J-2, J-8 and J-9 only

THE BOONE BAIT CO., Inc.
WINTER PARK, FLORIDA

Brown Brothers "Fisheretto"

In 1910 Sam Brown began making and selling fish lures in the basement of his family home in Osakis, Minnesota. On October 30, 1918, Sam filed for a patent for a fish bait or lure. Patent #1,331,618 was issued to him on February 24, 1920 (Plate 103). This new versatile fishing bait was named the "Fisheretto" and could be used as either a surface or underwater casting or trolling bait (Plate 104).

Sam Brown died in 1925, and his brothers Mike and Ed continued to carry on the lure-making business. The Brown brothers also made fish decoys, which they named "Dark House Fish Decoys." They were 5" long and had been modified from one of the four different Fisheretto casting lure shapes (Plate 105). It can be assumed that these dark house fish decoys were made from the modified convex belly model, machined flat in the belly area for attaching the side fins. Poured lead was used for ballast in both the head and center belly areas.

Side fins and tail were hand cut from galvanized sheet metal. There were two different side fin designs, and both were nail attached. There was one basic tail design. The tail was also nail attached after being inserted into a slit in the center rear of the wood body. The line tie was a simple eye screw at the top of the head or neck areas. Most eyes were either a convex metal washer or flat painted, but a few decoys with glass eyes have been found.

All casting lures and fish-spearing decoys were hand painted, but with some uniformity in different color combinations. Much paint flaking occurred because of galvanization of the metal.

The Brown Brothers business ceased operations in 1945, and the last living brother died in 1960.

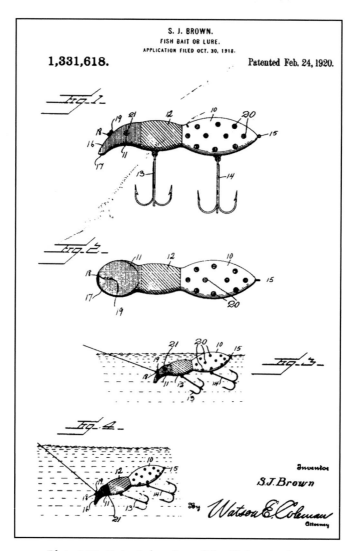

Plate 103. Patent drawing of the Fisheretto lure.

Plate 104. Two beautiful Fisheretto lures. Top: Concave belly model with washer eyes and front spinner. Bottom: Convex belly model with painted eyes and front spinner.

Plate 105. Two Dark House fish decoys. Top: Earliest angel wing side-fin model. Bottom: Model with 4 side fins.

Bru-Ell Decoys Manufacturers

Bru-ell Decoy Manufacturers business in Watkins, Minnesota, was started in 1943 as a joint husband-and-wife operation and still exists successfully today (Plate 106). Both Bruce and Helen Wakefield were born in 1915. They have been married over 65 years and have two sons. The decoy-making business was started out of necessity when Bruce was disabled by an accident and was unable to continue cattle farming and raising minks. The company name Bru-ell was adopted from Bruce's and Helen's names.

Bru-ell decoys are made from cedar wood and come in three sizes, a large 14" size (Plate 107), a medium 7½" size (Plates 108 and 110), and a small 3" inch size (Plate 109). Side fins are die-cut sheet metal on the most popular 7½" size and are template hand-cut sheet metal on the smaller 3" and larger 14" models. The tail component for all models is template hand cut sheet metal. Some examples have been found with side fins and tails of a textured sheet metal material. Side fins and tail are pressed into slits into the body. The tail is then nail attached, and the front set of side fins is secured with the pouring of the lead ballast. Ballast is lead poured into an oval hole at the frontal belly area.

Paint finishes are a variety of two colors of enamel paint, sometimes accented with glitter. Some paint finishes are realistic for a certain species. The side fins are usually painted the same color as the body. Tails on all examples I have seen have been painted silver, except on the smallest model which is painted white. Over the years their most popular seller has been the red and white paint finish, but some of today's best sellers are livelier colors, such as chartreuse or pink combinations. Eyes are off-the-shelf, white convex-shaped thumb tacks with a hand-painted black spot in the center, except the smallest model has no eyes. The line tie is always a nickel-plated eye screw, located in the frontal area of the back.

Bru-ell decoys were marketed in boxes only from about 1945 to 1950 (Plates 108, 109, 110, and 111). Helen Wakefield stated that the decision to drop the marketing boxes was because the decoys seemed to sell just as well without the expense of a box. Bru-ell decoys are distributed through manufacturing representatives and tackle and bait shops.

This author has high admiration for active seniors like Bruce and Helen Wakefield, still pursuing their business interest for some 57 years after its beginning. They are still manufacturing and marketing approximately 3,000 quality fish-spearing decoys annually.

Plate 106. Bruce and Helen Wakefield, founders of Bru-ell Decoy Manufacturers.

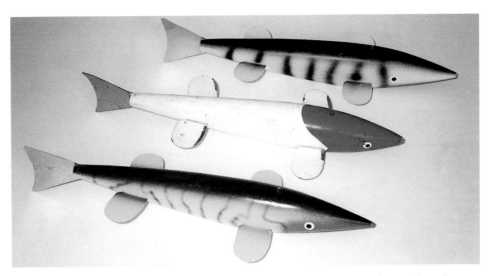

Plate 107. Three 14" long examples of the largest decoys manufactured and marketed by the Bru-ell Decoy Manufacturers.

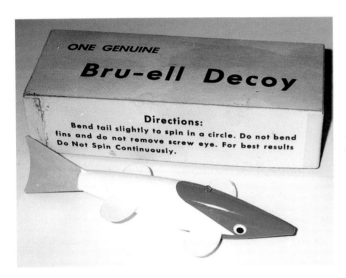

Plate 108. A beautiful 7½" long example of a Bru-ell decoy with the first marketing box used circa 1945.

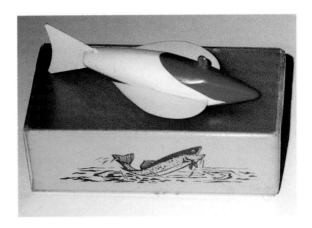

Plate 109. A pristine 2½" long example of the smallest decoy and marketing box manufactured and marketed by the Bru-ell Decoy Manufacturers, circa 1947.

Plate 110. Another mint condition 7½" long example of a Bru-ell decoy with textured metal side fins and tail, with a glitter accented paint finish, and the second marketing box used circa 1947.

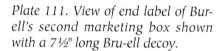

Plate 111. View of end label of Bur-ell's second marketing box shown with a 7½" long Bru-ell decoy.

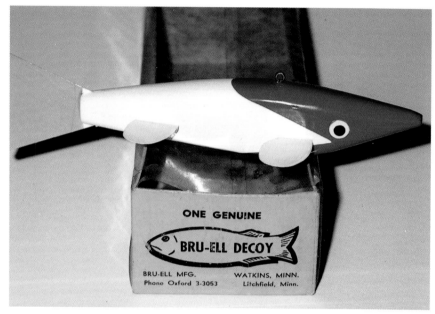

Carl Christiansen Lure Company

The Carl Christiansen Lure Company was formed in 1979 by Carl R. Christiansen (1958 – present) of Newberry, Michigan, a town in the central area of Michigan's Upper Peninsula (Plate 112). Carl, a self-taught carver and artist, realized at a young age that he was gifted with these special talents. As a young-ster Carl spent much time fishing, hunting, trapping, and camping with his father Hans. He also spent many vacations with his uncles Ervin "Butch" Schramm and Henry "Hank" Walters on the north channel of Lake St. Clair, near Algonac, Michigan. Both uncles were revered hunting and fishing guides with a background of market hunting and fishing as young men during the great depression of the 1930s. Carl learned quickly from his dad and uncles, and he

too became a proficient hunter, trapper, and fisher-man. Both Uncle Butch and Uncle Hank were excel-lent carvers and painters, making hundreds of waterfowl decoys, fish decoys, and fishing lures for their thriving guide services in both summer and win-ter. Observing and sometime helping his uncles, Carl soon found himself carving and painting his own decoys and lures at a very young age.

Carl married his wife Vickie of Pickfort, Michigan, in 1978 and had three sons by 1986. With this added responsibility of a family and since work was difficult to find in his area, Carl realized he would need a sta-ble income to give his family the quality of life he wished for them. Fortunately along with his God-given talents of being a gifted carver, artist, and inno-

70

vator, Carl is a very productive craftsman, which, as we all know, requires much patience and perseverance. Initially carving decoys and lures for hunters and fishermen, Carl soon discovered that the majority were going on to collectors' shelves, and even more frequently he was asked to do commissions of wildlife carvings and whimsical folk art creations for his clientele. Carl decided to establish a line of working commercial fish decoys and to make 30 different species in 3 different sizes. This decision was made because at that time only one manufacturer of fish decoys was still in Michigan, the K & E Company of Hastings, documented in this chapter on pages 111 – 114. Carl felt he could still take orders for his fishing lures and custom carvings from time to time as a needed change of pace.

Carl's first line of fish decoys had metal tails, but later decoys had wooden tails, because collectors seemed to prefer them (Plate 113). The added touch of a custom wooden slide-top box made by Carl's dad, Hans, also a craftsman, was admittedly done for marketing Carl's decoys to the collecting fraternity (Plate 114). The evolution of Carl's decoy design from a metal tail to wooden tail with only a slight change in form and paint makes his earliest work easy to recognize. Carl takes pride in the fact that his working decoys are and always have been designed and carved primarily for the fishermen. Collectors have complimented Carl by seeking the decoys for their aesthetic beauty.

The Carl Christiansen Lure Company (1979 – present) can be closely compared with the legendary Oscar Peterson's business in Cadillac, Michigan, 1920s – 1950s. Oscar Peterson was a prolific fish decoy and folk art carver for some 50 years. Carl, like Oscar, is a self-taught innovator, artist, and carver. Carl keeps his company on a small scale, choosing not to contract with outside distributors, keeping the business as somewhat a labor of love. Oscar Peterson's folk art, many one-of-a-kind creations, is highly sought after and commands large prices. Carl's many unique folk art creations are also prized and highly sought after by collectors (Plates 115, 116, and 117). I believe that Carl Christiansen is carrying on the traditions of the legendary masters such as Oscar Peterson, Bud Stewart, and his uncles Butch Schramm and Hank Walters.

Plate 112. Carl Christiansen with a dynamic 7-foot carving of a tiger muskie eating a perch.

Plate 113. Three early trout spearing decoys with metal tails by Carl Christiansen.

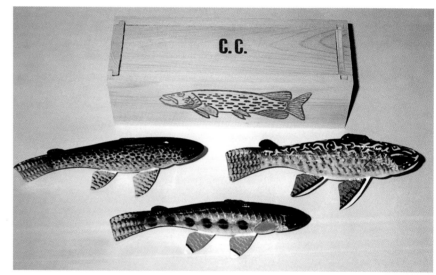

Plate 114. Three working trout fish-spearing decoys with wooden tail shown with a Hans Christiansen custom cedar wood slide-top box.

Plate 115. Four large whimsical bug fishing lures special ordered by a lure collector.

Plate 116. Lathe-turned, relief-carved flower vases, (upper right and left) pencil holder, (lower right) and toothpick holder (lower left) by Carl Christiansen.

Plate 117. Wooden fishing tackle box by Carl with incredible relief carvings of nine different freshwater fish on the top.

Creek Chub Bait Company

The Creek Chub Bait Company of Garrett, Indiana, was one of the earliest fishing tackle manufacturers in North America, founded in 1906 and operating more than 70 years.

One of the rarest lures produced by this early fishing lure manufacturer is their non-catalogued ice decoy (Plate 118). It is believed that the few examples known were produced in the 1920s. The body of the ice decoy was the same as the body of the Creek Chub Bait Company's Fintail Shiner lure, first produced in 1924. The Fintail Shiner is 3¾" long, with glass eyes, and the earliest models had cloth pectoral fins, dorsal fins, and tail (Plate 119). The fish decoy body utilized the same dorsal and tail fin cuts, but housed a die-cut metal dorsal fin and die-cut metal tail. No holes were drilled into the ice decoy body for the two belly hooks or line tie used for the Fintail Shiner, but for some unknown reason the slit for housing the diving lip

plate was cut into these decoy bodies. The decoy also had two small die-cut metal pectoral side fins. Ballast was lead poured into round holes drilled in the belly. The ice fishing decoy has glass eyes. Some of the Creek Chub Bait Company catalogued paint finishes which were first used on the Fintail Shiner lures have been found on the ice decoy. Most ice fishing decoy examples have been found with the red side scale finish, but some examples have been found with perch scale finish, and I have seen one example with golden shiner finish (Plate 120). A number of fish decoys have been found in a Creek Chub Bait Company fishing lure marketing box but have no catalog identification number which is typically stamped on the end of the marketing boxes (Plate 118).

There is evidence that the Creek Chub Bait Company experimented with developing an ice decoy in the early years of the company. A quality ice decoy

73

made from the Creek Chub Bait Company's first marketed lure, the "Wiggler," was discovered with the purchase of one of the earliest known fishing lure collections (Plate 121). The Walton collection was started in 1909, and was purchased in 1990 by longtime collector and historian Dan Basore. Much research into the Creek Chub Bait Company history and discussions with the last of the company's retired management led to the conclusion that the fish-spearing decoy found in the Walton collection was probably the Creek Chub Bait Company's earliest prototype of an ice spearing fish decoy.

In 1966 the Creek Chub Bait Company introduced a small 2", two-piece, die-cut metal jigging lure. (Plate 122). Although only advertised as a spin-cast-

ing jig bait, it was also used by ice fishermen as a jigging lure, and as an ice fishing decoy (Plate 123). Four holes were punched into the metal body. The front hole functioned as a simulated eye, the center hole in the dorsal fin was for a line tie, and the belly and tail holes allowed the attachment of removable hooks. The lure came in two plated finishes, catalogued 11-S silver and 11-G gold. The snap-on metal belly plate was always painted bright red. The front and rear double hooks were of the removable type. "Creek Chub" is prominently stamped on one side of the body. It was marketed in a clear plastic box with a brochure (Plate 122). This neat little minnow-shaped lure is also showcased in Chapter 2 (Plate 39).

Plate 118. The rare Creek Chub Bait Company's ice decoy in red side scale finish and its marketing box.

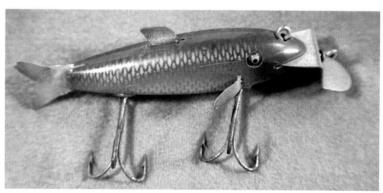

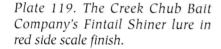
Plate 119. The Creek Chub Bait Company's Fintail Shiner lure in red side scale finish.

Plate 120. The Creek Chub Bait Company's ice decoy in the scarce perch scale finish.

Plate 121. Ice decoy from the Walton collection at bottom is believed to be an early Chub Chub Bait Company prototype ice decoy. It was made from an early no. 100 Wiggler like the example shown at top, also from the Walton collection.

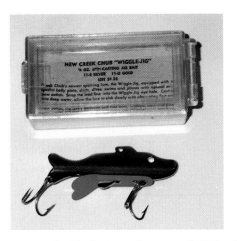

Plate 122. Creek Chub Bait Company's Wiggle-Jig lure with brochure and marketing box.

Plate 123. The Creek Chub Bait Company's Wiggle-Jig lure rigged by an ice spear fisherman to be used as an ice decoy.

Cy's Decoys

Cy's Fish-Spearing Decoys were manufactured and marketed by Cyrus D. "Cy" Halvorson (1905 – 1971) of Willmar, Minnesota (Plate 124). Through the years Halvorson was a sporting goods distributor, manager of The White House hamburger stand in Willmar, and an employee of the Great Northern Railroad. In 1954 he opened a sporting goods store called Cy's Tackle Box, also located in Willmar, which he operated until the time of his death in 1971.

Cy's wooden fish decoys were made in his home workshop. Most decoys found are 6" and 7½" long, but a few large examples 12" to 16" long have been found (Plates 125 – 129). Side fins were die cut from light-gauge metal, and the tails were hand cut to a template from a heavier gauge metal. All side fins and the tail were pressed into slits in the body and then nail attached. Ballast was lead poured into drilled

holes into the frontal belly area. Paint finishes, which included the side fins and tail, were of a variety of two-color spray-painted patterns, including some scale patterns. Some paint patterns were accented with glitter (Plate 128). Eyes usually were white or yellow painted thumb tacks accented with a hand-painted black dot in the center. Examples have also been found with black and white flat-painted eyes. Line ties were simple eye screws. Cy's Decoys have been found in two different marketing boxes. It is not known which of these boxes is the earliest. The red and white picture box is hand marked with a price of $1.35 (Plate 129).

Old-timers in Willmar recall seeing Cy Halvorson traveling the local route of bait, tackle, and sporting goods stores, merchandising his fish-spearing decoys from his station wagon which had a 4-foot wooden

fish decoy mounted on the roof as an advertisement. With Halvorson's many business ventures and his clever advertising ideas, he should be admired as one of our early entrepreneurs. Cy Halvorson's fish decoy business ended about 1963.

Plate 124. Cy Halvorson (left) and fishing partner Cliff Slore with four nice northern pike speared on Norway Lake, Minnesota, in 1946.

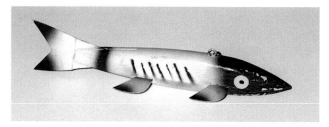

Plate 125. An example of Cy Halvorson's small 6" long fish-spearing decoy.

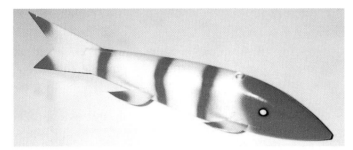

Plate 126. A beautiful 7½" long example of a Cy Halvorson fish-spearing decoy.

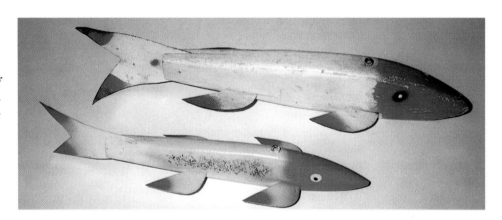

Plate 127. Two examples of large Cy Halvorson fish-spearing decoys. Top: Largest known 14" long, and bottom: 12" long.

Plate 128. Cy's Fish Decoys had a clever advertising slogan, "Made By a Fisherman–For a Fisherman." This is a 7½" example with a scale-accented finish and the marketing box showing the slogan.

Plate 129. This 7½" long example of a Cy Halvorson fish-spearing decoy has no scale pattern on the body. Notice the price of $1.35 marked on the plain marketing box.

Detroit Bait Company

It is believed that the Detroit Bait Company of Detroit, Michigan, started in business about 1920 with the filing of a patent for an artificial fishing bait eventually named the "ABC Minnow." This cleverly designed lure led to the successful marketing of other conventional fishing lures and an ice-spear fishing decoy. Patent No. 1,477,864 was granted to a man named George W. Bolton of Detroit, Michigan, who was sole owner of the Detroit Bait Company (Plate 131).

The initial patented ABC Minnow was a 5" long wooden, glass-eyed, round-nosed, three treble-hooked floating fishing bait with six interchangeable different colored backs (Plate 130). A diver model of the ABC Minnow was accomplished by simply cutting the nose area of the floater at a 45° angle. The glass eyes were left off this model and it had only two treble hooks. The ABC Simplex Minnow fishing bait and the ABC Ice Decoy were made from the initial wooden lathe-turned body of the ABC Minnow (Plate 132). The Simplex Minnow lure had a die-cut metal tail inserted into a vertical slit cut into the rear end of the body and then nail attached. A second method for attaching the tail was to screw the tail to the body (Plate 133). The overall length of the Simplex Minnow, including the metal tail, was 5". The ABC Minnow fish

decoy has been found in three sizes, 5", 6¼", and 8" (Plates 133 and 134). The metal tail and the way it was attached were the same for the ABC Ice Decoy and the ABC Simplex Minnow.

The ABC Ice Decoy is found with two side fins on the 5" size and four side fins on the 6½" and 8" sizes. Each metal side fin was hand cut to a template and had an upstanding flange with two drilled holes for screw attachment to the body. Ballast was lead poured into a single large drilled hole in the frontal body area. Line ties have been found with both a simple eye screw with a flat washer and an inch worm-type, die cut and shaped from light-gauge metal, giving the spear fisherman three different tether line-attaching areas (Plate 133). The glass eyes are quality fishing lure type. Paint finish is always white body with a red head. Side fins and tails are usually painted body color white, but examples have been found unpainted (Plate 133, top).

It is not known whether George W. Bolton sold the Detroit Bait Company or sold interest in his company. Marketing advertisements of the ABC Minnow have been found under two other company names, ABC Bait & Mfg. Co. and Detroit Sporting Good Co. The last known advertisement of the ABC Minnow was dated 1937.

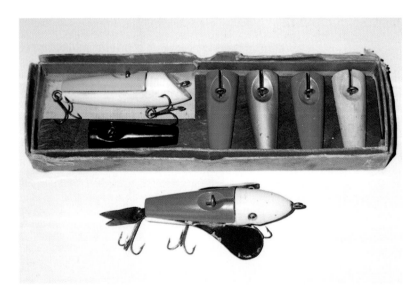

Plate 130. Two examples of the ABC Minnow Lure. Top: The underwater model in a marketing box with six different color interchangeable backs. Bottom: The floater model. The added metal side fins and tail component made by a fisherman turned this floating fishing lure into a jigging lure or fish-spearing decoy with cheater hooks.

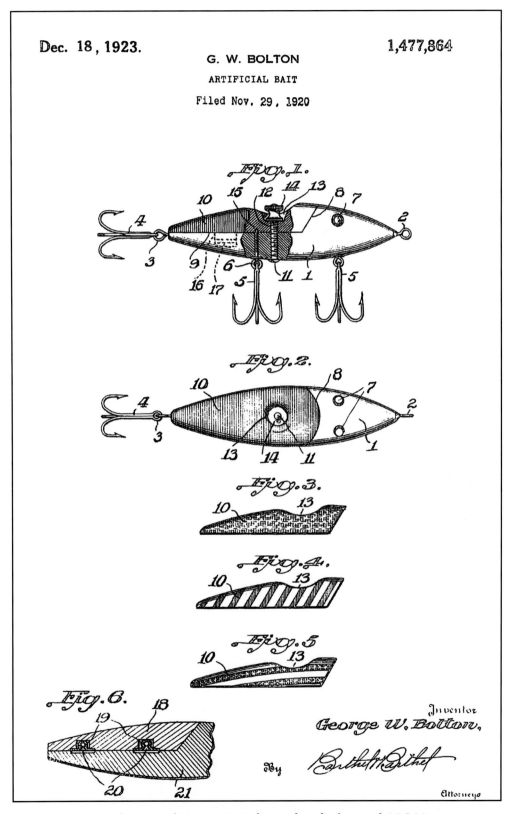

Plate 131. Patent drawing of George W. Bolton's cleverly designed ABC Minnow.

Plate 132. Notice that the ABC Minnow fish decoy (top) has no hooks, but the ABC Simplex fishing lure, (bottom) has two treble hooks and no side fins.

Plate 133. Top: Example of a 5" long ABC Ice Decoy with screw-attached tail, two unpainted side fins, and an inch worm-type line tie. Bottom: Example of a 6¼" long ABC Ice Decoy with an inserted nail-attached tail, four painted side fins, and an eye screw and washer line tie.

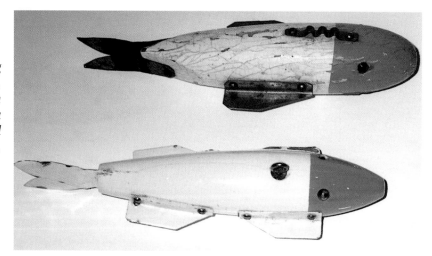

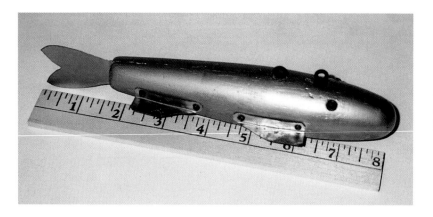

Plate 134. An example of the rare 8" long ABC Ice Decoy in solid gold paint finish.

Franklin Discher Decoys

Franklin Discher was born in 1906 in Port Austin, Michigan, located on Lake Huron on Saginaw Bay (Plate 135). He was a hunter and fisherman all of his life. In 1935 he moved to Bay City, Michigan, a larger city also located on Saginaw Bay about 50 miles southwest of Port Austin. It was in that year that Discher began making fish decoys. All of his decoys were made from white pine. Most of the wood came from discarded wooden shipping pallets from the Bay City General Motors Chevrolet auto plant where he worked.

All Franklin Discher decoys are patterned after the shape of a smelt. There are four sizes: 3¾", 4", 5" and 6½", with some small length variations. Forms of the four different sizes show great uniformity in proportions (Plate 136). Fins were usually made of tin, hand cut to templates, with the two smallest sizes. Sometimes the 5" size had two side fins and a small fin located on the back just in front of the start of the tail. The largest size decoy and sometimes the 5" decoy have a five-fin pattern, with two more side fins near the front of the tail. The high location of all side fins give Franklin Discher decoys an upside-down look.

Discher painted his decoys with at least ten different color combinations, using enamel paint. Most decoys had either three or four colors. The base body color is either silver or white. The heads are a different color from the frontal area of the belly and the base body color. The gills are accented in a different color, and the flat-painted eyes and open mouth were also painted in another color. These bright multicolored decoys were unique to Michigan decoys of that time period. Ballast was lead poured into a rectangular-shaped hole in the belly, then filed and sanded to the convex shape of the belly.

It is estimated that Franklin Discher marketed several thousand decoys from 1935 to 1950 at outlets from Port Austin and around the complete shoreline of Saginaw Bay, all the way to Ossinike, Michigan, on the northeastern shore of Lake Huron. A large wholesale hardware company in Bay City, Michigan, distributed the decoys statewide.

In 1939, both commercial and sport fishermen from the Midwest came to Saginaw Bay to fish for the most prevalent fish, the walleye. By 1941, their catches had decreased by about 90%. The fishermen then turned to fishing by hook and line for perch, and their spearing decoys were put aside. With this declining sale of his fish decoys, Franklin became frustrated with his business and turned to other interests. Still Franklin Discher decoys were popular enough to remain on the market until 1950. Discher died in 1985, never knowing the desirability of his sleek, superb swimming Saginaw Bay attractors in the fish decoy collecting world.

Plate 135. Franklin Discher (1906 – 1985).

Plate 136. A great group of four-colored Franklin Discher fish decoys showing four different sizes.

Duey's Decoys

Duane "Duey" Johnston, born in 1934, is the founder and sole owner of Duey's Decoys of New York Mills, Minnesota (Plate 137). This venture was formed in 1989 when Johnston was unemployed, and he admits that his company was born out of necessity to stay alive. With expertise gained starting at the age of 12 when he began ice spear fishing with his grandfather on Detroit Lake and continuing for many years, Johnston developed his great line of ice spear fishing decoys. He turned two rooms of his house into workshops and today has difficulty keeping up with orders from both large sport shops and individual sportsmen. The decoys are sold to sporting good outlets and bait dealers in Minnesota, Michigan, North Dakota, and Wisconsin.

Today Duey's Decoys offer 26 different models, including his creation of a rattling model, his best seller (Plate 138). A hollow chamber in the decoy's belly area contains a few BB shot, and this added feature make his decoys that much more deadly. The addition of spinners, flashers, and plastic curly tails also serve to make Duey's decoys more dynamic attractors.

Johnston's wife Nancy paints the decoys. Each may receive anywhere from five to nine coats of paint. An all-metal decoy was designed and marketed for about a year in the early 1990s, but Duey's wooden models are more popular, so the metal design was dropped from his inventory (Plate 139). As Duey's packaging label states, a challenge is presented to the customer that if he spears a fish 14 pounds or larger, he is given a free Duey's decoy. This promotion costs Duey about 35 decoys each year, testifying to the success of the decoys (Plate 140).

In this modern era of high tech mass production, we are fortunate to have a product that, although deemed commercial, makes the buyer feel that each Duey's decoy purchased was custom made especially for him or her.

Plate 137. Duey Johnston at work in his shop.

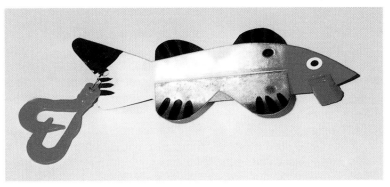

Plate 139. Duey Johnston's metal decoy with plastic curly tail attractor.

Plate 138. Duey Johnston's rattling decoys with metal flasher attractors.

DUEY'S DECOYS

MINNESOTA'S FINEST • DEPENDABLE • DURABLE • DEADLY

Rt. 2, Box 252, New York Mills, Minnesota 56567

7" CRAPPIE

Handcrafted In Minnesota From Native Pine

ENJOY A GREATER FISHING EXPERIENCE WITH A DUEY RATTLE DECOY.

Congratulations & Thank You for purchasing a **DUEY DECOY**. These decoys are tested in Northern Minnesota by FISHERMEN; and are the result of over 40 years of spearing and research. Enjoy the lively action with moving parts, bright colors, and today's progressive designs. **(Over)**

The rear fins can be adjusted for "Dive" or "Sail". For more dive, turn the rear of the fins down. For less dive or sail, turn the rear of the fins up. The bent tail gives you a small or large circle. Do **NOT** adjust the front fins. NOT PREADJUSTED.

When you spear a fish 14 lbs. or over, mail me a picture of the fish *with the decoy. Include this tag* with the picture, and I will forward a free decoy. *Limit 1. May be used for promotions.*
Enjoy fishing and good luck.

Phone
218-837-5024

Duey Johnston

DECOY DUEY

Hang this decoy with a small finish nail thru the tailhole.

Help Preserve Spearing - Join The Minnesota Darkhouse and Angling Association

CAUTION: Large fish (northern pike, muskie, 30 lbs. plus) have been known to attack this lure! Not for use by timid fisherfolk! Serious trophy hunters only!

TAKE OUR YOUTH FISHING & TEACH CONSERVATION

Plate 140. Duey's Decoys packaging label, with fishermen's challenge.

Edson's Fish Lures

The "Fish Fooler," a combination casting, trolling, and fish decoy lure, was invented by Madison Edson of Grayling, Michigan (Plate 141). Madison Edson was born in 1906 and grew up in northwestern Michigan. He was employed by the famous Bear Archery Company in Grayling, Michigan, for over 20 years, and was instrumental in the development of their aluminum target and hunting arrows. An avid fisherman and hunter as a young man, he quickly learned what it took to fool fish into biting. In the early 1950s Madison invented and started manufacturing the Fish Fooler.

The Fish Fooler body was made from four separate components that were die cut from aluminum sheet stock. It came in only one size, 5⅝" long, and was fish-shaped, jointed with two split rings at about center to hold the front and rear sections together, and cleverly designed also to limit the amount of their movement. Three treble hooks were attached with split rings, two at the middle area of the front side component, and one at the top area of the tail. The eyes were a flattened split shot sometimes painted red. The Fish Fooler had four drilled or punched holes at the head area. These were for line attachments for casting, trolling, jigging, or ice spear fishing (Plate 142). When the rearmost hole was used as a line tie and the treble hooks were removed, the Fish Fooler made a dynamic swimming fish decoy in a relatively horizontal attitude (Plate 143). The Fish Fooler was machined to a shiny random texture aluminum finish, which refracted much when it was in the water.

The Fish Fooler was marketed in a tan-colored two-piece cardboard box with a brochure at a cost of $2.00 (Plates 142 and 144). The Fish Fooler was marked "EDSON'S FISH FOOLER PAT.APPLD.FOR," but a patent has not yet been found.

Plate 141. Madison Edson (1906 – 1965).

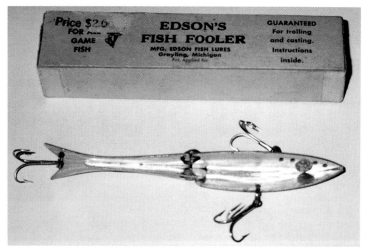

Plate 142. The Fish Fooler lure with marketing box.

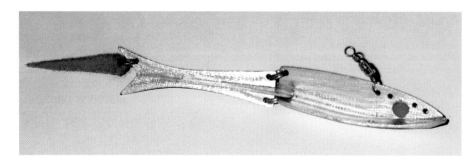

Plate 143. The painted eye model rigged as an attractor for ice spear fishing as found in an ice fisherman's decoy box.

Through tests made by average fishermen, Edson's Fish Fooler is believed to be the greatest fish fooler ever invented. With a little practice one gets the natural action of a live minnow. Best results are obtained by drifting and easing along and over weed beds. Do not try to work Lure too fast. After the cast, move your rod forward, swing back to starting point and reel up line. This gives Lure a chance to go down. Then Repeat. Lure can be skipped on the surface to simulate feeding minnows. When trolling for trout in deep water, wire line will take Lure to proper depth — If water current is too swift use a trolling triangle and weight about six feet from Lure.

For fishing in rivers where current is steady, fish the deep holes by weighing line so weight rests on the bottom. Lure will work and stay above the bottom. BE SURE AND USE A GOOD LINE AND LEADER.

Good Luck and More Fish

EDSON FISH LURES,
Grayling, Michigan

P. S. —— Edson's fishing contest pays off. Take a picture of your catch, mail it to Edson's Fishing Contest, Grayling, Michigan, and get entry blanks.

Plate 144. The Fish Fooler box brochure.

Enterprise Manufacturing Company/Pflueger Bait Company

One of the largest early manufacturers of quality fishing tackle in North America was the Enterprise Manufacturing Company of Akron, Ohio. Ernest F. Pflueger and Ferdinard Schumacher co-founded the company in 1881. Both company names, Enterprise Manufacturing Company and Pflueger Bait Company, are synonymous with quality products from this prolific tackle manufacturer, backed by many historical references.

The first documentation of a fish-spearing decoy in fish form was sometime between 1887 and 1892. This decoy was molded in solid rubber and came in four sizes, 2", 2½", 3", and 7". These were exactly the same as the "Admiral" and the "Muskallonge Trolling Minnow" lures manufactured by the Enterprise Company. They undoubtedly shared common molds with the fish spearing decoys (Plates 145 and 146).

The ballast of the fish decoys was internal, and the line tie was a wire form at the front of the dorsal fin anchored into the ballast. The earliest models had integral molded pectoral and anal fins, and in 1898 a one-piece die-cut metal side fin was added at the front molded pectoral fin area through a slit cut into the lower front of the body (Plates 147, 148, and 149). This side fin addition was designed to give the decoy a more controllable swimming mode. The quality multicolor blended paint finish over the realistic detailed molded fish form made these decoys look alive in the water. Molded protruding eyes were painted two colors, a yellow or a white pupil with a black iris. These decoys were also marketed in both a luminous silver paint finish and a non-luminous silver paint finish

(Plate 150). These silver paint finish decoys seem to be much scarcer than the multicolor realistic paint finish decoys. The 2", 2½", and 3" decoys were packed one dozen per box. The 7" model came in its own box, a solid maroon-colored, two-piece cardboard box with an identifying end label (Plate 151).

An advertisement of a non-fish-form fish decoy device appeared in the 1900 catalog and was called "Pflueger's Fishing Castle." This spherical wire cage was hinged and held minnows or other live bait plus a light. A number of fishing lines were attached with hooks for live bait or artificial hooked baits. The patent drawing for this unique fishing decoy is shown in Plate 2.

The first catalog advertisement of a wooden fish spearing decoy was found in the 1905 catalog (Plate 147). The catalog mentions two sizes, 3½" and 5" in length. The 5" decoy is shown in Plate 152 but no examples of the smaller 3½" size have yet been found. A note indicated that the wooden decoys were not carried in stock but would be made to order. Because these early wooden fish decoys were a special order item only, they are quite rare. It is believed that the larger red cedar decoy body was also used as the body of the circa 1911, five-hook Monarch Underwater Muskallonge Minnow lure with modification. This modification was achieved by leaving material at the rear of the body during the lathe body-shaping operation, creating a longer body length (Plate 153).

The decoy had no side fins. A die-cut metal tail was inserted into a slit cut into the tail area and was attached with a single brass pin. The tail was painted

the same color as the body. Ballast lead was poured into holes drilled in the belly area. The eyes were glass-eyed fishing lure type. Some decoys had a green back blending to a silver belly, and others had a plain solid silver paint finish. Both models had three hand-painted gill marks. The line tie was a simple eye screw. The 3½" models were packaged one dozen to a box, and the 5" model came in its own box. This was probably the same style two-piece maroon cardboard box that was used to market the solid rubber decoy. I have not seen an example of this box with an end label for a red cedar body ice decoy, but some surely must exist.

A few rare examples of a frog fish-spearing decoy made by the Enterprise Manufacturing Company that were not in their catalog have been found. This critter decoy has the same body as the 3" Satin Cork casting frog lure that was first introduced in their 1900 catalog (Plate 154). The wire extending through the lure body that served as dual-function line tie and hook hanger, along with the hooks, was left off the casting lure and was replaced for the ice decoy with a lead weight for ballast at the center of the belly, and a wire form line tie in the middle of the back, which allows the attachment of a tether line for swimming the ice decoy. Paint finish was a hand-painted realistic natural frog finish. This rare item was not catalogued and probably like the red cedar fish-spearing decoy was a special-order item only (Plate 154).

The record of this prolific manufacturer of quality fishing tackle of all types is unsurpassed. The Enterprise Manufacturing Company/Pflueger Bait Company were innovators in the world of both fresh and salt water fishing tackle in their 80 years of existence before going out of business in 1972.

Plate 145. The 2" "Admiral" lure (No. 7) from the Enterprise Manufacturing Company.

Plate 146. The 7" Muskallonge Trolling Minnow lure (No. 819) from the Enterprise Manufacturing Company.

PFLUEGER ARCTIC-DECOY MINNOW

Used principally for fishing through the ice and are ballasted and constructed to dart when pulling on the line to which they are attached and which is done to attract the fish.

PRICE EACH

No.		Sizes, Inches	3⅝	5	7
*862	Red Cedar Body—Silver Belly—Green Back		.75	1.00	....
949	Soft Rubber Body—Silver Belly—Green Back		...	....	1.25

Packed—Wrapped in silver tissue paper and one in a fancy card box.

NOTICE—This mark * preceding the Stock Number, Name, Size or Price of the article indicates goods NOT carried in stock, but will be made to order.

See **Page 4** for our Unlimited Guarantee on *PFLUEGER BULL DOG* Brand Goods.

Plate 147. An advertisement for an Enterprise Manufacturing Company, Pflueger fish-spearing decoy with the added metal side fins.

Plate 148. Two beautiful, pristine condition examples of Enterprise Manufacturing Company fish-spearing decoys. Bottom: Earliest finless model, circa 1887 – 1892. Top: Later metal side-fin model, circa 1898.

Plate 149. Top: Pflueger Monarch Underwater Muskallonge Minnow lure. Bottom: Pflueger fish spearing decoy which used the same rubber molded body.

Pflueger's Fish Spearing Decoy Minnows

MADE OF PURE SOFT RUBBER

	Sizes........	2	2½	3	7
No. 947 Luminous Soft Rubber, Decorated......................					
" 948 " " " Plain Silver......................					
" 949 Non-Luminous, Soft Rubber, Decorated					
" 950 " " " " Plain Silver....					

Packed—Sizes 2, 2½ and 3 inch, one dozen in a box, 7 inch one in a box.

MADE OF CEDAR WOOD, WATERPROOFED

	Sizes	3½	5
No. 860 Luminous, Cedar Wood, Decorated			
" 861 " " " Plain Silver....			
" 862 Non-Luminous, Cedar Wood, Decorated...			
" 863 " " " " Plain Silver...			

Packed—Size 3½ inch, one dozen in a box, 5 inch one in a box.

The above scene represents a fisherman in his movable "dark house" in the act of spearing fish through the ice, using a Decoy Minnow. The Decoy is painted true to life, and being weighted and balanced with a lead core it dances merrily by simply pulling on the line to which it is tied. It furnishes great sport to those that indulge in this class of fishing.

Plate 150. An advertisement from an Enterprise Manufacturing Company catalog showing all models, sizes, and color finishes of Pflueger fish-spearing decoys marketed.

Plate 151. The marketing box end label for a No. 949, 7", non-luminous finish fish-spearing decoy.

Plate 152. Model 862 fish-spearing decoy in the 5" size. The red cedar body has a green back and silver belly paint finish.

Plate 153. Top: Pflueger fish-spearing decoy. Bottom: Pflueger Monarch Underwater Muskallonge Minnow lure.

Plate 154. Top: Pflueger Satin Cork Frog lure. Bottom: Non-catalogued Pflueger frog fish-spearing decoy.

Fish Bust'r

Very little is known about the origin of the "Fish Bust'r" fish-spearing decoy (Plate 155). It was distributed by a division of P & F Products, Incorporated, located in Crosby, Minnesota. The estimated time period of these decoys is the 1960s. They were marketed in a clear plastic bag with an orange paper label (Plate 156). The Fish Bust'r decoys next appeared in a clear plastic bag with a white paper label and were marketed from a post office box in Baxter, Minnesota, which is located about 20 miles southwest of Crosby in central Minnesota (Plate 157).

The Fish Bust'r decoys came in three sizes, 5", 7", and 9" long (Plate 155). They are very simple in design, flat on all four sides, made from rectangular

shelf stock. The head and tail areas were band sawed and sanded to shape. The front and rear side fins and tail components were one-piece sheet metal hand cut to a template and then nail attached. Ballast was lead poured into a oval-shaped cavity in the frontal belly area. Paint finishes were two colors spray painted and always finished with gold or silver glitter. Eyes were hand painted with two colors. The line tie was a simple eye screw always located in the head area.

The author hopes that the origin of the Fish Bust'r can be better documented from readers' knowledge of this fairly recent but little-known Minnesota fish-spearing decoy.

Plate 155. Three examples of the Fish Bust'r fish spearing decoy Top: 9" long; middle: 7" long, bottom; 5" long.

Plate 156. The packaging of the Fish Bust'r decoy with the P & F Products Inc., Crosby, Minnesota label.

Plate 157. The packaging of the Fish Bust'r decoy with the Baxter, Minnesota post office box label.

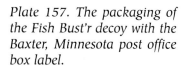

James Heddon's Sons Company

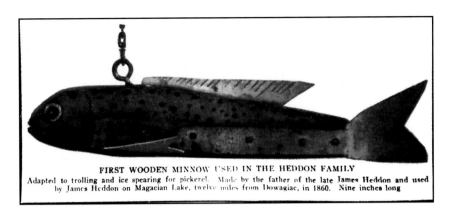

FIRST WOODEN MINNOW USED IN THE HEDDON FAMILY
Adapted to trolling and ice spearing for pickerel. Made by the father of the late James Heddon and used by James Heddon on Magacian Lake, twelve miles from Dowagiac, in 1860. Nine inches long

Fig. 158. This illustration was published in the American Angler, Vol. 3, #1, May 1918.

There is documentation of the Heddon family making ice decoys in the 1860s. The sight of fish attracted to decoys and their willingness to attack them led to the next logical step of attaching hooks to these minnow-shaped lures, and the Heddon company was born (Plate 158). The Heddon Company began in 1902 with Jim Heddon and his two sons, Charles and William, working out of their home in Dowagiac, Michigan (Plate 159). Soon the Heddons relocated, renting a floor in a downtown building in Dowagiac. By 1907 a new larger operation was needed. Their operation enlarged and expanded many times until 1983, when the company was finally sold to the Pradco Bait Company of Fort Smith, Arkansas, and relocated there, where today it is still a flourishing business.

Today Heddon Company lures have become the most popular company sought by fishing lure collectors. The availability of this company's products, the romance of its origin, the aesthetic beauty in both form and paint patterns, and the highest quality of craftsmanship are all instrumental in attracting thousands of collectors.

The spearing decoys manufactured by the Heddon Company follow an evolution of design with seven different models being manufactured from 1913 until 1935. I have listed these seven decoys in their order of design and my rationale for their subtle and major redesigns in the life of the Heddon Company spearing decoys. It is significant to note that the design changes in form, paint patterns, and colors are the means to identifying the seven different decoys manufactured during the life of the Heddon Company at Dowagiac, Michigan. The six wooden models of these decoys, Period 1 through Period 5A, were predominantly made from both red and white cedar wood, but some of the earliest models were made

from gum wood. The buoyancy of these woods can be slightly different and vary from tree to tree. Therefore the number of concealed belly weights (ballast) in most Heddon decoys ranges from three to six. The function of the lead ballast is to make the decoy sink in the water in a relative horizontal attitude but to have a near neutral buoyancy for sensitivity in swimming in the water. The seventh model, Period 6, the last decoy manufactured by the Heddon Company, was made from early plastic, with steel and lead components.

Fig. 159. James Heddon (1845 – 1911), founder of the Heddon Company.

Plate 160. Period 1, "The Woodtail Fourpoint" in fancy mottled green back with white belly finish.

Period 1

The Woodtail Fourpoint, circa 1912, 5½" overall length, has glass eyes. All examples found have hand-painted gill marks, single eye screw line tie with a box swivel, nickel-plated brass dorsal fin, anal fin, and side fins. Fins have been found unmarked but have also been found marked in script "Heddon's Dowagiac" (Plate 160). Colors are fancy molded green back with white belly and imitation early vertical bar perch. The earliest reference for this first Heddon decoy was found in a February 1913 *Hunter, Trapper, Trader* magazine (Plate 161). This early advertisement showed only two side fins, but most examples found have four side fins, thus the terminology "The Woodtail Sixpoint" commonly used by collectors (Plate 162). There is no documentation of a Heddon Company box for this decoy at this time. It can be assumed the initial two- or four-side fin design was revised to the Batwing design for Period 2 to allow the decoy to be fished in a more dynamic swimming mode.

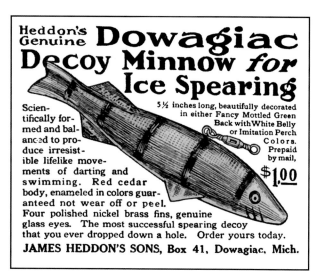

Plate 161. Advertisement from Hunter, Trapper, Trader magazine, February 1913, for "The Woodtail Fourpoint."

Plate 162. Side view of Period 1 "Woodtail Sixpoint" in imitation vertical bar perch finish.

Period 2

The woodtail batwing, commonly referred to by collectors as "The Woodtail Batwing," circa 1913, is 5¼" in overall length with glass eyes. All examples have been found both with and without hand-painted gill marks, single line tie, nickel-plated brass dorsal and anal fins and pinned two-positioned adjustable nickel-plated bass side fins, giving the fishermen the ability to change the glide pattern and speed of the decoy while it is being swum during spear fishing (Plates 163 and 164). Side fins are marked in script "Heddon's Dowagiac." Colors are fancy mottled green back with white belly and imitation vertical slant bar perch (Plate 165).

There is documentation of a Heddon Company box for this decoy. The box is marked ICE-L on the end, and the top has a downward diving bass (Plate 166). The decoy was issued in 1912. It was believed that the revision of the design of the Woodtail Batwing (Period 2) was due to an unacceptable scrap rate during manufacturing because of the coarse grain of the cedar wood bodies at the fragile wooden tail area. Replacing the wooden tail with a light-gauge metal pinned tail designed for Period 3 gave the fisherman the ability to adjust the swim pattern by bending the curve of the tail. This allowed the decoy to be swum in either a wide or a tight circle.

Plate 163. Side and bottom views of Period 2 "Woodtail Batwing" in vertical bar imitation perch finish.

Plate 164. "The Woodtail Batwing" with side fins in the maximum outward adjusted position.

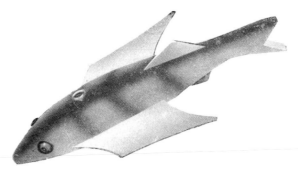

HEDDON'S "DOWAGIAC" DECOY ICE MINNOW
For Fishing through the Ice

Length over all 5¼ inches; weight 2 1-2 ounces. Has metal fin on either side and at top and bottom, of nickeled and polished brass. Made of Wood, with twisted tail, which gives it a decidedly lifelike swimming motion when raised and lowered in the water. Has glass eyes and is enameled and finished with the same excellence of the Heddon's Bass Minnows. Finished in either Fancy Green back with White belly or imitation Perch colors.

Plate 165. Early catalog advertisement of Period 2 "The Woodtail Batwing" in vertical bar imitation perch finish from 1913 H.H. Michaelson of New York, New York sporting goods catalog.

Plate 166. Two-piece diving bass cardboard box marked ICE L for Periods 2, 3, and 4 ice decoys.

Period 3

The pinned metal-tailed batwing, referred to by collectors as "The Pintail Batwing," circa 1916, is 5⅜" in overall length, with glass eyes (Plate 167). All examples found have hand-painted gill marks, and a new four-looped pigtail line tie, giving the fisherman the ability to have greater maneuverability while swimming the decoy. The decoy has flanged, nickel-plated, brass screw-attached batwing-type side fins. The side fins are marked in script, "Heddon's Dowagiac." The colors are fancy mottled green back with white belly and imitation slant bar perch. The box for this decoy is assumed to be the same as for the Period 2 decoy, although at this time I have no documentation of one being found. It is believed that changing the attaching mode of the nickel-plated brass metal tail component from insertion into a vertical slit with a pin at the rear center of the tail area in the body to a two-split flanged metal tail, with a four-screw attachment design, for Period 4 was introduced to reduce the scrap rate during manufacturing.

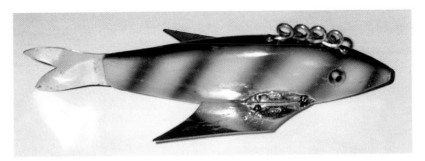

Plate 167. Period 3 "The Pintail Batwing" in imitation slant bar perch finish.

Period 4

The split metal-tail batwing, commonly referred to by collectors as "The Metal Tail Batwing," circa 1917, is 5⅜" in overall length, with glass eyes, three or four looped pigtail line ties, and flanged screw-attached, nickel-plated brass batwing-type side fins (Plate 168). Side fins are marked in script "Heddon's Dowagiac." The nickel-plated brass tail is no longer put into a slot in the body. It has been split to have two flanges that are screwed to the outside of the body with two screws on each side of the body. Colors are fancy mottled green back with white belly and imitation slant bar perch. Once again the box for this decoy can be assumed to be the same as for Period 3 and 4 (Plate 169). This decoy has been found in a number of colors not catalogued for this ice decoy (Plates 170 and 171). Examples have been found both with and without hand-painted gill marks. It is believed that the revision of the batwing-type side fins to the "Fourpoint" design, Period 5, simplified the design and lowered manufacturing cost, since there were no longer unique left and right side fins required.

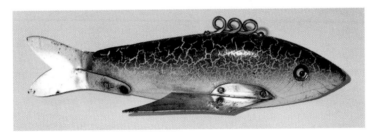

Plate 168. Period 4 "The Splittail Batwing" in fancy mottled green back with white belly.

Plate 169. Rare hi-box (1⁹⁄₁₆" in height), only one known to exist. Box is marked ICE MINNOW YELLOW-PERCH, found with slant bar imitation perch decoy shown in Plate 170.

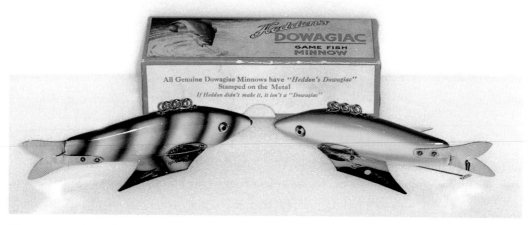

Plate 170. Slant bar imitation perch (left) and Rainbow (special order color) Splittail Batwing decoys with hi-box.

Plate 171. Period 4 "The Splittail Batwing" in a special-order Heddon color, green scale finish.

Period 5

The split metal-tail fourpoint, No. 400 series, referred to by collectors as "The Metal-Tail Fourpoint," circa 1920, is 5⅜" in overall length and has glass eyes, an inch worm line tie, new flanged, screw-attached, nickel-plated brass fourpoint type side fins. Side fins are marked in script, "Heddon's Dowagiac" (Plate 172). The new fourpoint-type side fin design was initially designed and introduced for the model 1600 Deep Diving Wiggler in 1915 (Plate 173). Using this hardware led to substantial tooling cost and complexity savings for the company. The split nickel-plated brass tail has the same design and attaching mode as the Period 4 tail design. The colors were fancy mottled green cracked back, rainbow, green scale, and yellow perch. Shiner scale finish was added in 1925 and white body with red eyes, perch scale, and natural scale finishes were added in 1927 (Plates 174 and 175). This decoy has been found in a number of Heddon Company colors not catalogued for this decoy (Plate 176). Examples have been found both with and without hand-painted gill marks. The box for this decoy has been found in both the upward jumping and downward diving bass style boxes, marked with the 400 series (Plates 176 and 177). A few early examples of this decoy in vertical bar perch scale finish have also been found in these same boxes, but are marked ICE-L.

No. 400 Series "Ice Decoy"

No. 400 SERIES—Ice decoy minnow for spearing. Best attractor ever devised for spearing through the ice. Tail may be bent to control circular swimming. Body length 4½ in. Weight 8½ oz. In the following select colors:

400	Green cracked back.	409D	Green scale.
401	Rainbow.	409L	Perch Scale.
402	White body, red eyes.	409P	Shiner Scale.
409A	Yellow Perch.	409R	Natural scale.

Dozen $18.00

Plate 172. A 1927 Heddon advertisement for the Period 5 "The Metaltail Fourpoint" ice decoy.

Plate 173. Installation comparison of Metaltail Fourpoint side fin hardware on the No. 400 "Ice Decoy" versus the No. 1600 "Deep Diving Wiggler."

Plate 174. Complete color set of "The Metal Tail Fourpoint" ice decoys and the two different style boxes in which they were marketed.

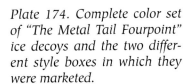

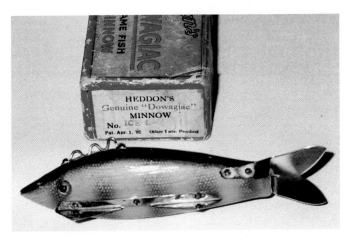

Plate 175. Period 4 The Splittail Batwing in the first version of Heddon's early perch scale with two-piece diving bass cardboard box in which it was found.

Plate 176. "The Metal Tail Fourpoint" in Goldfish scale finish, a special-order color with original box.

Fig. 177. Two-piece jumping bass box with a generic label for the Period 5 ice decoy.

Plate 178. This picture depicts the evolution of the form, hardware, and imitation perch pattern from Period 2 (top) to Period 5 (bottom).

Period 5A

The Split Metal Tail Fourpoint hardware on a No. 4 Heddon modified Coast Minnow body is referred to by collectors as "The Musky Decoy," circa 1920, is 6" in overall length, with glass eyes (Plates 179 and 180). Examples have been found both with and without hand-painted gill marks, inch worm line tie, and flanged screw-attached nickel-plated brass fourpoint-type side fins. Side fins are marked in script, "Heddon's Dowagiac." The split nickel-plated brass tail is the same design and attaching mode as the Period 5 tail design. Colors are assumed to be the same as for the split metal tailed fourpoint, although only some of the eight catalogued colors have been found. No documentation of a Heddon Company box for this decoy has been found at this time.

Plate 179. "Coast Minnow" No. 4, 5" in overall length, introduced in 1914, in yellow, red, and green spot finish.

Plate 180. "The Musky" decoy (top) in perch scale finish and the "The Metal Tail Fourpoint" (bottom) in perch scale finish.

Period 6

The Spook, No. 450, referred to by collectors as "The Spook Decoy," circa 1931, is 5" in overall length and is made of molded plastic, with painted eyes, a hole through the body line tie, and flanged rivet-attached stainless steel side fin and tail component (Plate 181). Side fins and tail are unmarked. The oval-shaped, screw-attached lead ballast base is always painted in a green crackleback finish and is always marked "Heddon Ice Spook" on the bottom. Colors are white and red, perch scale, shiner scale, and natural scale. Gill areas on this decoy are painted red blush on all found examples. The box for this decoy is the same as that for period 5 except that the box is marked No. 450 series (Plates 182 and 183).

Plate 181. "The Ice Spook" decoy in shiner scale finish (top) and natural scale finish (bottom).

Plate 182. Two-piece jumping bass cardboard box for Period 6 ice decoy.

Heddon "ICE-SPOOK"—No. 450 Series

To Swim in a circle:- Bend Tail-Flukes right or left.
To Dive Shallow:- Bend tips of Horizontal Fins slightly upward.
To Dive Deep:— Bend tips of Horizontal Fins downward.
Combinations of different actions can be obtained by experimenting with different bending fin and tail.

Length 5 in. Weight 2 oz.

Made in colors:
452 White and Red   459P Shiner Scale
459L Perch Scale   459R Natural Scale

James Heddon's Sons, Dowagiac, Michigan

Printed in U. S. A.   Patents pending on both mechanical features and material.

Heddon "ICE-SPOOK"—No. 450 Series

True "Fish-Flesh" Appearance

Transparent and Indestructible in Construction and Finish

Here's an Ice Decoy that you can make cut all kinds of luring capers to bring the big ones to your spear. Just bend slightly, the tips of the horizontal fins, or the tail-flukes, at different angles, and you have a real "performer."

The "ICE-SPOOK" will dive deep or shallow; will swim in a circle, right or left, wide or narrow; and even dive and rise in a spiral. Fins are of Stainless Steel, and give an enduring flashing lure to the bait. They are guaranteed not to break.

(See instructions on other side)

Plate 183. The front and back sides of "The Ice Spook" box brochure.

Here are two examples of Heddon lures in fish form that with a slight modification would have been great fish decoys. These casting lures are among some of the most popular with Heddon collectors.

Plate 184. "Black Sucker" No. 1300, 5¾" in overall length, black sucker finish, introduction date 1911.

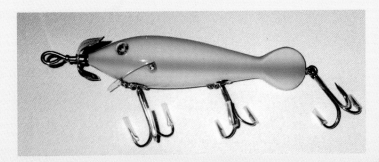

Plate 185. "Spindiver" No. 3000, 4½" in overall length, rainbow finish, introduction date 1918.

Herter's Inc.

George Herter incorporated the Herter's Company from a small fly-tying supply operation sometime during the 1930s. It became a major distribution firm of sporting items, mailing over a million catalogs annually and filling 3,000 to 4,000 orders per day. Six retail stores were located in the Midwest, with the headquarters in Waseca, Minnesota.

The Herter's catalog, unlike most sporting supply catalogs that simply listed products and prices, also gave detailed instructions on how to achieve the best results using their products. Products were also accompanied by many customer testimonials and great photographs of successful results. A number of examples of the Herter's Company's marketing descriptions are in Chapter 2.

Fish decoys were only advertised in the Herter's 1964 and 1965 catalogs. It has been documented that the Randall Decoy Company supplied the Herter's

Company with their fish spearing decoys. They were supplied in two different lengths with four different color patterns (Plate 186). Several other high quality commercial decoys have been attributed as being marketed by Herter's Inc., but no documentation to substantiate the origin of these decoys has been found at this time (Plate 187).

The Herter's Company was a major supplier for fishermen, hunters, trappers, taxidermists, and gunsmiths for over 40 years. When competition from larger retail stores led to declining sales, the company was sold to a investment firm in 1977. Today the Herter's trademark is held by Northern Hydraulics, which is also a hunting and fishing supplier with its main facility located in Beaver Dam, Wisconsin. They presently operate retail stores in Minnesota.

HERTER'S SPEAR HOUSE SPEARING DECOYS

All Herter spearing decoys are hand made and hand painted. We make only the tried

and proven models and finishes selected from our many years of spearing experience.

All decoys are made from selected wood specially treated for lasting finish. The fins are a die cast alloy that can be bent to change the action. Bend the back fin down slightly for fast or up for slow.

Colors: (1) Red head white body (3) Orange body black spotted (4) Tiger (5) Perch. Shpg. wt. 1 lb. each.

No.	Length	Each	Per 3	Per 12
AK7N	8"	$1.02	$2.90	$10.92
AK7N1	10"	1.20	3.41	12.78

Plate 186. A 1965 Herter's, Inc. catalog advertisement for 2 sizes of fish-spearing decoys in 4 different color finishes.

Plate 187. Top: Two examples of quality commercially made decoys that have been attributed to the Herter's Company. Bottom: Another quality decoy that has been attributed to the Herter's Company.

Hoseney Woodcarvings

The Hoseney Woodcarvings Company was founded by Donald Hoseney (1934 – 1988) of Washington, Michigan (Plate 188). Don started his company in 1986 as a part-time venture while still working for General Motors Automotive Company as an industrial illustrator. With a full retirement in sight within a couple of years, Don's plan was to work semi-retired making fishing lures and fish decoys as a labor of love. A fatal illness in 1988 canceled his dream.

Don's October 1986 catalog reveals the versatility in his carvings of both fish and critter lures and decoys (Plates 189, 190, and 191). A custom dovetailed wooden slide-top box with Don's company logo and matching decoy or lure serialized number could be ordered for an additional cost (Plates 192, 193 and 194). Like the legendary master lure and decoy carver Bud Stewart of Flint, Michigan, Don advertised to custom carve and paint any lure or decoy the fisherman designed. Don very much admired the versatile Stewart. Stewart's accomplishments are also documented on pages 155 – 159. Don also collected Bud's work and was intrigued by his famous early folk-art period spotted paint finish (Plate 293). After years of experimenting, Don perfected the process and introduced his "Albino Spotted Frog" fish spearing decoy (Plate 195). These are some of the scarcest of Don's lures, for like Bud Stewart lures, every spot had to be individually painted, which was very time consuming.

Don's frog fish-spearing decoys and casting frog lures are considered by many fish lure and fish decoy collectors as the ultimate frog lures to collect (Plates 195, 196, and 197). The scarcest catalogued items made by Don were the mouse fish spearing decoy, the spotted Albino frog fish decoy, and the diving bufflehead duck fish spearing decoy (Plates 195, 198, and 199). Because they were only made on a part-time basis for a few short years, Don Hoseney's fishing lures and decoys are highly prized by collectors everywhere.

Plate 188. Donald Hoseney (1934 – 1988).

OCTOBER 1986

MY CARVINGS ARE MY OWN DESIGNS AND ARE SIGNED, NUMBERED AND REGISTERED IN THE OWNER'S NAME. THE FLYROD LURES AND 2⅜ INCH FISH DECOY ARE ONLY SIGNED AND REGISTERED. ALL ITEMS ARE CARVED IN ONE PIECE.

I WILL CARVE ON ORDER ANY ITEM A COLLECTOR WANTS.

THE BOXES ARE MADE OF SOLID WOOD WITH JOINTED CORNERS AND SLIDING COVER LIKE THE OLD ONES. THE COVER LOGO WILL INCLUDE THE NUMBER OF THE FROG OR NAME OF THE LURE. THE BOXES ARE AVAILABLE IN VARIOUS SIZES FOR ALL CARVINGS EXCEPT THE LARGE FISH DECOYS.

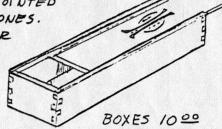

BOXES 10⁰⁰

FROG DECOYS

THE FROG DECOYS ARE MADE AS WORKING DECOYS, LEAD WEIGHTED AND FINISHED WITH VARNISH.

THE SMALL FROG, MODEL B AND MODEL KB IN STANDARD PAINT IS GREEN WITH WHITE BELLY AND BLACK SPOTS, ALSO AVAILABLE IN SPECIAL ORDER COLORS.
THE OPTIONAL GLASS EYES ARE TAXIDERMIST GLASS FROG EYES.

SMALL FROG
4 IN PAINTED EYE 40⁰⁰
5 IN PAINTED EYE 60⁰⁰
GLASS EYES 25⁰⁰

MODEL B 8 INCH
100⁰⁰ PAINTED EYE
125⁰⁰ GLASS EYES
BOX 10⁰⁰

MODEL KB 7¾ INCH
125⁰⁰ PAINTED EYE
150⁰⁰ GLASS EYES
BOX 10⁰⁰

THE "ALBINO SPOTTED FROG" HAS A WHITE BODY WITH NATURAL LOOKING BLACK SPOTS – A SPECIAL FINISH – AND IS AVAILABLE IN TWO SIZES. THE GLASS EYES ARE STANDARD AND ARE FISHING PLUG TYPE EYES.

5 INCH 100⁰⁰

8 INCH 150⁰⁰

MORE ITEMS ON THE BACK

Plate 189. Hoseney Woodcarvings catalog October 1986, page 1.

FISH DECOYS

THE FISH DECOYS ARE CARVED AND PAINTED REALISTICALLY WITH CURVED BODY AND TAIL. ALL HAVE TAXIDERMIST GLASS EYES. THEY ARE MADE AS WORKING DECOYS WITH METAL FINS AND LEAD-WEIGHTED. FOR DISPLAY THEY CAN BE SUSPENDED BY HOLES IN THE TOP FIN OR SIT UPRIGHT ON ITS FLAT BELLY.

- PUMPKINSEED 6 INCH 150⁰⁰
- WALLEYE 11 INCH 160⁰⁰
- LARGEMOUTH BASS 11 INCH 160⁰⁰
- BROOK TROUT 10 INCH 175⁰⁰

THE 2³⁄₈ INCH FISH DECOY IS A RAINBOW TROUT WITH METAL SIDE FINS, CURVED BODY AND TAIL AND WEIGHTED WITH LEAD.
PRICE 25⁰⁰   WOOD BOX 10⁰⁰

MOUSE DECOY

150⁰⁰

THE MOUSE DECOY IS 5 INCHES LONG HAS A BROWN-BLACK BACK AND WHITE BELLY, BLACK GLASS BEAD EYES, LEATHER EARS & TAIL, MONO WHISKERS AND SEPERATE FRONT LEGS WHICH ARE ATTACHED WITH BRASS "L" RIG HARDWARE. LEAD WEIGHTED.

FLYROD LURES

FROG 25⁰⁰
BLACK BEAD EYES
GREEN OR SPOTTED
BROWN

MOUSE 25⁰⁰
BROWN W/BLACK BEAD EYES
WHITE W/RED BEAD EYES

MINNOWS 20⁰⁰
• PUMPKIN SEED
• PERCH
• RAINBOW TROUT

TURTLE 30⁰⁰
"SPECIAL SPOTTED" SHELL
YELLOW & GREEN
W/ YELLOW BEAD EYES

THANKS
Don Hoseney

Plate 190. Hoseney Woodcarvings catalog October 1986, page 2.

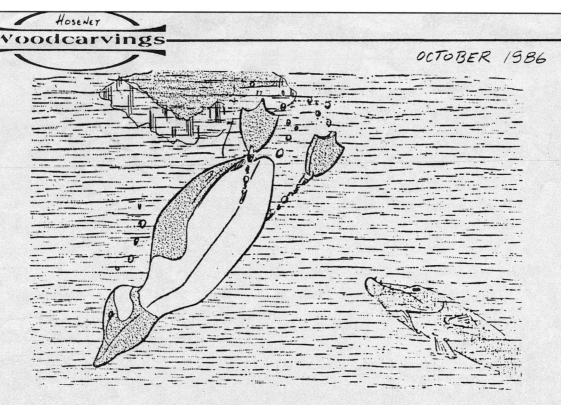

OCTOBER 1986

THE DIVING DUCK SPEARING DECOY

Considered by some collectors as "The Ultimate Decoy" the Bufflehead Duck original is a crossover between duck shooting decoys and fish spearing decoys. The original is featured in the Kimball's Book "The Fish Decoy".

The rarity of this one-of-a-kind decoy warrants reproducing. To protect the value of the original this copy is slightly smaller in size, bill to tail 10¼ inches. Details of the original, carving technique, incised markings, hardware and painting have been carefully reproduced. Each decoy is signed, numbered and registered in the owner's name. The body is carved of basswood and the feet of hard maple. A wire hanger to suspend the duck and feet in diving position is included.

PRICE $180⁰⁰

THANKS
Don

— **DON HOSENEY** • 60812 Waschull Drive • Washington, Michigan • 48094 • Phone (313) 781-3872 —

Plate 191. Hoseney Woodcarvings catalog October 1986, page 3.

Plate 192. *Custom wooden serial numbered boxes and mouse lures.*

Plate 193. *Custom wooden serial numbered boxes and frog lures.*

Plate 194. *Hoseney Woodcarvings custom wooden serial numbered box with matching serial numbered 6-inch Brown Trout fish decoy.*

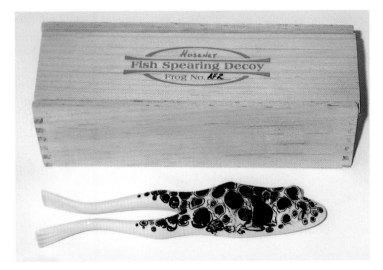

Plate 195. *Hoseney Woodcarvings 5" "Albino Spotted Frog" fish spearing decoy with matching serial numbered marketing box.*

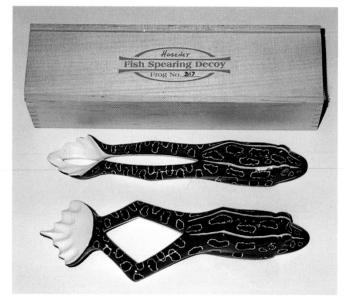

Plate 196. Hoseney Woodcarvings 8" gliding and 7¾" kicking frog fish spearing decoy with serial numbered marketing box.

Plate 197. Hoseney Woodcarvings special-order 8" gliding frog fish spearing decoy in a beautiful white and red spotted paint finish.

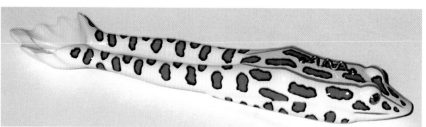

Plate 198. Top and bottom views of Hoseney Woodcarvings rare 5" signed and serial numbered mouse fish spearing decoy.

Plate 199. Hoseney Woodcarvings unique 10¼" diving bufflehead duck fish-spearing decoy. The idea for this unique diving duck fish-spearing decoy came from the original made and used in 1940 by the legendary Lake St. Clair, Michigan spear fisherman Gordon "Pecor" Fox of Mt. Clemens, Michigan. Top picture shows bufflehead in diving position with wire form made by Don Hoseney and marketed with each decoy for collector's display.

Jenkins Decoys

The provenance of the beautiful fish spearing decoys known as the Jenkins Decoys is documented only by word of mouth. Veteran collectors of fishing-related items in the state of Iowa attribute their origin to a man with the last name of Jenkins who resided in Marshalltown, Iowa. It is believed the Jenkins decoys were mostly made and marketed in the 1940s. Fish spearing has never been legal in Iowa, so most of the Jenkins decoys were probably marketed in Minnesota, where spearing fishing is legal and a very popular winter sport. Many Iowans go to Minnesota to fish in both summer and winter.

The Jenkins decoys have been found in only one size, 5¾" long (Plate 200). The wooden body has a flat bottom and is of a generic fish form. Four side fins, dorsal fins, and the tail were hand cut from a template of light-gauge metal. The side, dorsal, and tail fins were pressed into slits cut into the wood body, with the front side fins anchored by the lead ballast. The rear side fins and tail were nail attached. Ballast was lead poured into an oval-shaped cavity in the frontal belly area. The line tie is a U-shaped wire pressed into drilled holes in the frontal back area.

Paint finishes are a combination of spray painting and hand painting. The body and all fins and tail were spray painted the base decoy color. The head, the tips of all five fins, the body side slashes, the spots beneath the side fins, three spots on the belly, and

stippling on the tail were all hand painted (Plate 201). The eyes were two colors, black and white, hand painted. Examples of the Jenkins decoys have been found in only one paint pattern, but in four different color combinations (Plate 200). One solid-color painted example with thumb tack eyes has been found (Plate 202).

It is the author's hope that more information will be forthcoming about this beautiful, quality-made commercial fish-spearing decoy produced in the non-spear-fishing state of Iowa.

Plate 200. Three examples of the Jenkins fish decoy in three different color paint finishes.

Plate 201. A view of the beautiful combination spray painted and hand-painted Jenkins fish decoy showing both the side and the bottom.

Plate 202. An example of a tack-eyed Jenkins fish decoy with a solid color paint finish.

K & E Tackle, Inc.

The K & E Tackle, Inc. name was officially incorporated in 1969, but the company was really born in the late 1950s. Kenneth "Ken" Sprague (1933 – present) of Hastings, Michigan, designed and produced lures for himself and his friends in the basement of his home. By the late 1960s K & E Tackle, named for Ken and his wife Evelyn, began selling their lures through a Michigan sporting goods distributor. By 1969 their business had grown to a point where Ken had to make a decision between the fishing tackle business and his job as a machinist. He decided to take his chance in the fishing tackle manufacturing business, producing lures full-time. His wife Evelyn assisted him in all phases of the business. Through the 1970s the company expanded their line of lures as their popularity grew throughout the Great Lakes and upper Midwest.

In 1983 the K & E Tackle Inc. made its first major acquisition when it purchased the assets of the Bear Creek Bait Company of Kaleva, Michigan. The Bear Creek name along with their popular high-quality ice spearing decoys and related ice fishing items became a division of the K & E company. The history of the Bear Creek Bait Company founded in 1946 is documented earlier in this chapter.

The decoys being produced by the Bear Creek Bait Company at the time of the K & E company purchase were the Type III and Type IV noted in the Bear Creek Bait Company history (Plate 203). The Type III Bear Creek Bait Company models, which are presently being produced by the K & E company, are a 4¾" long sucker and a 6" long pike. All are hollow plastic with integral solid plastic side fins and have an integral lead ballast and are marketed in a variety of color finishes (Plate 204). The Type III 6" sucker model first marketed by the Bear Creek Bait Company was also

produced and marketed by the K & E company until sometime during the year 2000. With the wearing of the tooling in the side fin area, the K & E company produced a small number of Type III sucker decoys with die-cut metal side fins (Plate 205). This metal side fin model was produced only for a short time and is no longer available. The Type IV Bear Creek Bait Company models presently being produced come in three different body forms. An 8" long perch is available in a variety of paint finishes, natural large mouth bass, natural rainbow trout, and natural brown trout paint finishes. Both a 9" long sucker and a 10" long pike come in a variety of paint finishes. All of these hollow-bodied decoys have screw-attached die-cut metal side fins. The ballast is achieved by the water that fills the decoy through holes in the body when the decoy is submerged (Plate 206). These decoys are marketed in a plastic bag with a printed paper label (Plate 207).

K & E Tackle has acquired many more companies producing both salt and freshwater fishing lures and tackle since buying the Bear Creek Bait Company in 1983. Recently the "STOPPER" name was added to the original K & E name. The K & E/Stopper Tackle Company now produces over one million ice lures a year, as well as a wide variety of open water lures and related items. K & E/Stopper was the first manufacturer to sell ice spear fishing decoys on the Internet. These popular, effective decoys can be seen by visiting www.stopperlures.com.

Ken and Evelyn Sprague retired from the business in 1998 (Plate 208). Their three children continue to work at the K & E/Stopper Tackle Company, carrying on the family tradition.

All our Bear Creek spearing decoys are hand assembled and painted for the highest quality available today. We use our popular epoxy coating as a finishing touch to insure that the paint will remain intact for years of spearing pleasure with your favorite style. All decoys are poly bagged with a header and are available in the following sizes and colors:

6" PIKE
PLASTIC FINS

ORDER NO.	COLOR
S-10	Natural Pike Finish
S-20	Red Head Finish
S-30	Perch Finish
S-31	Fluorescent Finish
S-32	Pearl/Pink Eye Finish

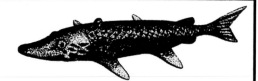

6" SUCKER
METAL FINS

ORDER NO.	COLOR
S-50	Natural S...
S-60	...
S-7(..)	...ish Finish
S-71(..)	Fluorescent Finish

NOT AVAILABLE

8" PERCH
METAL FINS

ORDER NO.	COLOR
S-40	Natural Perch Finish
S-41	Red Perch Finish
S-42	Fluorescent Finish
S-48	Glow

9" SUCKER
METAL FINS

ORDER NO.	COLOR
S-90	Natural Sucker Finish
S-91	Red Head Finish
S-92	Gold Fish Finish
S-93	Fluorescent Finish
S-94	Silver Natural Finish

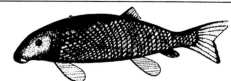

10" PIKE
METAL FINS

ORDER NO.	COLOR
S-80	Natural Pike Finish
S-81	Muskellunge Finish
S-82	Red Head Finish
S-83	Gold Fish Finish
S-84	Fluorescent Finish
S-85	Pearl/Pink Eye Finish

4³/₄" SUCKER
PLASTIC FINS

ORDER NO.	COLOR
S-15	Natural Sucker Finish
S-16	Red Head Finish

LARGE MOUTH BASS

- Natural Large Mouth paint pattern
- 8" Length, Metal fins

ORDER NO: S45
PACKAGED: 1 per poly bag & header

RAINBOW TROUT

- Natural Rainbow Trout paint pattern
- 8" Length, Metal fins

ORDER NO: S46
PACKAGED: 1 per poly bag & header

BROWN TROUT

- Natural Brown Trout paint pattern
- 8" Length, Metal fins

ORDER NO: S47
PACKAGED: 1 per poly bag & header

DECOY PINS
These handy metal pins allow quick changes of your lure whether it is live or artificial. The Wrap Around model is specifically designed to keep minnows alive longer for more live action. Packaged one per poly bag, 12 per master carton.

ORDER NO: DP-1 (piercing model)   DP-2 (wrap-around model)

PIERCING

WRAP AROUND

STOPPER ICE FISHING LURES

Plate 203. A fish decoy advertising page from the present K & E/Stopper Tackle Company marketing catalog.

Plate 204. Three different K & E/Stopper Company Type III solid plastic fish decoys. Top: 6" sucker in gold fish finish. Middle: 6" pike in natural pike paint finish. Bottom: 4¾" sucker in red head paint finish.

Plate 205. The K & E company Type III 6" long modified sucker decoy with metal side fins.

Plate 206. The three different forms of K & E/Stopper Tackle Company Type IV hollow plastic fish decoys. Top: 10" pike in muskellunge paint finish. Middle: 9" sucker in natural sucker paint finish. Bottom: 8" perch in natural perch paint finish.

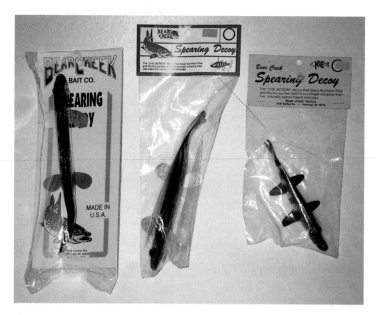

Plate 207. Three examples of different packaging used by the K & E/Stopper Tackle Company for marketing their fish-spearing decoys.

Plate 208. Ken and Evelyn Sprague, founders of the K & E Tackle, Inc., with daughter Kathy Howes, current vice president of the K & E /Stopper Tackle Company.

Kohler's Ice Decoys

The ad shown here is the only documentation of this early commercial quality-made Kohler's ice spearing decoy that I have found. This decoy was advertised in a Farwell, Ozmun, Kirk and Company wholesale hardware catalog (Plate 209). This company also manufactured metal products, paints, and varnishes and was located in St. Paul, Minnesota. Because the same catalog advertised a Heddon & Sons Bait Companies Four Point ice spearing decoy first produced in 1920, we can approximately date the advertised Kohler's ice decoy.

The Kohler's ice decoy was advertised in only one size, 6½" long, and had a round wooden body with carved gills and an open mouth. This catalog illustration also reveals what appear to be die-cut metal side and dorsal fins and tail components. Eyes appear to be domed metal tacks or glass eyes. The ballast design is unknown. The line tie assembly was a simple eye screw with box swivel. The paint finish advertised in the catalog for this decoy was solid silver with red accent paint on the carved gills and around the side fins. The wholesale price per one dozen decoys was $12.00, which was double the price of the popular Heddon & Sons Company fish decoys advertised in the same catalog as Dowagiac ice decoys.

The unusual characteristics of this decoy's design and paint finish make it easily recognizable, yet the author and a number of other long-time fish decoy collectors have yet to see an example. The mystery of why this sleek early fish decoy is so rare makes it a challenge to avid collectors to add an example to their collection.

Plate 209. The Farwell, Ozmun, Kirk and Company catalog advertisement for both the Kohler's ice decoy (top) and Heddon and Sons Bait Company ice spearing decoy (bottom).

Martin Kroph Decoys

Very little is known about Martin Kroph's commercial decoy. Kroph lived in Whitehall, Michigan, which is located in the west central area of Michigan's Lower Peninsula. These decoys were only manufactured in the mid-1950s, and it is said that they were only marketed for two to three years because of their poor swimming capability (Plate 210).

The only model was 7½" long. It had a solid aluminum die-cast body with a curved tail, integral dorsal and anal fins, and integral molded gills, eyes, and mouth. The side fins were made from one piece of light gauge metal, cut with a template into a round-shaped component. This one-piece side fin was attached by inserting it into a horizontal slit cut through the body. The paint finish was a combination of both spray and hand painting. The various multi-colored spray-painted finishes were always accented with a lateral line made by hand painting multicolored dots. The side fins were spray painted with the body color on top and the lighter belly color on the bottom. The eyes were hand painted black and yellow, and the gill and mouth areas were hand painted in red. The line tie was an off-the-shelf cotter pin molded into the center back area of the body.

The marketing price for these decoys was $1.50, and a number have been found marked with that price. The design of this solid aluminum die-cast decoy is very similar to the design of the Sletten Manufacturing Company decoys documented on page 149, leading one to wonder if the earlier Sletten decoy inspired the design and manufacturing of Martin Kroph decoys.

Plate 210. Two beautiful examples of Martin Kroph fish-spearing decoys.

Kurtis Katch-All Lure

The versatile "Kurtis Katch-All" lure was invented by Louis A. Kurtis (1905 – 1992) of Detroit, Michigan (Plate 211). He invented the Kurtis Katch-All lure in 1957, and it was patented in 1966 as a birthday gift by his son, Dr. Louis T. Kurtis, who is also an avid hunter and fisherman. The patent was titled "Bait Holder" and was filed on November 9, 1964, and numbered 3,284,945 (Plate 212). The Kurtis Katch-All instructions recommended foremost the use of dead or frozen smelt as bait, for the use of live smelt was illegal at the time. Smelt is one of the favorite forage fish of most freshwater fish including pike, muskie, bass, and lake trout.

The Kurtis Katch-All lure was developed because of the difficulty in hooking fish with conventional single or double-hook lures. With four treble hooks and an optional rear double hook, this lure improved the catch ratio greatly. The Kurtis Katch-All kept the smelt in the proper position and contained all solid materials within the bait. The fish isn't warned when the smelt is mouthed before being swallowed, which is the only way the fish will take a bait lying still in the water.

The Kurtis Katch-All lure was die cut from solid brass sheet stock and then plated. Lures came in one size only, 4" long, not including the front gang treble hook assembly or the optional rear double hook. They were packaged in a hard clear plastic snap-lock container, and each package included instructions for using the bait (Plates 213 and 214).

The versatility of the lure is truly incredible, because not only could it be still fished, but it could be cast and slowly retrieved with excellent results. It could also be jigged, bobber fished, and fished through the ice by jigging. It also could be used as a fish decoy through the winter ice with frozen or freeze-dried smelt or bait fish by removing the hooks (Plate 215).

Plate 211. Louis A. Kurtis (1905 – 1992).

Plate 212. Patent drawing of the Kurtis Katch-All lure.

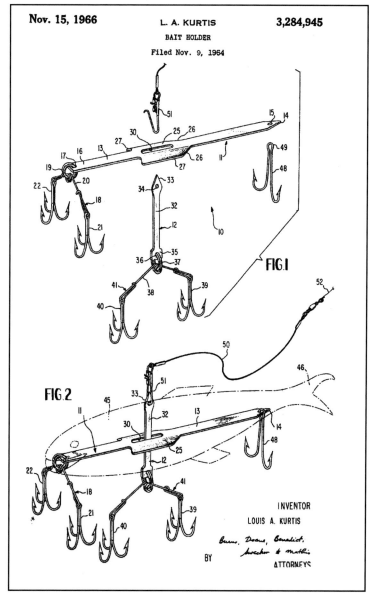

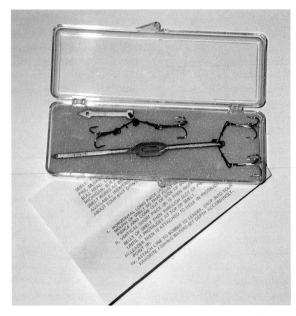

Plate 213. Example of the Kurtis Katch-All lure
with brochure and marketing box.

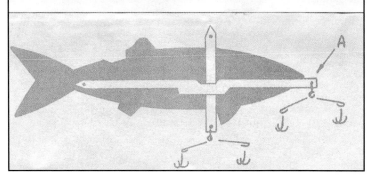

INSTRUCTIONS FOR USE: "KURTIS KATCH-ALL"

SMELT: FAVORED FOOD OF MOST FISH, PARTICULARLY
PIKE, MUSKIE, BASS, LAKE TROUT, WHITE FISH, COHO AND
BULL HEAD. LIVE SMELT IS ILLEGAL IN CANADA &
MICHIGAN, BUT FORTUNATELY FROZEN OR FREEZE DRIED
SMELT WORKS AS WELL. IN THIS STATE THE BAIT IS ALWAYS
AVAILABLE, INEXPENSIVE AND EASY TO KEEP. NO WORRY
ABOUT YOUR BAIT DYING AND BECOMING WORTHLESS.

I. HORIZONTAL LONG PIECE (A) INSERTED FIRST INTO
MOUTH OF SMELT SO THAT POINT OF LONG PIECE WILL
PIERCE AND COME OUT OF SIDE OF SMELT NEAR TAIL.
II. VERTICAL SHORT PIECE (B) IS THEN INSERTED THROUGH
BELLY OF SMELT THEN THROUGH SLOT OF PIECE (A)
UNTIL IT PROTRUDES AT TOP OF SMELT.
III. LEADER THEN IS ATTACHED TO HOLE IN PROTRUDING
POINT (B).
IV. ATTACH LINE TO BOBBER TO LEADER, DROP INTO YOUR
FAVORITE FISHING WATERS-SET DEPTH ACCORDINGLY.

Plate 214. The Kurtis Katch-All box brochure.

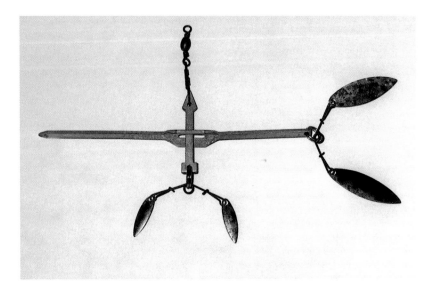

Plate 215. The Kurtis Katch-All lure as found in a spear fisherman's decoy
box, rigged for ice spear fishing by removing the 4 treble hooks and
replacing them with flashers. The lure is then inserted into a bait fish.

Lakco Quality Tackle

Lakco Quality Tackle is one of the few active makers and distributors of ice spear-fishing decoys today. These great swimming wooden-bodied attractors are an excellent buy on today's market. Lakco Quality Tackle is a division of Lake Country Products of Isle, Minnesota. The ice spear fishing decoys manufactured and marketed by Lakco Quality Tackle were designed by John I. Funkhouser (1945 – present) of Isle, Minnesota (Plate 216). An avid outdoorsman, John's experiences spear fishing as a young man with his father led to his designing a simple but very functional fish-spearing decoy for the Lake Country Products Company (Plate 217). These decoys were first marketed in 1995 in three sizes and seven finishes.

These decoys are made from select white pine and come in three sizes, 6", 8", and 10" long. The bodies are flat and a generic fish shape. The side fins and tail are die-cut from 0.032 thick sheet metal. The one-piece front and rear side fins are pressed into broached slits in the lower body and are spray painted the same color as the body during the spray-painting operation. The unpainted metal tail is pressed into a slit sawed into the rear of the body area and then nail attached after painting. The bright unpainted metal tail serves to reflect light while being fished. The ballast is lead poured into an oval cavity at the frontal belly area, which in turn locks the front fin in place.

The body and side fins are spray painted in six different two-color and three-color paint finishes and then clear-coated for waterproofing. Eyes are die-cut from black and silver reflector tapes and are bonded in the head area before the clear coating operation. The line tie is a simple nickel-plated eye screw.

The decoys are packaged in a plastic bag with a printed paper label (Plate 218). Lacko Tackle Company fish spearing decoys are marketed in bait and tackle shops and sporting good stores throughout the midwestern United States.

Plate 216. John I. Funkhouser (1945 – present), designer of the Lakco fish spearing decoy.

Plate 217. Three examples of Lakco fish spearing decoys. Top: Largest 10" long model. Bottom: Two examples of the 6" long model with different paint finishes. Note the light-reflecting quality of the bright metal tails.

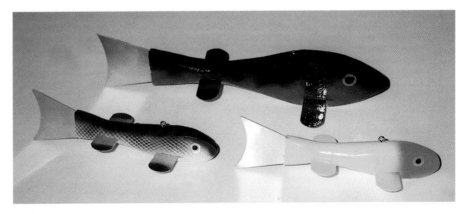

Plate 218. A plastic bag with a paper label is used to market the Lakco fish-spearing decoys.

Lee's Decoys

Lee's Decoys were produced by LeRoy "Lee" Carlson (1936 – present) of Coon Rapids, Minnesota, an engineer with the Honeywell Corporation. The designing, manufacturing, and marketing of his unique airplane-shaped fish spearing decoys was a successful part-time business venture for Lee Carlson in his hometown of Coon Rapids (Plate 219).

The Lee's Decoys came in three sizes. The smallest was 3½" long, including the tail hair, and weighed ⅞ of an ounce. The medium-sized one was 4½" long, including the tail hair, and weighed 2 ounces. The largest size was 6" long, including the tail hair, and weighed 4 ounces (Plate 220). The molded lead body of these decoys has a round cross section on the smaller model and an oval cross section for the medium and larger size models. The one-piece rectangular side fin was die-cut metal and was anchored into position with the molding of the solid lead body. There were two punched holes at both outside ends of

the side fins to attach a bright metal spinner blade at final assembly as an added attractor. The line tie was a looped wire anchored in place during the body molding operation. The ballast of the decoy is the overall weight of all its metal components. Most decoys were spray painted two colors, but some solid color examples have been found. The eyes are hand painted black and white. The artificial tail hair is bonded to a molded stem at the rear of the body. The tail hair was dyed to match the color of the head, but for decoys in a solid color, the tail hair is a natural white.

Lee's Decoy were marketed stapled on a 4" x 7" colorful sales card, covered with clear plastic (Plate 220). They were marketed in area tackle stores and bait shops and sold for about $2.00 each. Lee's Decoys went out of business in 1988, but during their two short years of existence, approximately 300 decoys were marketed.

Plate 219. An example of a Lee's Decoy in its swimming position as the fish see it.

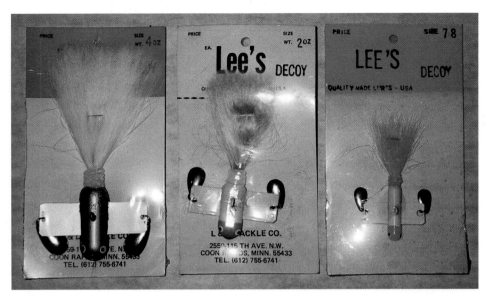

Plate 220. Examples of the three sizes of Lee's Decoys, each in its marketing packaging. Left: largest 6" long decoy; center: 4½" long decoy; right: 3½" long decoy.

Macatawa Bait Company

Tony Smith, born in Holland, Michigan, in 1945, founded the Macatawa Bait Company in Holland, in 1979 (Plate 221). He is considered one of the most clever innovators of custom fishing lures and fish decoys, both working and decorative (non-working). Smith frequently cannibalizes and modifies old hardware from discarded fishing lures and decoys. He is a master at integrating this old hardware into his creations, but he also designs and manufactures his own hardware when required. His unique fish and critter lures and decoys, sometimes whimsical, are coveted by collectors of both vintage and recent items. Tony's creations are so desirable because of their unusual forms and paint patterns (Plates 222 and 223).

Smith married Holly Kalkman of Holland, Michigan, in 1980, and they have two daughters. He has a full-time job as a civil engineer with the city of Holland, located in southwestern Michigan. This industrious engineer, designer, and carver has a second career year-round as owner and manager of the Macatawa Bait Company.

Tony can be compared with Michigan's legendary lure maker, the late Bud Stewart, one of the finest makers of commercial lures and fish decoys, documented later in this chapter. The parallel is that Bud Stewart was one of the few custom lure makers of his day, as is Tony. It was not uncommon to sit and visit with Bud while he was carving, sanding, or assembling a lure or fish decoy. Likewise, Tony visits with friends while carving, sanding, or assembling a unique creation behind his table at one of the many lure or sporting collectible shows that he attends while demonstrating his beautiful work. He, like Bud, is very prolific and is always glad to accept the challenge of any custom design, whether for a working or decorative decoy, with or without a vintage look (Plate 224).

I believe Macatawa Bait Company will always remain a small operation because of the perfection in both the design and finished products required by Tony himself. We are fortunate to have the Macatawa Bait Company for custom ordering of baits and fish decoys just as the fishermen did in the 1940s through 1990 from the now-gone Bud Stewart Bait Company of Michigan.

Plate 221. Tony Smith displaying some of his decoys at a sporting collectible show.

Plate 222. A beautiful brown trout spearing decoy with antiqued paint finish.

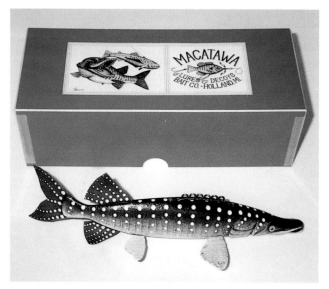

Plate 223. A realistic northern pike spearing decoy with Tony's unique paint finish.

Plate 224. A custom-order praying mantis carving by Tony Smith with his distinctive box.

Marv's Wood Products

The founder and sole owner of Marv's Wood Products is Marvin Leo Cekalla (1941 – present) of Little Falls, Minnesota (Plate 225). Marvin is a retired barber by trade and owns a lumber and casual furniture making business in Little Falls. With a passion for hunting and fishing year-round and being a metal and woodworking craftsman, Marv was a natural to design and manufacture the combination fish-spearing decoy and fishing lure that he named "The Intruder" (Plate 226). Marv credits the success of this versatile lure to information passed down from his grandfather. As a young man, Marv's grandfather, an immigrant from Poland who came to America in 1870, lived near and fished in the upper Mississippi River. He recalled seeing the Native Americans successfully netting fish using very thin fish decoys with various patterns of specific colors. Marv recalled his grandfather drawing these patterns in the sand for him. He kept this information in the back of his mind and used it to design, test, and market his Intruder lure. The Intruder was designed as both an ice fish-spearing decoy and a year-round open water attractor. The Intruder decoy comes in only one size, 9" long. The body shape is hand cut from 0.035 thick sheet metal, and the body is slightly twisted to give the decoy an

erratic swim pattern. A slit and a notch are cut in the tail area to allow the fisherman to bend the tail to desired swimming dynamics. A hole is drilled at the center of the back area to attach a snap swivel for a

Plate 225. Marvin Leo Cekalla.

123

tether line. A hole the same size is drilled at the center of the belly area to attach a sucker pin to add a live sucker or chub minnow as an added attractor (Plate 227).

The decoy bodies are spray painted to desired color, and then the head and tail areas are dipped in paint in complementary colors. An accent of blood red paint is hand painted at the bottom rear corner of the tail as an added attractor. A triangular shape of colorful waterproof tape is added to each side of the body, and a half-circle of metallic light-reflecting waterproof tape is added to both sides in the head area to simulate gills. Two hollow plastic eyes with a white pupil

and a dynamic moveable iris are bonded to each side of the decoy's head area. The decoy is packaged in a plastic bag with directions on how to fish the Intruder (Plate 228). The Intruder comes in three color patterns, called the "Shady Lady," the "Sandy Hawk," and the "Streetwalker" (Plate 226).

The Intruder was first marketed in 1991 and is still being marketed today. Most are sold through local bait stores and tackle shops, but some are marketed by mail order. They are produced in Marv's home shop, and approximately 400 – 600 have been successfully marketed at this time.

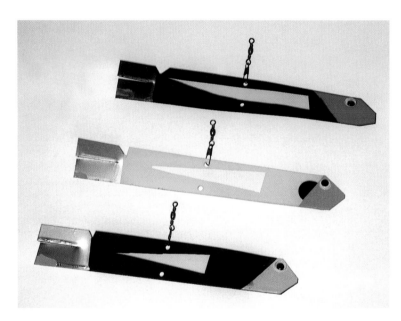

Plate 226. The three different color patterns for the Intruder. Top: "Shady Lady" model; middle: "Streetwalker" model; bottom: "Sandy Hawk" model.

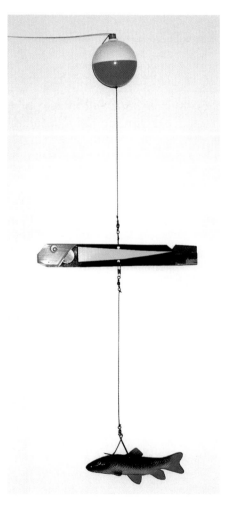

Plate 227. The Intruder rigged for open water fishing with a bobber, sucker pin, and chub minnow.

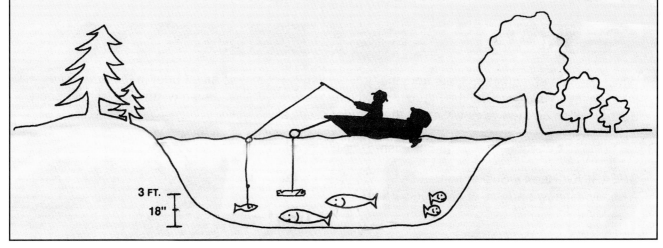

Intruder · FOR BEST RESULTS:

When used as an attractor, 3 feet from the bottom, fish react to it as an intruder in the area. They will try to eat everything around the Intruder ... which means your bait ... even when they're not hungry. Bobber action on the waves will make the Intruder come alive.

ANGLING: Put the Intruder on a line with a large bobber, adjust depth to 3 feet from the bottom (15' to 20' from boat or dock is ideal). Fish in a 20' radius from the Intruder.

SPEARING: Hook a Sucker Minnow 12"-14" below the Intruder. A decoy minnow harness or clip works great!

Good Luck!

3 FT.
18"

Plate 228. An example of the Intruder's packaging, with directions on how to fish it.

McCormick Decoys

Little is known about Vernon "Vern" McCormick, the maker of the McCormick fish-spearing decoys. McCormick (1917 – 1988) lived in the small town of Allegan, Michigan, which is located in the southwestern part of Michigan's Lower Peninsula. Vern McCormick was a woodworker by trade, employed at a casket making plant in Allegan. He had a reputation for being an excellent fisherman, especially on the winter ice. At that time period, the early 1940s, the larger Allegan area lakes were known for large pike and muskie which spear fishermen pursued.

It is believed that one of Vern McCormick's spear fishing friends, a man named Erie Wolf, was responsible for designing and perfecting a very successful pike and muskie spearing decoy and that Vern McCormick

decided to copy and market it commercially around 1940.

The McCormick decoy was made only in one size, 9" long (Plate 229). This larger-than-normal fish decoy size was typically used when pursuing larger fish, such as pike and muskie. The body had a generic form, always with a metal tail. The tail was hand cut to a template from light-gauge metal and nail attached. The side fins were a one-piece transparent plastic component, assembled through a horizontal slit in the body and then nail attached. The transparent side fin was assembled before the painting operation and then masked off during painting. This clever transparent side fin was to give the fish decoy a more lifelike appearance, with the side fins being inconspic-

uous to the fish. The ballast was lead poured into a cavity in the frontal belly area and then filed and sanded to the belly shape. Eyes were off-the-shelf convex-shaped thumb tacks accented with a hand-painted dot in their centers. The line tie was a simple eye screw painted during the body painting operation. The two-color paint finishes were both spray painted and hand painted. The base color was spray painted on the bodies, and then vertical stripes or a dot pattern was hand painted over the base color (Plate 230).

A number of examples have been found finished with a silver or gold foil, with accent dots or dashes hand painted on the foil. The tail was sometimes painted the same color as the body and sometimes left unpainted. The mouth is flat, hand painted on all decoys. McCormick decoys were marketed in local bait and tackle stores in the Allegan area. Stories of large fish being speared using them are still being told today, half a century or more later.

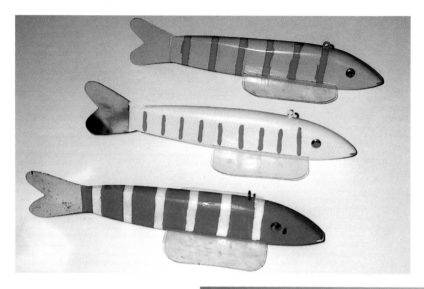

Plate 229. Three examples of McCormick fish decoys with the typical vertical stripe paint finishes.

Plate 230. An example of a McCormick fish decoy with the dot paint pattern.

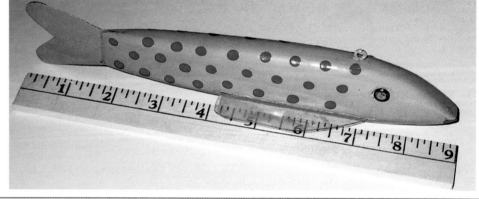

Minnetonka "Tonka" Baits – Schipper Manufacturing

The Minnetonka "Tonka" Bait Company was founded by brothers Ithel A. Schipper (1919 –1986) and Darel Schipper (1926 – present) in their home town of Wayzata, Minnesota, in 1944 (Plate 231). In 1947 Darel bought out his brother Ithel and became sole owner of the company. Shortly after buying out his brother, he changed the name of the company to Schipper Manufacturing because the name Tonka Baits was being used by a local bait shop in Wayzata. On August 8, 1946, Ithel applied for a patent for an ice spear-fishing decoy, and patent no. 2,557,516 was granted on June 19, 1951 (Plate 232).

The Tonka – Schipper fish decoys were made in two sizes, 5¾" and 8" long (Plate 233). The wooden bodies were a generic fish form proportionally the same, except an open mouth was sawed into the head of the larger model. The front and rear one-piece side fin components were die cut from sheet metal. The larger front and smaller rear side fin components were attached to the body, loaded into a horizontal slot cut into the lower body from the front to the rear fin location. The horizontal slot was then filled with a waterproof wood filler. The front side fin was anchored by the lead ballast, but the rear side fin was nail attached. The tail was also die cut from sheet metal and nail attached. The ballast was lead poured into an oval cavity at the frontal belly area. The line tie is a light-gauge worm-shaped wire form, giving the spear

fisherman three different tether line points. The line tie was assembled through two drilled holes in the back, one close to the head and another anchored by the lead ballast. The earliest decoys were two-color dip painted. Later decoys were spray painted in a variety of finishes. Eyes are hand painted in two colors. The earliest decoy were stamped "TONKA BAITS, WAYZATA, MINNESOTA. PAT. PEND." (Plate 234). The later decoys are marked SCHIPPER MFG. PAT.#2,557,516 (Plate 235).

Schipper decoys were marketed by Sears Roebuck stores throughout all the major cities of the Midwest and also through local area hardware and sporting good stores. The large decoy models sold for about 80 cents each and the smaller models for about 60 cents.

The Schipper Manufacturing Company went out of business about 1977 when demand for fish spearing tackle was waning. Since 1998, Darel Schipper has produced a few decoys to satisfy collector demands. He always signs these decoys "D. Schipper."

Plate 231. Darel and Ithel Schipper, founders of the Minnetonka "Tonka" Bait Company.

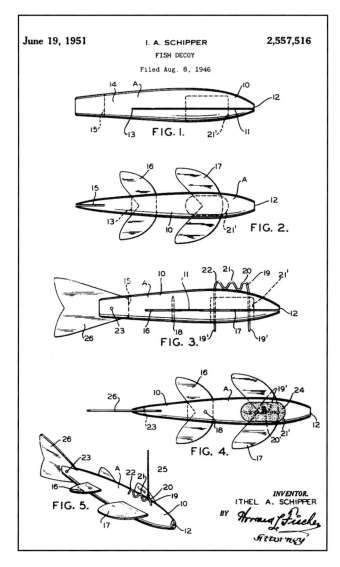

Plate 232. The patent drawing for the Tonka – Schipper fish decoy.

Plate 233. Three examples of Tonka – Schipper fish decoys. Top: 8" long fish decoy; bottom: two examples of the 5¾" long fish decoy with different finishes.

Plate 234. The belly identification stamp of the early Tonka fish decoy.

Plate 235. The belly identification stamp on the later Schipper fish decoy.

Moonlight Bait Company/Paw Paw Bait Company

Founded in 1908 in Paw Paw, Michigan, by Horace Emery Ball and Charles E. Varney, the Moonlight Bait Company was another early successful fishing tackle manufacturing company. They manufactured and successfully marketed a versatile line of quality fishing lures during the life of the company. In 1923 there was a dramatic change in the Moonlight line due to the merger of the Silver Creek Novelty Works of Dowagiac, Michigan, with the Moonlight Bait Company. The new company was called the Moonlight Bait and Novelty Works and was located in Paw Paw, Michigan. The final chapter of the Moonlight Bait Company began with its sale to the Paw Paw Bait Company, also of Paw Paw, Michigan. This was around 1927, but incorporation did not take place until 1935 when the Moonlight Bait Company officially became the Paw Paw Bait Company.

A number of Moonlight Bait Company catalogs have been found, the earliest dated 1913. None of the catalogs found so far have advertisements for an ice decoy, but collectors of lures from the Moonlight Bait Company of Paw Paw, Michigan, speculate that the two commercially made fish-spearing decoy examples shown in Plate 236 were made by the Moonlight Bait Company. In Plate 237 the 6½" long decoy (bottom) attributed to Moonlight Bait Company, but not shown in their catalog shows a great similarity of design to the larger 7½" long catalogued Paw Paw Bait Company decoy (top). Similarities include body form, location of all die-cut metal fins and tail, a round head brass nail at the nose, and line tie, ballast, and eye locations that are proportionally the same.

Moonlight Bait Company lures were always manufactured with glass eyes or flat-painted eyes, but most Paw Paw lures have painted tack eyes. The two examples in Plate 236 have glass fishing lure-type eyes used by the Moonlight Bait Company. It is not known whether these two examples have been overpainted by spear fishermen or were originally hand painted by the manufacturer. One of these examples was found in Michigan and the other in Minnesota, both with very similar paint finishes.

The Paw Paw Bait Company marketed three different style ice decoys in a variety of colors in the company's 35-plus years of existence (Plate 238). The first ice decoy marketed by the Paw Paw Bait Company was the largest, 7½" long, which is 1" longer than the attributed Moonlight Bait Company decoy and was first advertised in their 1929 catalog (Plates 239 and 240). Other differences between the attributed Moonlight Bait Company decoy and the first marketed Paw Paw Bait Company decoy are the glass eyes used by Moonlight in contrast to Paw Paw Bait Company's painted convex tack eyes. There were also the shape differences of the die-cut metal side fins and tail. Side fins, dorsal fin, and tail were pressed into slits in the wooden body on all three styles of decoys. The tail was pressed into a slit at the very rear of the body and then nail attached. Ballast was lead poured into three round drilled holes in the belly. The line tie is a simple eye screw. Side fins and the dorsal fin have been found in two different shapes in this model only (Plate 241).

The second and most common style ice decoy found made by the Paw Paw Bait Company was the 5⅛" wooden tail model (Plate 242). The four die-cut metal side fins were the same as the smaller type side fins used on the large 7½" Paw Paw Bait Company ice decoy. The die-cut metal dorsal fin is a new design. Ballast is poured lead into three round holes drilled in the belly. Eyes are two-color painted convex tacks. There was a variety of finishes, most also used on the company's fishing lures. Line tie was a simple eye screw and convex washer. A few examples of an open mouth model have been found (Plate 243). This decoy is identical to the aforementioned 5⅛" long wooden tail model, except for the open mouth design which replaces the pointed nose with brass nail design, and the different tail form.

The third and rarest ice decoy made by the Paw Paw Bait Company was the 3¼ " decoy with wood tail (Plate 244). This decoy was not catalogued, but it is believed that it was marketed in 1929 about the same time that the 5⅛" wood tail model was introduced. This little minnow-like fish decoy was the same in form as the 5⅛" wood tail model with the exception of size, no dorsal fin, and only one ballast hole. It has only been found in one color, a green perch finish.

Plate 245 shows a group of quality made Moonlight Bait Company and Paw Paw Bait Company fishing lures in fish form that had potential to be great fish decoys.

129

Plate 236. Two glass-eyed fish decoys with metal tails attributed to the Moonlight Bait Company.

Plate 237. This photographic comparison reveals the similarity of design from the attributed Moonlight Bait Company decoy (bottom) and the catalogued Paw Paw Bait Company decoy (top).

Plate 238. The 3 different style ice decoys marketed by the Paw Paw Bait Company. Top: 7½" metal tail model. Middle: 5⅛" wood tail model. Bottom: 3¼" wood tail model.

Plate 239. A 1929 advertisement from a Paw Paw Bait Company catalog for their first decoy, a 7½" fish decoy.

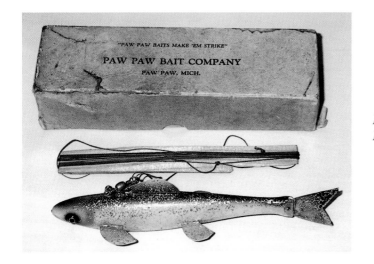

Plate 240. The earliest 7½" ice decoy by the Paw Paw Bait Company with its box.

Plate 241. Later 7½" ice decoys by the Paw Paw Bait Company with a larger side fin design.

Plate 242. The 5⅛" ice decoy by the Paw Paw Bait Company shown in 5 different paint finishes.

Plate 243. An example of the Paw Paw Bait Company's rare open mouth 5⅛" ice decoy.

Plate 244. The rare 3¼" ice decoy by the Paw Paw Bait Company shown in green perch finish.

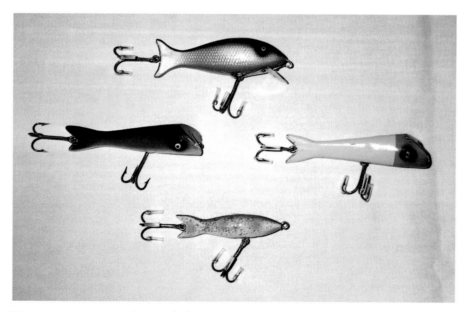

Plate 245. A group of Moonlight Bait Company and Paw Paw Bait Company fishing lures that, with slight modification, would have been great fish-spearing decoys. These casting lures are some of the more popular ones with Paw Paw and Moonlight Company lure collectors.

Martin Pestrue Decoys

Martin Pestrue (1884 – 1953) of Standish, Michigan, was another of Michigan's early makers of commercial fish decoys. Standish is located just a few miles inland from Lake Huron's Saginaw Bay, one of Michigan's best summer and winter fisheries. There is much documentation of market fishing in Saginaw Bay right up to the Depression era of the 1930s.

The Martin Pestrue Decoys came in only one size, 6" long. The earliest model was made from wood in about 1930 (Plate 246). In about 1935 the same shaped decoy appeared in a solid molded form from an early plastic material. It is believed that a body mold was made, using an early wood bodied decoy as a pattern to create the molding tooling for the solid molded plastic model. The wood versus plastic decoys are so similar that only the wood grain of the body reveals the material composition difference (Plate 246). The Martin Pestrue decoys are thin with full curved bodies and resemble a small smelt. A single side fin was die cut from metal and used at all four side fin locations. The dorsal fin was hand cut to a template from metal. The side fins and dorsal fin on the wood model are pressed into slits in the body. The side fins and dorsal fin on the plastic model are anchored into position during the molding of the body. Ballast is lead poured into a single drilled hole in the frontal belly area on both models. The line tie is two drilled holes in the dorsal fin.

There are two hand-painted finishes, both referred to as the "Saginaw Bay Spot-tail." The first is a solid silver body and head with a red hand-painted spot on the tail, hand-painted gills, and hand-painted yellow and black eyes. The second paint finish is a solid silver hand-painted body with a red hand-painted head and tail, a yellow hand-painted spot on the tail, and hand-painted yellow and black eyes (Plate 247). The decoys were marketed on a hand-cut, hand-painted cardboard display board usually signed in script on the back "M. Pestrue, Standish" (Plates 248 and 249). The Saginaw Bay Spot-tail decoys were sold in local bait and tackle shops and also through Bay City Hardware and Woods Sporting Goods stores.

Plate 246. An example of Martin Pestrue's earliest wood bodied "Saginaw Bay Spot-tail" fish-spearing decoy. Note the wood grain visible through the body paint.

Plate 247. The two different paint finishes of Martin Pestrue's "Saginaw Bay Spot-tail" fish-spearing decoys.

Plate 248. Two marketing cards of Martin Pestrue's Saginaw Bay Spot-tail fish-spearing decoys. Note the solid silver paint finish on the left and the red and silver finish on the right.

Plate 249. The back side of a Martin Pestrue fish decoy marketing card with his signature.

Oscar Quam Company

Oscar Quam (1887 – 1967) was born in a log cabin near New London, Minnesota. He grew up on the family farm on the shores of Mud Lake in southwestern, Minnesota. Oscar Quam's father owned the Great Northern Hotel in nearby New London. The great hunting and fishing in the area brought many sportsmen to the hotel. Oscar became a hunting and fishing guide for these visitors while still in his teens. After graduating from the University of Minnesota Agriculture School, Oscar took over the family cattle farm and chicken hatchery. In 1910 Oscar started a hunt club on a small island, referred to as Crane Island, located just off shore from the Quam farm. The stock market crash in 1929 caused Oscar to lose the family farm, but the hunt club still flourished until the early 1940s. After losing the farm, Oscar moved his family to Minneapolis. He eventually was able to purchase and operate three area Texaco service stations.

While still operating the stations, he started a sideline business making and marketing waterfowl decoys and also duck, goose, and crow calls, advertising in many different sporting magazines. He eventually produced a catalog for mail orders as demand increased.

It was in one of these earliest catalog that Oscar advertised a fish decoy called "Fish House Minnow." He also advertised a cleverly designed combination jig stick and ice tester with a wooden sheath (Plate 250). The fish decoy came in two sizes, a large size at 75¢, and medium size at 60¢. I have not yet seen an example of this decoy or the combination jig stick and ice tester, so at this time the size, paint finishes, and methods of construction are unknown. These items surely exist in the field but remain anonymous due to their low volume production and lack of markings for identification.

Plate 250. The early catalog advertisement of the Oscar Quam fish decoy and the combination jig stick and ice tester, circa 1940.

Randall Decoy Company

George Randall (1921 – 1979) was the founder and sole owner of the Randall Decoy Company of Willmar, Minnesota. As a young man he made fish-spearing decoys and fish spears for himself and his friends. After graduation from high school, he found employment with the Burlington Northern Railroad as a machinist and inspector. At the start of World War II, he entered the service as a Navy Seabee. He returned from active duty in 1946 and went back to work for the railroad until the rail yards closed in Willmar in the late 1950s. George began making spears and fish decoys in his workshop next to his home on Eagle Lake near Willmar, Minnesota. In 1960 George moved to Spicer, Minnesota, and in 1963 he purchased a restaurant there. George used the basement of the restaurant for his spear and fish decoy business, and the upstairs became the Randall Cafe. In about 1969 George sold the restaurant and bought an old blacksmith shop in Spicer and moved his spear and decoy business there, employing a number of local people at the height of his business.

The Randall fish decoy and spear catalog flyer (circa 1960s) revealed that the company marketed four different models of wooden-bodied fish decoys (Plate 251). The best seller was a generic form of decoy called the "Deluxe Decoy," which came in 4 different sizes and 10 different paint pattern finishes (Plate 252). A decoy in sucker form, called the "Golden Sucker," came in four sizes and only one paint pattern (Plate 253). A decoy in pike form, called both "Natural Pickerel" and "Red Head Pickerel," came in one size and two different paint patterns (Plate 254). A wooden tail decoy in panfish form, called the "Sunfish," came in one size and two paint patterns (Plate 255). This small 5" model has also been found with a metal tail, but this version was not in the catalog (Plate 256). The wooden bodies of all four models were flat sided. The four side fins on all models, except for the large 16" model, were made of one piece of molded lead, which also functioned for ballast and had the marketing price molded into it. The largest 16" model had a similar side fin and integral ballast design, but was of a two-piece design (Plate 257). All side fins were nail attached. The tail was die-cut from light-gauge sheet metal and nail attached, after being pressed into a slit at the rear of the body. Only the small panfish model had an integral curved wooden tail. There were a total of 15 different catalogued multicolored spray-painted paint finishes on these wooden models, but some other finishes, including an unpainted natural finish, have been found. These were probably special-order finishes and thus were not in the catalog. Eyes were integrally machine carved into the head area and were spray painted with two colors. Side fins were painted the

same color as the body, and the tail was partially painted the body color. Line ties were nickel-plated eye screws.

One other non-catalogued narrow flat-sided little wooden 2¼" long decoy was made by the Randall Decoy Company (Plate 258). The two metal side fins and metal tail were hand cut to a template. The side fins were pressed into slits in the body and anchored by the ballast. The tail was pressed into a slit at the rear of the body and then nail attached. Ballast was lead poured into a cavity in the frontal belly area. Paint finish was always red and white. Eyes were integrally circle punched and hand painted with a black dot. The line tie was a simple eye screw. These little minnow-like decoys are sometimes referred to as perchers because of their popularity with spear fishermen pursuing perch, whitefish, and tullibees. The earliest wooden body Randall Company fish decoy can be recognized by what is referred to by collectors as "undercut gill model." These undercut gills are a result of the belly being cut away to the gill area (Plate 259).

It is believed that the Randall Company started making a solid aluminum die-cast fish-spearing decoy sometime in the early 1970s. This first model was probably designed as a cost-saving version over the earlier wooden models (Plate 260). This die cast model had four side fins and is found only in one size, 7½" long. Very few of this first four-fin, aluminum die-cast model were made because of poor swimming quality. A short time later, a second solid aluminum die-cast model was designed, manufactured, and marketed with excellent results. It was much narrower with angel wing side fins, and featured a bendable tail (Plates 261 and 262). Examples have been found in four sizes, 6", 8", 10" and 12" long. The side fins, the dorsal fins, gills, eyes, and line tie hole were integrally molded on both models. There were six different color finishes for both of these die-cast models, mostly spray painted in two colors, and some scale pattern finishes have been found as well. Eyes are hand-painted with a black dot on both models. No ballast was needed because of the specific gravity of the die-cast metal body. Both models were marketed in a plastic bag with a printed paper label (Plate 263). This decoy is believed to be the last fish-spearing decoy designed and marketed by the Randall Company.

The Randall Company was a very successful business venture for George Randall. The large number of Randall spears and fish decoys still being used today by spear fishermen is a testimonial to their quality and desirability. A few months after George Randall died in 1979, the Randall Decoy Company was sold to the Paschke Company of Spicer, Minnesota, who were manufacturers of gardening equipment. The

Paschke Company marketed Randall design spear and sucker pins under the name Randall-Paschke

Spears but did not market fish decoys.

Plate 251. The Randall Decoy Company catalog flyer of fish decoys.

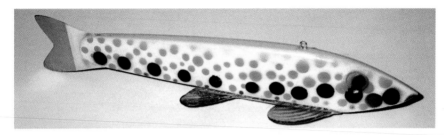

Plate 252. The Randall Decoy Company's generic form "Deluxe Decoy" in the beautiful Red Dot finish.

Plate 253. The Randall Decoy Company's Golden Sucker decoy in the 10" size.

Plate 254. The two large 16" pickerel decoys made by the Randall Decoy Company.

Plate 255. The Randall Decoy Company 5" long sunfish decoys with marketing box in crappie finish (right) and bluegill finish (left).

Plate 256. The Randall Decoy Company 5" sunfish decoy with metal tail and bluegill finish. This version of the decoy is not in the catalog so may have been a special order.

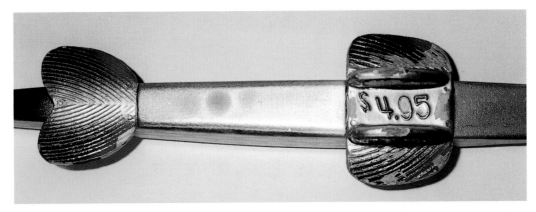

Plate 257. A view of the bottom of two-piece side fin design on the large 16" pickerel decoy. Note the marketing price is molded into the front side fin.

Plate 258. An example of the non-catalogued, smallest 2¼" Randall decoy shown with the catalogued largest 16" Randall decoy.

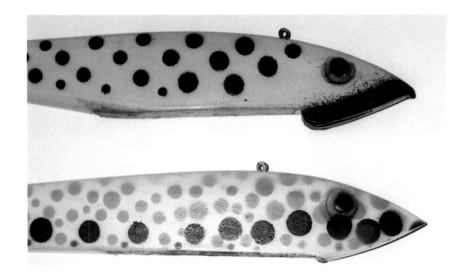

Plate 259. A body form comparison of the Randall Decoy Company, earliest undercut gill model fish (top), later model fish decoy (bottom.)

Plate 260. An example of the first aluminum die-cast fish decoy with four side fins made by the Randall Decoy Company.

Plate 261. The angel wing aluminum die-cast fish decoy in four different sizes made by the Randall Decoy Company.

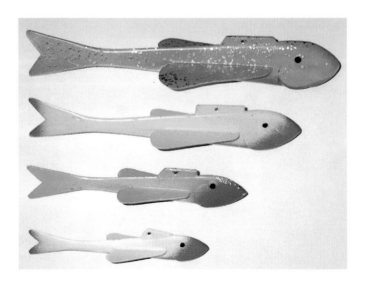

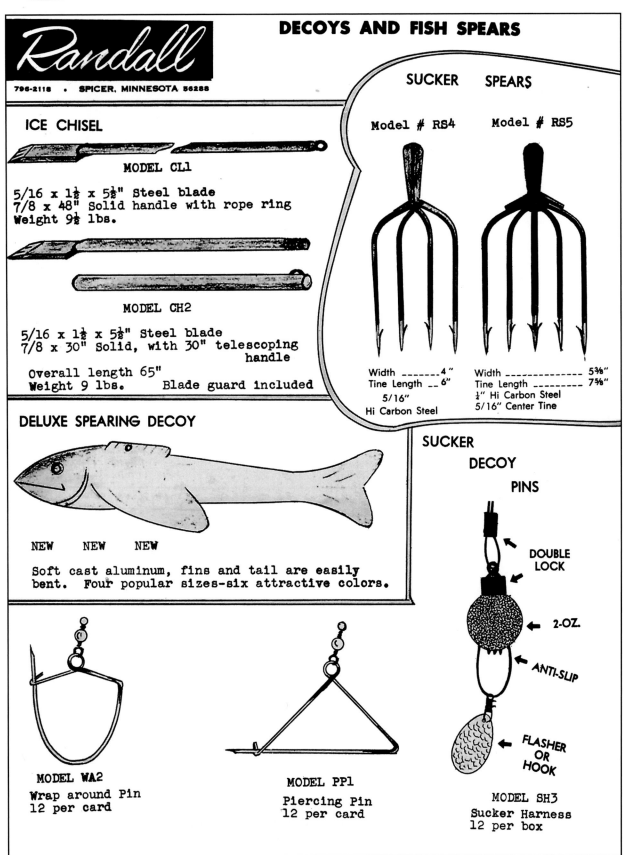

DECOYS AND FISH SPEARS

Randall

796-2118 • SPICER, MINNESOTA 56288

ICE CHISEL

MODEL CL1

5/16 x 1½ x 5½" Steel blade
7/8 x 48" Solid handle with rope ring
Weight 9½ lbs.

MODEL CH2

5/16 x 1½ x 5½" Steel blade
7/8 x 30" Solid, with 30" telescoping handle

Overall length 65"
Weight 9 lbs.   Blade guard included

SUCKER   SPEARS

Model # RS4   Model # RS5

Width ------- 4"   Width ------------ 5⅜"
Tine Length -- 6"   Tine Length -------- 7⅜"
    5/16"   ¼" Hi Carbon Steel
Hi Carbon Steel   5/16" Center Tine

DELUXE SPEARING DECOY

NEW   NEW   NEW

Soft cast aluminum, fins and tail are easily
bent. Four popular sizes-six attractive colors.

SUCKER DECOY PINS

DOUBLE LOCK

2-OZ.

ANTI-SLIP

FLASHER OR HOOK

MODEL WA2
Wrap around Pin
12 per card

MODEL PP1
Piercing Pin
12 per card

MODEL SH3
Sucker Harness
12 per box

Plate 262. An advertising catalog flyer for the angel wing, side fin, cast aluminum fish decoy.

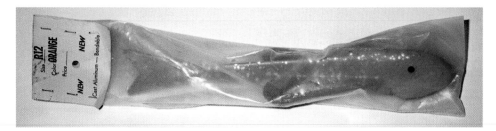

Plate 263. The marketing package for the angel wing aluminum Randall Decoy Company fish decoy.

Reigstad Decoys

Oliver Reigstad (1910 – 1979) and his wife Olga of Duluth, Minnesota, were a husband and wife team of fish decoy makers. All of their decoys were produced from 1957 through 1964 as a side business while Oliver worked for the Erie Mining Company on a barge in Duluth Harbor on Lake Superior (Plate 264). His job responsibilities allowed him time to work, carving and sanding approximately six fish decoy bodies daily.

Reigstad then brought the finished bodies home, where he poured lead into three drilled holes in the frontal belly area for ballast. Four metal template-cut side fins and a template-cut tail were inserted into slits in the body. Oliver's wife Olga painted all the decoys. There were a variety of two-color paint finishes, most with the body and side fins one color and the head and tail another color. The three bestsellers were

of a red and white, green and white, and black and white paint finish. Many decoys had multicolored glitter added to the decoy while the paint was still wet. This gave the decoys eye appeal for marketing and eye appeal to the fish (Plate 265).

The eyes of the decoys were a shelf item, convex-shaped painted thumb tacks of various colors. Most were gold, red, or yellow and then accented with a hand-painted black dot by Olga. The line tie was always a simple nickel-plated eye screw. The decoys were marketed in a plain gray, two-piece cardboard box, with both top and bottom marked REIG'S FISH DECOY (Plate 266). The decoys were of one size, 7¼" long, and were sold for $1.00 each.

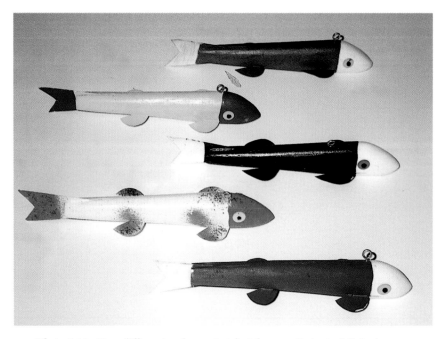

Plate 264. Five different color paint finishes on Reigstad fish decoys.

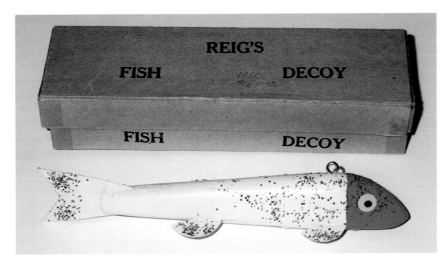

Plate 265. This red and white Reigstad fish decoy with glitter was a best-seller.

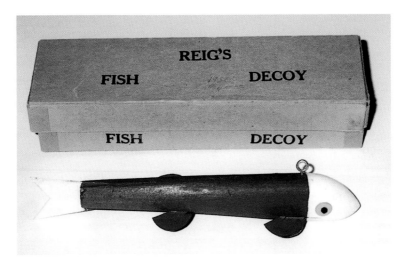

Plate 266. The very plain Reigstad fish decoy marketing box with a beautiful example that's never been in the water.

Jay B. Rhodes Fish Decoy

Jay B. Rhodes of Kalamazoo, Michigan, was a well-known inventor at the turn of the twentieth century. By 1904 he had made over 100 inventions and patented many of them, most unrelated to fishing items. Jay Rhodes was owner of the Kalamazoo Fishing Tackle Manufactures of Kalamazoo, Michigan. In 1905 he sold the rights to his fishing items and all his fishing manufacturing equipment to the William Shakespeare, Jr. Company, also located in Kalamazoo. This sale included the future great-selling Rhodes Perfect Casting Minnow and the Rhodes Mechanical Frog lures.

Jay B. Rhodes' name appeared once again on a fishing-related item in 1919, 14 years after the sale of his company to William Shakespeare, Jr. He was assigned patent no.1321850, granted on November 18, 1919, and titled "Lure or Decoy" (Plate 267). This beautiful 7" long ice spear fishing decoy is in bass form and is a two-piece aluminum die casting (Plate 268). The upper and lower halves overlapped in the gill area and were held together by a single screw, located at the approximate center of the belly area, and then attached into a threaded area of the top section. A subtle curve was designed into the rear of both the upper and lower sections. This allowed the decoy to swim in a counterclockwise direction.

The patent drawing shows one-piece angel wing-type side fins of transparent material. This side fin was designed to be held in place by having the upper and lower sections screw attached together. This was a clever idea, for the patent states, "The side wings or fins, being transparent, are invisible or inconspicuous in the water so that the lure has a *very* life like appearance." The only example that I have seen had no side fins, possibly removed by the fisherman. It also had no side hooks as shown in the patent drawing, and the example I saw had no provisions for side hook attachments. Perhaps the hooks and side fins shown in the patent drawing were deleted for production. The hollow design of this decoy allowed it to be filled with both buoyant material and ballast. The buoyant material used in the example shown is two separate components of wood, and ballast is lead shot encased in paraffin wax. The flat thin strip of lead material shown may have been added by the fisherman or possibly at production final assembly (Plate 269). The patent reveals that the ballast was designed to be placed in the lower front area for proper location of the center of gravity for ideal swimming quality of the decoy. The eyes are two-color quality glass fishing lure-type eyes. The line ties are drilled holes into the dorsal fin. The decoy was unpainted except for red accent paint at the gill area and on the pectoral fins and anal fin. I have heard of only one other example of this decoy being found, this one also in Michigan. The strength and quality of design and assembly of this metal decoy indicate it should have had a great survival rate, but because only two examples have been found to date, probably very few were made.

Plate 267. The patent drawing of the beautiful, realistic Jay B. Rhodes fish-spearing decoy.

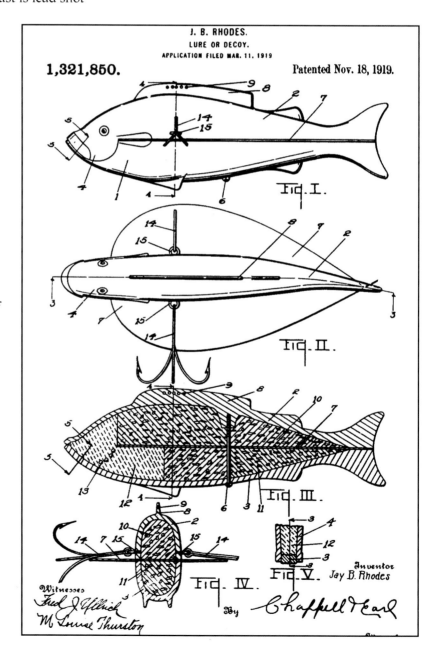

Plate 268. The lifelike Jay B. Rhodes attractor as the fish viewed it.

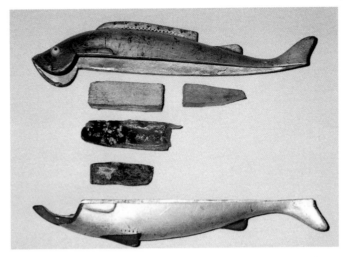

Plate 269. An inside look at all the components making up the cleverly designed Jay B. Rhodes fish-spearing decoy.

Ripley's Decoy Minnow

Horace E. "Slim" Ripley was born in Riceville, Iowa, on November 21, 1891. He married Lucy Hendricks in 1911 and in 1920 they moved to Alexandria, Minnesota. A house painter by trade, Slim Ripley (Plate 270) started making fish-spearing decoys in 1927 to help supplement his income. The business became a family affair, with one daughter helping paint the decoys and a second daughter folding and stamping the decoy boxes.

Slim Ripley's decoys were fairly uniform in size, form, and paint patterns. The metal side fins, dorsal fin, and tail were hand cut, but very uniform, indicating that shapes were scribed from templates. The typical size was 5¼" with dual colors accented by dots and dashes and flat painted eyes (Plate 271). Ballast was lead poured into a frontal, rectangular-shaped belly cavity, then filed and sanded flush to the flat belly. A number of Slim Ripley decoys were marked "RP" in paint on the lead ballast. The line tie was a simple single U-shaped wire form pressed into the back of the decoy body. Many of Slim Ripley's decoys were marketed in hardware stores in both Alexandria and Minneapolis, Minnesota.

Slim Ripley retired to Florida in 1954. He passed away at the age of 84 on August 30, 1976.

Plate 270. Slim Ripley (1891 – 1976).

Plate 271. *Typical Slim Ripley decoy box with the decoy minnow marketed in it.*

Plate 272. *Two Slim Ripley decoy minnows in different trout-like color paint finishes.*

D.C. Rivet's Decoys

The founder and sole owner of D.C. Rivet's Decoys was Dennis C. Rivet (1868 – 1947) of Bay City, Michigan. Bay City is located on Lake Huron's Saginaw Bay, which is one of the best summer and winter fisheries on the Great Lakes. Dennis Rivet was a fireman by profession for Bay City, eventually becoming the chief of the Bay City Fire Department. Many of the D.C. Rivet's fish decoys were made by Dennis and other firemen at the fire station while they were waiting for the next fire run.

The majority of D.C. Rivet's fish decoys made were small minnows, ranging from 2¼" long to 4" long (Plate 273), but a number of large 4½" to 8" long examples have been found (Plates 274 and 275). The wooden bodies are round with a generic minnow fish form, always with wooden tails. The gills were realisti-

cally hand cut, the mouth was a simple saw cut, and the eyes were drilled. A few fish lure-type glass eye examples have been found but were probably special order (Plate 276). Almost all examples found have a textured scalelike finish, from the gills rearward to the start of the tail area. This uniform texturing into the soft wood body was accomplished by hand with a rolling knurling tool. Two small angel wing-shaped side fins were hand cut to a template from light-gauge metal. All decoys, whether large or small, had a dorsal fin hand cut to a template from light-gauge metal. The largest decoys found have an added small anal and adipose fin hand cut to a template from light-gauge metal. Ballast is lead poured into an oval-shaped cavity in the frontal belly area, which also serves to anchor the side fins.

Paint finishes are hand done and range from two colors to four colors. Many examples found have partially unpainted natural wood heads. Others have a series of accent dots painted on the top of their heads. Also a few examples have been found with gold or red accent spots or dashes hand painted on the body sides. Side and all other fins are usually painted silver, but some are painted the body side color or are left unpainted. The line tie is a single handmade copper wire loop, probably anchored into the ballast

D.C. Rivet's decoys were marketed not only in Saginaw Bay area bait stores and tackle shops but also by Morley Brothers, the largest hardware distributors in Michigan at that time. The Morley Brothers hardware distributors marketed D.C. Rivet's fish

decoys in marketing boxes (Plates 277 and 278). The majority of D.C. Rivet's fish decoys were marketed between 1925 and 1938, the golden years of ice spear fishing in Michigan.

The popularity of the small minnow-like fish decoy used on Saginaw Bay can be traced as far back as the early market fishermen, who spear fished mainly for perch, walleye, and whitefish. There is documentation of horse-drawn wagons making daily rounds on the winter ice of Saginaw Bay, picking up the catch of the day from the market fishermen. Many of the market fishermen had sleeping lofts in their fishing shanties, staying out on the winter ice for weeks at a time.

Plate 273. Six examples of the smaller D.C. Rivet's minnow fish decoys.

Plate 274. Four examples of larger D.C. Rivet's fish decoys. Top to bottom: 5¾" long to 4¼" long.

147

Plate 275. An example of the largest 8" long D.C. Rivet's fish decoy.

Plate 276. An example of a 6" long D.C. Rivet's fish decoy with glass eyes.

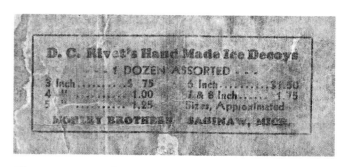

Plate 278. A Morley Brothers, Saginaw, Michigan, distributing box label for one dozen D.C. Rivet's fish decoys of assorted sizes with recommended retail prices.

Plate 277. An example of an unused D.C. Rivet's minnow fish decoy in a generic Morley Brothers marketing box.

Sletten Manufacturing Company

Kermit Sletten (1911 – 1959) was born in Willmar, Minnesota. After serving his country in World War II, Kermit returned to Willmar in 1946. He started the Sletten Manufacturing Company in his garage and shortly converted it into a plant to solely manufacture fish-spearing decoys. He later expanded the business by moving to a larger building at the nearby fairgrounds. Kermit not only designed all of his own decoys but also designed all the tooling to manufacture his decoys. Six different species of fish decoys and one critter, a combination fishing lure and fish spearing decoy called "The Water Bug," were manufactured and marketed by the Sletten Company.

All fish decoys were solid aluminum die castings. The fish decoy species were a 3¾" sunfish, a 4¼" crappie, a 5½" chub, a 6½" perch, a 7" pickerel, and a 7" pike (Plates 279 and 280). All species had an offset metal tail, an integral dorsal fin, and integral molded eyes, mouth, and gills. A horizontal slit was cut into the body at the anal area to attach a .060 thick one-piece template-cut sheet aluminum side fin. These were marked K. Sletten, Willmar, Minn. Pat.Pend. The side fins came in two different sizes and shapes. The smaller size was used on the sunfish, crappie, and chub species. The larger size was used on the pike, pickerel, and perch species. A single hole was drilled into the dorsal fin for a line tie. There were a variety of spray-painted finishes. Many simulated realism of the species. Eyes were always hand painted black and white. Each decoy was marketed in a cellophane bag

with a brochure on how to fish the decoy, along with the unassembled side fin component (Plates 281 and 282).

The Water Bug was a combination casting, still fishing, and fish-spearing decoy lure (Plate 283). Like the fish decoys, it was a solid aluminum die casting. The Water Bug critter lure was 3½" long and had integral molded eyes, mouth, dorsal fin, and an offset rudder-type fin at the rear. It also had a small finlike protrusion with a drilled hole at the lower head area for attaching a split ring and treble hook. The dorsal fin also had a drilled hole for a tackle line hook-up or a conventional fish decoy line tie. The rear rudder-type fin also had a drilled hole to attach a split ring and treble hook. The two split rings allowed the hooks to be removed if desired when using the Water Bug as a spear fishing decoy. A horizontal slit was cut into the rear of the body to insert the side fins, and the Water Bug used the same smaller size side fin as the fish decoys. There were a variety of spray-painted finishes. Unlike for the fish decoys, the side fins of the Water Bug were painted the same color as the body. Eyes were always hand painted black and white.

Each Water Bug was marketed in a small tan cardboard box stamped Water Bug, Sletten Mfg. Co. Willmar, Minn., and came with a brochure about the numerous ways to fish this versatile critter lure (Plates 283 to 287).

Plate 279. The Sletten Manufacturing Company's fish-spearing decoys. Top: Chub; center: crappie; bottom: sunfish.

Plate 280. Three versions of the Sletten Company's fish spearing decoys. Top: Pike; center: perch; bottom: pickerel.

Sub Surface Lures may be had in an assortment of colors, sizes and types. They are cast of aluminum to prevent rusting, have an adjustable fin and are designed for greater speed and action. They come in natural colors and shapes which make excellent lures even though they are not in motion. The tailfin is in a fixed position to guide each lure in circles of varying diameters ranging from approximately 15 inches to 4 feet, depending upon the type of lure used.

INSTRUCTIONS

1. Do not attempt to bend or adjust tailfin. Each type is designed to travel in circles of different diameters according to their size.

2. If fin loosens, tighten by making punch mark in the center of the fin.

3. If slot is too tight to insert fin, run an ordinary hacksaw blade thru slot.

4. It is very important to have adjustable fin in proper position. A few minutes of experimenting will soon determine this for you.

Plate 281. Sletten Company advertising brochure for the lures.

USE A COMPLETE SET

For best results in winter fishing, we suggest the use of a complete set of lures which consists of the following types—

PICKEREL — PERCH — PIKE CHUB — CRAPPIE — SUNFISH

You have purchased a lure of quality and one that will give you much service and good results. Ask your dealer to show you the complete set, they are varied, realistic and active.

Manufactured By

K. SLETTEN
WILLMAR, MINNESOTA

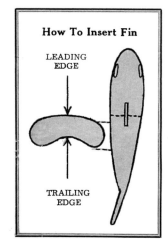

How To Insert Fin

LEADING EDGE

TRAILING EDGE

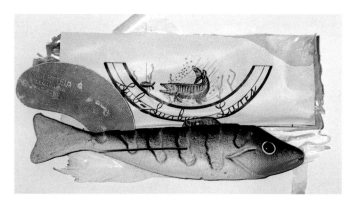

Plate 282. The Sletten Company decoys came in a cello-phane bag containing the decoy, side fin, and brochure.

Plate 283. Sletten Company advertising brochure for the Water Bug lure.

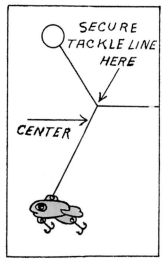

Now! YOU CAN "STILL FISH" *with* MOVING ARTIFICIAL BAIT!

A new creation in the angling market

The Water Bug

The WATER BUG is always in season, whenever or wherever there is fishing—The Water Bug is designed for year around fishing in coastal or fresh waters. It is also designed for surf-casting, still fishing, drop line fishing from boats, wharfs, piers, bridges, etc. Likewise it is an excellent bait for northern territories where it may be used during winter months for angling thru the ice or as a decoy in sheltered or dark house spearing.

SUGGESTIONS FOR USE

If the Water Bug is used for dropline or still fishing the line should be provided with a swivel. An upward or downward movement of the line is all that is required to put the Water Bug in action.

For casting—attach the Water Bug to a bobber with the length of line desired for fishing. Use a bobber of 2½ inch diameter or larger. Secure the tackle line to the bobber line at a point about 3 inches off center, towards the bobber. This hitch will permit the Water Bug and bobber to be reeled to the top of the tackle pole with the bobber just above the Water Bug. This arrangement will prevent the hooks from becoming fouled in the bobber line.

The natural movement of the bobber over waves, swells or rough water is all that is necessary to give the Water Bug action to attract the carnivorous fish.

K. SLETTEN, Willmar, Minn.

Plate 285. The Sletten Company Water Bug rigged for ice spear fishing. Note the added attractor of a shiny spinner blade.

Plate 284. The Sletten Company Water Bug and marketing box.

Plate 286. The Sletten Company Water Bug rigged for surf casting.

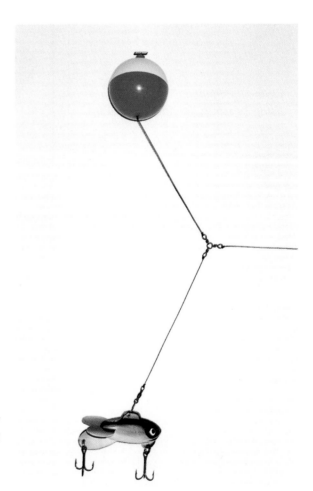

Plate 287. The Sletten Company Water Bug rigged for still fishing utilizing a large bobber.

South Bend Bait Company

The South Bend Bait Company was founded in 1910, and their first and only ice decoy was introduced in their 1923 – 1924 trade catalog (Plate 288). This was the only catalog that ever documented their ice decoy. The decoy utilized the wood body of the South Bend Company Muskie Trolling Minnow catalog no. 956, first introduced in 1912 (Plate 289). The ice decoy, like the Muskie Trolling Minnow, has five belly weights, but they are not in line as designed and implanted in the Muskie Minnow body. Instead they are staggered, not only for ballast but to balance this unique attractor that has no tail and no side fins. Fish decoys of this type were not designed to be swum in a circle. They became dynamic when the fisherman

twisted the tether line and let the decoy turn as it unwound against the resistance of the water. Also this finless decoy became an attractor to spear many curious fish by being jigged up and down by the spear fisherman. Either way the South Bend ice decoy was mighty attractive to the fish.

The assigned catalog number was 258 and it was available in only two colors: 258SF scale finish, green blend (Plate 290) and 258RHA red head and aluminum body (Plate 291). This decoy came only in one size, 5¼" in overall length, had glass eyes, and was marketed in the same box as the Muskie Trolling Minnow (Plate 290).

Plate 288. The page from the South Bend Company 1923 – 1924, No. 46 trade catalog showing their ice decoy.

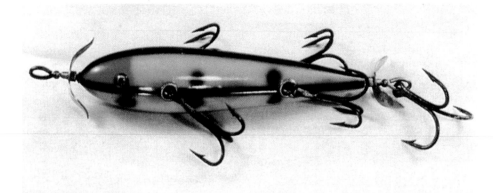

Plate 289. The South Bend Muskie Trolling Minnow No.956Y(1) in yellow hex paint finish.

Plate 290. The South Bend ice decoy No. 258SF in scale finish, green blend, with box in which it was marketed.

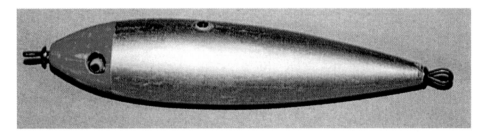

Plate 291. The South Bend ice decoy No. 258RHA with red head and aluminum body paint.

The Bud Stewart Tackle Company

The factory era of the Bud Stewart Tackle Company began in 1940, but this unique company was really born as a cottage factory operation in a chicken coop in Flint, Michigan, in 1930. That time frame is commonly referred to as the "Folk Art Period" (1930 – 1940). At that time Elman "Bud" Stewart was an unknown decoy maker who promoted the sale of his handmade, one-of-a-kind fish decoys out on the winter ice of the many inland lakes around the southern Michigan city of Flint (Plate 293). During the summer months he used the same marketing ploy, demonstrating his casting and trolling lures to fishermen, both fishing from the shore or in a boat out on the lake. His reputation and success as an outstanding fisherman helped immensely to sell his lures. When demand outweighed supply, the Bud Stewart Tackle Company was born.

This "Factory Period" lasted 40 years (1940 – 1980). It began in the spring of 1940 with the leasing of a 2,500-square foot building behind the family home in Flint, Michigan. The first employees were Bud's fishing friends with the largest complement of employees being 16 in 1956 (Plate 292). The earliest company brochure shows a variety of lures and decoys already being made. The mid to late Factory Period was when the greatest number of Bud's fish and critter spearing decoys were marketed. Many were special order, but most were sold off the shelf (Plates 294 and 295). The Bud Stewart Tackle Company also advertised and produced a larger variety of fish spearing critter decoys than any other company, both off the shelf and custom-ordered. The most popular critter decoys were ducklings, muskrats, and frogs. Other critter decoys produced were snakes, salamanders, and turtles.

The Bud Stewart Tackle Company was the only company during this time period to advertise that they would custom-make decoys and fishing lures for their customers (Plates 296 and 297). This is the reason why many one-of-a-kind examples are found by today's collectors. The most common fish decoy species marketed were sucker, pike, and perch. Most were carved and painted to a specific species. Most fish decoys had a scale pattern, but examples of solid color and multicolored decoys are sometimes found (Plate 298). Many special-order color patterns included multicolored glitter on the belly area, sometimes on the fins and tail. This glitter Bud found was a great added attraction, for it reflected much of the light coming through the ice.

Decoys from this period have been found as small as 1½" in length to as large as 15" long. The ratio of wooden tail versus metal tail models was about 40%

to 60%. The eyes were almost always of a convex painted tack type. Only a few decoys with glass eyes have been found; these were special ordered. The hardware was off-the-shelf bait propellers and spinner blades. Sometime these blades were cut in half for a different action. One unique design feature on some of Bud's fish decoys was a set of moveable spinner blades at the pelvic fin area of the body. These blades made the decoy very dynamic with the slightest movement (Plate 299). Numerous Stewart decoys of this period were rigged with an eye screw at one of the front pectoral fins and were called a crippled rig. When jerked by the spear fisherman, the decoy would turn over, making it appear crippled, wounded, or dying (Plate 299). A lathe-turned, round-bodied decoy was manufactured for about one year but was dropped from the line because Bud was unable to perfect its swimming action (Plate 300).

Another unique design was a combination fish decoy and casting bait called the "Jerk Minnow for Jerks." It was basically a fish decoy with a curved tail, a front and rear revolving propeller, a belly- and tail-rigged treble hook, and a set of stationary side fins. It had a conventional fish decoy line tie and also a tie at the front propeller for casting. It was finely tuned to swim in small circles with the propellers revolving as added attraction when being fished as an ice decoy. It could also be cast and retrieved as a underwater minnow or be jigged near the bottom from an anchored or drifting boat or fished through the ice. It was truly one of the most versatile fishing baits ever devised. Most examples found are 2½" to 3" in length and have a perch finish (Plate 301).

The final period is designated the "Collector's Period" (1980 – 1999). This period commenced with Bud's retirement, which, like that for many active people, evolved to a semi-retired status. Bud thought he would be like the proverbial cowboy who rides off into the sunset, but the public's demand for his beautiful, unique custom lures would not allow this to happen. With the establishment of the National Fishing Lure Collector's Club, the interest in collectible fishing tackle increased tremendously and with it a renewed desire from collectors to obtain examples of Stewart's lures and decoys. With this renewed interest and appreciation of his work, Bud was encouraged to come out of retirement and once again transform his ingenious ideas into what we refer to as the Collector's Period lures and decoys (Plate 302). These special quality baits and fish decoys were all hand carved, painted and tested for performance by Bud. Some of the baits and fish decoys of this period are glass-eyed, but the majority are still painted tack eyes. The hard-

ware used was the late Factory Period vintage. Extra time was spent on the paint patterns, with many reflecting the Folk Art Period spotted and swirl patterns that are most popular with today's collectors. These baits favor more medium to lighter colors with multicolored hues. Because many designs were one-of

a-kind, examples from this period of Bud's work are especially exciting and desirable. For these reasons along with their beautiful form and paint, Bud Stewart fish decoys are highly sought after by collectors (Plate 303).

The Stewart Cripples - - Different - - Proven for 16 Years

STEWART'S CRIPPLED MOUSE!

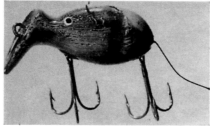

SIDE VIEW

TOP VIEW

Stewart's Crippled Mouse!

The Pedegreed Mouse with Papers—Notice how body rolls to the left giving a lop sided crippled effect. Hollow headed easy to plunk, yet a Real Action Surface Killer on a straight retrieve. Where can you get features like this? That is why Each Crippled Mouse is guaranteed (with guarantee paper) to be the Best Action Mouse Today!

Eye appeal—sure, see one today! Has everything. Boxed 12 in container, including real picture of news-clipping for a Compact Counter Display. Retail $1.25. Regular jobbers discount.

100 Series
P.G. 100—Plain Grey
G. 100—Grey
R.S. 100—Red Head Spotted
B.S. 100—Black Spotted
B.W. 100—Black and White
Also Specials

STEWART'S CRIPPLED WIGGLER!

SIDE VIEW

TOP VIEW

Stewart's Crippled Wiggler!

We won't spend a lot of time describing the features of the Crippled Wiggler. Notice Contortion Shape, like a minnow laying on its side, wiggles like nothing you have ever seen. You havn't seen a wiggle until you've seen the Crippled Wiggler. Made and proved for 16 years a killer! Made in a finish that is entirely different; the sweetest selling lure out. See one! 2 sizes—large and small.

B.S. 200—Brown Spotted
R.W. 200—Red and White
Y.S. 200—Yellow Spotted

Both Crippled Wiggler and Crippled Mouse are advertised in leading magazines. The World's Best Action Lures or **Double Money Refund!**

STEWART TACKLE
1032 ANN ARBOR ST.   FLINT 3, MICHIGAN

STEWART'S SSS MINNOW

(Stewart's Shiny Shiner)

A metal two piece, different Minnow Shaped Lure that even looks like a minnow —actually two minnows in one—sweet action. See one. Retail 85c.

Stewart's Crippled Sucker and Crippled Perch Decoys

Can be made to go any direction, any circle, large or small, sail beautifully. Made in a Flashy Eye-Appeal finish that is entirely different. Each tested for correct balance; ride right, try them—'nuf said!

Proved and Tested for 16 Years—Not a new untried over-nite lure!

Plate 292. Earliest Bud Stewart Tackle Company brochure advertising early Factory Period lures and ice decoys.

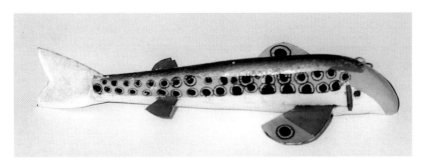

Plate 293. Folk Art Period sucker decoy.

Plate 294. Mid-Factory Period pike decoy.

Plate 295. Examples of duck, turtle, snake, salamander, and frog decoys by the Bud Stewart Tackle Company.

BUD STEWART is a custom Bait Maker, making and Experimenting Full Time for over 20 years and has actually experimented with more various different lures than any Ten Companies or persons alive.

IF YOUR IDEA OF A LURE CAN'T BE MADE, SEND A SKETCH TO BUD AND HE WILL REFINE AND MAKE THE BAIT. Example- you wanted a perch two inches or two feet, sucker, frog duck or what have you.

Twenty Years full time at Lure Making, over 3000 DIFFERENT models of lures have come from the Knife of Stewart, yes they are hand carved to perfection. Any action you wish can now be captured, and here is the only place in the Country that will devise for you what you want. All you do is explain your problem, let Stewart send you a lure to challange your problem. He specializes in spinning and Muskie - Works of art. His Muskie Sucker is the real thing - both surface and under water.

Plate 296. The Bud Stewart Tackle Company was the only bait company that challenged the fisherman to design his own bait and color pattern, as shown in the mid-Factory Period brochure.

Plate 297. Factory Period baby muskrat critter decoy.

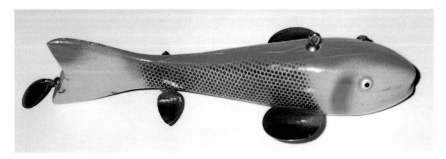

Plate 298. Mid-Factory Period colorful generic fish decoy.

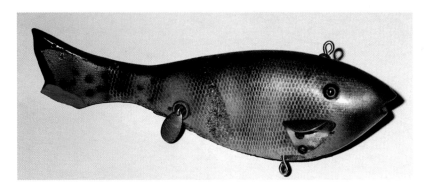

Plate 299. Example of dynamic moveable rear side fins and secondary cripple line tie.

Plate 300. Example of rare lathe-turned sucker decoy.

Plate 302. Example of an incredible Collector's Period panfish decoy with Bud's unique spotted finish.

Plate 301. Top: Versatile combination decoy and casting and jigging lure. Middle: Decoy utilizing same body as top lure. Bottom: Example of Bud's smallest perch minnow decoy.

Plate 303. Elman "Bud" Stewart (1912 – 1999) holding a Factory Period decoy during an interview with the author.

Art E. Storrs Decoys

Art E. Storrs of Le Center, Minnesota, made commercial fish, frog, and mouse fish-spearing decoys from 1930 to 1950. His fish decoys were 5½" long with bass form (Plate 304). The side fins, dorsal fin, anal fin, and tail were hand cut of light-gauge metal from templates. Ballast was lead poured into a rectangular hole at the frontal belly area. The decoys had two- and three-colored spray-painted enamel finishes. Eyes were flat painted in one or two different colors and in some cases there were no eyes. Line ties were a simple eye screw.

Art E. Storrs also made and marketed many frog fish-spearing decoys commercially (Plate 305). His frogs were 5" in length. The side fins and rear feet on the early models were hand cut from templates from sheet copper. The front side fins of his earliest frog decoys had notched trailing edges. Ballast was lead poured into an oval cavity into the frontal area of the belly. Each frog had a hand-painted white belly with green back and natural black and yellow frog spots. Eyes are two-color yellow and black flat painted. The line tie was a simple eye screw. Most of the frog decoys were stamped with ink "Made by A.E. Storrs" on the belly (Plate 306). His fish decoys were not stamped. Commercial critter decoys of any kind are rare, but judged by the number of the frog fish-spearing decoys found, this model must have been a successful venture for Storrs.

He also made and marketed a mouse fish-spearing decoy. His mouse decoy is considered very rare, for only a few have ever been found (Plate 307). This mouse decoy was 5½" in overall length, including the 2" tail. The legs, tail, and ears were hand cut from sheet copper. Ballast was lead poured into an oval-shaped cavity at the frontal belly area. Finish was hand-painted brown with white belly and black ears and tail. Eyes were flat-painted black, and the mouth was flat-painted white. The line tie was a simple eye screw. Most examples of these great fish, frog, and mice fish-spearing decoys have been found in Minnesota.

Plate 304. Examples of Art E. Storrs' fish decoys in three different paint finishes.

Plate 305. Two examples of Art E. Storrs' frog fish-spearing decoys. Top: Earliest with rounded side fins and metal rear feet, circa 1940. Bottom: Later version with angular side fins, circa 1950.

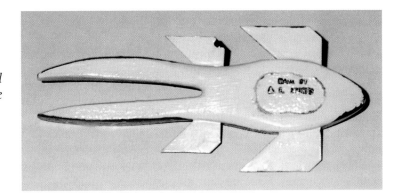

Plate 306. View of Art E. Storrs commercial marketing stamp on the bottom of the decoy shown at the bottom in Plate 305.

Plate 307. Example of Art E. Storrs' rare mouse critter fish-spearing decoy.

Titloe Heights Bait Manufacturer

William C. "Ole" Oldenburg of Gaylord, Minnesota, was the founder of the Titloe Heights Bait Manufacturer Company. The company was named after Lake Titloe on which the city of Gaylord is located in south central Minnesota.

Ole Oldenburg applied for a U.S. patent in 1935 for his lure, which he named the "Ole" 3-Way Fish Lure (Plate 308). The three examples shown in Plate 309 were most likely predecessors that later evolved into the patented model shown in Plate 308. It is believed that Ole Oldenburg marketed these earlier models from his home to local fishermen. These earliest models have been found in three different sizes: 4¾", 6", and 6½" long.

The body and angel wing-shaped side fins were hand cut from a template from 0.030 thick light-gauge sheet metal. The two side fins were attached with two rivets through drilled holes in the upstanding flange of each side fin, and matching holes in the body. The ballast was a molded lead rectangular-shaped component, with a slit cut in the center area. It was then crimped onto the lower head area. Paint finishes on these early examples were hand painted with two colors. On all of these earlier examples, the body color was light gray, with a small area of the head and tail painted red, blue, or black. The eyes were of duck decoy type, that is, quality molded two-color glass on a single wire. The wire from each eye was then thread-

ed through a hole in the head area, twisted together, then cut and bent over at the top of the head. A rubber-type sealer was then placed around the periphery of the wire between the eye and body to seat the eyes and also to prevent rusting of the wire. Line ties on these early examples are six drilled holes at the top of the back, located just behind the head. The later patented model was advertised as a fish-spearing decoy, a jigging lure, and a conventional casting or trolling lure (Plate 310). The body was 0.065 thick sheet aluminum, machine cut to shape. With the next operation the tail area was curved, which allowed the decoy to swim in a circle while being spear fished or to swim erratically while being jig fished, cast, or trolled. The angel wing side fins were 0.035 thick sheet metal die cut to shape. The patent models were smaller than the earlier models and have been found in three different sizes: 4¾", 4", and 2½" long. Only the largest 4¾" size is marked PAT.PENDING (Plate 311).

The two side fins were attached with two rivets through drilled holes in an upstanding flange of each side fin and matching holes in the body. No ballast component was needed for the patented models because the weight of the body, side fins, and eye components added up to an ideal weight to submerge and swim the decoy. The eyes were molded lead inserted into a hole in the head area, convex shaped

to an approximate half circle on both sides of the body. Nine holes were drilled into the body of the patent model. The three holes at the center of the back were line tie-attaching holes, with the two smaller examples having four line tie-attaching holes. The smaller hole at the nose area was a line tie-attaching hole for casting or trolling the lure. The larger hole in the nose area and the hole at the lower tail area functioned for attaching the lure hooks and split rings. As with the earliest examples, only the 4¾" patent example has provisions for the split ring and hook attachments. This leads me to believe all other sizes would

be out of proper balance with the additional weight of hooks and split rings.

The finishes were spray painted in two-color paint patterns, either red and white, blue and white, black and white, or green and white. Gills and mouths were spray painted on smaller models. The eyes were two-color spray painted yellow and black. The patent 4¾" model was marketed in a cardboard box with two treble hooks and attaching split rings, a brochure describing the three different methods for fishing this versatile lure, and a mail-order blank (Plate 311).

Plate 308. The "Ole" 3-Way Fish Lure with its marketing box.

Plate 309. Three examples of Ole Oldenburg's earliest glass-eyed fish-spearing decoys.

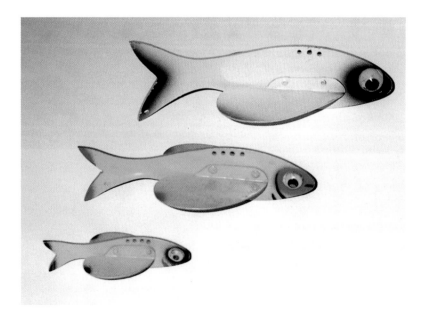

Plate 310. Three examples of Ole Oldenburg's later models. Top: 4¾" long. Middle: 4" long. Bottom: 2½" long.

The "OLE" 3-WAY FISH LURE

A Tried and Tested Fish Lure Which Is a Proven Success

Manufactured Under U. S. Patent Office Serial Number 762989, Series
of 1935, By the "Titloe Heights" Bait Manufacturer, Gaylord, Minnesota.

Feature Number "1"

Feature Number "1"

The Lure serves as an excellent Decoy for spearing fish through the ice in a dark house. When used for this purpose, detach the treble hooks from the body by way of the slip on rings and attach your decoy line to one of the three holes in the top of the body of the Lure, suitable to your adjustment, as illustrated in the picture to the left. Sink the Lure in the water to a suitable depth, then by gently raising and lowering the line the Lure will maintain a continuous circular movement in the water, within a radius of several feet. This is the action demanded by skilled fishermen and always gives the best results.

Feature Number "2"

For your fishing through the ice in a shelter or out in the open, the Lure will serve just as well as when spearing in a dark house. For this type of fishing, attach the treble hooks in the two large holes in the mouth and tail of the Lure by way of the slip on rings and attach your line in one of the three holes in the top of the body of the Lure, suitable to your adjustment, as illustrated in the picture to the right. When adjusted in this manner the same action and results will be obtained as described in Feature Number "1."

Feature Number "2"

Feature Number "3"

For summer fishing, the Lure also serves as an excellent bait when trolling or casting. To use the Lure for this purpose, fasten your line in the hole in the mouth of the Lure and attach the treble hooks if they have been detached. The wings of the Lure are flexible and can be adjusted to produce the various actions which you may desire. Try tilting the right wing downward and the left wing upward to obtain best results. See illustration in the picture to the left. The Lure also serves well in the summer for drop fishing. When drop fishing the line should be attached at the top of the body of the Lure as shown in Feature Number "2" and should be operated in the same manner.

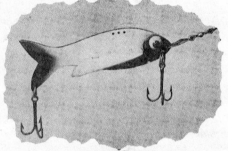

Feature Number "3"

The "3-Way" Feature has made this Lure famous. The Lure is constructed of metal material, and is approximately 4¾ inches in length, weighing approximately 2 ounces. It is beautifully decorated in colors and is equipped with two treble hooks which are attachable and detachable from the main body of the Lure by way of slip on rings.

The colors and prices of the Lure are as follows:

NUMBER	COLOR	PRICE
No. 501	Red and White	$1.50
No. 502	Blue and White	1.50
No. 503	Black and White	1.50
No. 504	Green and White	1.50

This Lure is sold direct by the Manufacturer only. To be assured that your Lure will reach you in time for your winter fishing this year, place your order now. All orders will be filled in the order in which they are received. Enjoy a successful season of fishing with the "Ole" 3-Way Fish Lure.

Titloe Heights Bait Manufacturer,
Gaylord, Minn.
...................................., 194........

Enclosed, herewith, please find currency, draft, money order, in the amount of $..........................., for which please send me......................."Ole" 3-Way Fish Lures, in the following colors:.......................................

Name.......................................

Address.......................................

Plate 311. The brochure and mail order blank for the patented "Ole" 3-Way Fish Lure found in the box with the lure.

Tru-Fish Decoys

One of the cleverest innovations for decoying fish to the fisherman is the unique attractor manufactured by the Tru-Fish Decoy Company of Waukegan, Illinois. The Tru-Fish decoy was invented and designed by Malcolm Layson (1920 – present) of Waukegan, Illinois (Plate 313), who was granted United States patent no. 4,550,518 on November 5,1985 (Plate 312). Layson, an avid fisherman, conceived the idea for this year-round fish attractor while fishing for crappie. Observing how the crappies fed sporadically, coming and going from time to time, he devised this attractor called the Tru-Fish decoy. The Tru-Fish decoy looks like an actual school of live fish, but in reality it is actual fish photographed and printed on a sheet of clear plastic. Since Malcolm is an artist who owned his own graphic art business before retiring, he was a natural to design and manufacture this unique attractor. The original fish design image was of a school of 8" to 10" long perch, first marketed in 1961 (Plate 314). The second design marketed was of a school of crappie. Later designs were bluegill with seaweed, crappie feeding on minnows, bass feeding on minnows, perch in seaweed feeding on minnows, and a large school of swimming minnows.

Malcolm's first design was marketed in a clear plastic celluloid carrying tube with red plastic end caps. The tube contained all the necessary items required to fish the Tru-Fish decoy (Plate 315). The printed mylar sheet with the schooling fish design was 18" x 22" in size. Three bell sinkers were to be attached with rubber bands to the bottom of the mylar

and functioned to sink the mylar sheet. Two transparent bobbers were to be attached with rubber bands to the upper two corners to suspend the mylar sheet upright. The Tru-Fish decoy could be fished either suspended or on the lake bottom, depending on the size of the sinkers. A tether line with a large bobber was attached to one of the immersed corner bobbers to keep the Tru-Fish decoy in the same location (Plate 314). Also included were directions on how to fish the decoy in both open water and under the winter ice (Plate 316).

Later patent revisions included a larger mylar sheet 28" x 40" and the addition of a sealed ⅜" diameter, 18" long clear hollow plastic floatation tube attached to the top of the mylar decoy. This replaced the two transparent bobbers.

The last patent revision is using the decoy carrying tube, for a live bait tube and attaching it to the top of the Tru-Fish decoy floatation tube. At your fishing location, fill the tube approximately ⅓ to ½ full from minnow bucket or lake water. Next add your choice of legal live bait, minnows, night crawlers, wigglers, etc. Secure the functional end cap with holes in it. This allows lake water to fill the tube as you lower it to the pre-determined depth. This live bait tube is a great fish attractor and keeps fish around the decoy longer, enhancing your fishing results (Plate 317). The Tru-Fish Decoys are currently marketed through mail order only. The Tru-Fish Decoy's success is backed by many letters of testimony from fishermen.

Plate 312. The first patent drawing of the Tru-Fish decoy.

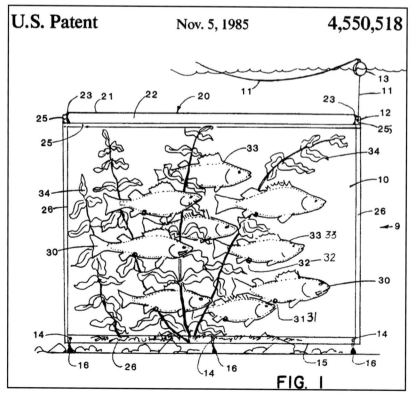

Plate 313. Malcolm Layson (1920 – present), inventor of the Tru-Fish Decoy, out on the winter ice for a day of ice fishing using his decoy.

Plate 314. A simulation of the Tru-Fish decoy being fished.

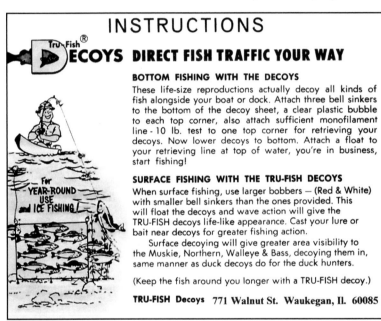

Plate 315. The Tru-Fish decoy with carrying tube and all related items.

INSTRUCTIONS

Tru-Fish® DECOYS DIRECT FISH TRAFFIC YOUR WAY

BOTTOM FISHING WITH THE DECOYS

These life-size reproductions actually decoy all kinds of fish alongside your boat or dock. Attach three bell sinkers to the bottom of the decoy sheet, a clear plastic bubble to each top corner, also attach sufficient monofilament line - 10 lb. test to one top corner for retrieving your decoys. Now lower decoys to bottom. Attach a float to your retrieving line at top of water, you're in business, start fishing!

SURFACE FISHING WITH THE TRU-FISH DECOYS

When surface fishing, use larger bobbers — (Red & White) with smaller bell sinkers than the ones provided. This will float the decoys and wave action will give the TRU-FISH decoys life-like appearance. Cast your lure or bait near decoys for greater fishing action.

Surface decoying will give greater area visibility to the Muskie, Northern, Walleye & Bass, decoying them in, same manner as duck decoys do for the duck hunters.

(Keep the fish around you longer with a TRU-FISH decoy.)

TRU-FISH Decoys 771 Walnut St. Waukegan, Il. 60085

Plate 316. The Tru-Fish decoy directions for how to fish the decoy both in open water and under the winter ice.

MUSKIE, NORTHERN, BASS & WALLEYE FEED ON PERCH . . . BLUEGILL AND CRAPPIE FEED WITH PERCH!!!

ICE FISHING WITH THE TRU-FISH DECOYS

Always roll decoy from top toward bottom, this keeps the sinkers free to automatically unroll it.

For ice fishing just place decoy sheet flat on the ice and proceed to accordion fold it — (Careful not to crease the sheet), insert sinkers thru ice hole first and feed in your retrieving line freely until it reaches bottom. For floating the TRU-FISH DECOYS* use smaller sinkers.

Ducks go for decoys AND FISH DO TOO!

*(Keep the fish around you longer with a decoy)

LINES FISH TRAFFIC FROM EVERY DIRECTION

RUBBER BANDS PROVIDED TO SECURE BOBBERS & SINKERS

NOTE:
TIE A LOOSE LOOP THRU ALL GROMMETS

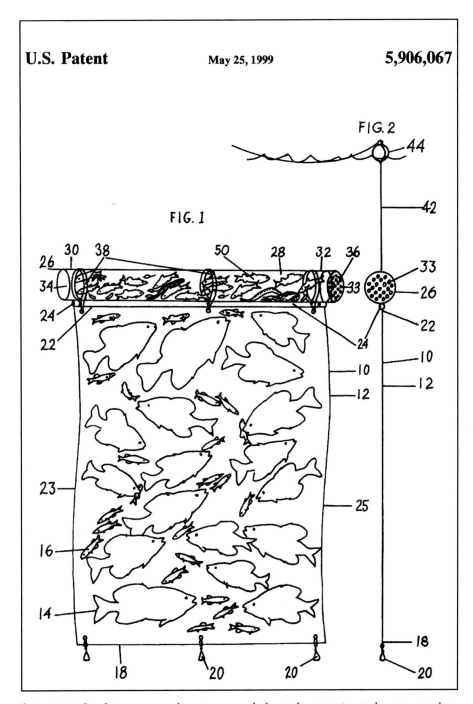

U.S. Patent   May 25, 1999   **5,906,067**

FIG. 2

FIG. 1

Plate 317. This later patent drawing reveals how the carrying tube was used as an added attractor to the Tru-Fish decoy. Live minnows, crawdads, or night crawlers inside the plastic tube supporting the mylar sheet prove to be a mighty fine attractor.

Harry L. Way Decoys

Harry L. Way of Muskegon, Michigan, was born in 1901. His working life, starting at age 15, was spent mostly in metal shops in the Muskegon area and spanned about 50 years. His transition into woodcraft began during his layoff during the Great Depression of the 1930s. His income came solely from manufacturing quality furniture, mostly beautifully made cabinets and desks, from his basement workshop. It was during that time that he started making fish decoys for spear fishing enthusiasts (Plate 318). By his own estimate he had produced about 400 to 500 fish-spearing decoys by the early 1960s. He marketed most of his fish decoys from his home workshop and some from local stores (Plate 319).

Harry's decoys varied in length and were basically in two different shapes. One was a bass form and the other a sleek pike form. Metal side and dorsal fins and tail were hand cut from a template and inserted into slits in the body. Ballast was lead poured into an oval hole in the frontal belly area. Eyes were mostly domed nickel-plated upholstery tacks, but some were off-the-shelf painted thumb tacks. A few examples without eyes have been found. The bodies were spray painted, in both multicolor and solid colors. Side and dorsal fins and tail were not painted on most examples, but there were a few exceptions, usually a solid red paint finish. The gill and mouth areas and sometimes the periphery of the eyes were accented in red paint on most examples. The line ties were a simple eye screw. The earliest decoys made by Harry were initialed H.W.

Harry Way passed away in the early 1970s and has to be admired for his ingenuity and entrepreneurship during the Depression when there was no welfare to care for the jobless.

Plate 318. A beautiful early example of a Harry L. Way fish-spearing decoy.

Plate 319. A store display board of Harry L. Way decoys for sale. The open slits indicate decoys that have been sold.

Albert "Bert" Winnie Decoys

Albert "Bert" Winnie (1874 – 1935) of Traverse City, Michigan, was the older brother of Art Winnie (1880 – 1966) also of Traverse City. Both were barbers in Traverse City who cut hair every day and fished almost every evening. They were both accomplished fishermen, fly tiers, and lure makers. Their most popular selling lure was the Stump Dodger. The Stump Dodger lure came in a variety of sizes and was designed and patented on August 15, 1913 and assigned patent no. 784,957. This lure was made from 1912 to 1935 (Plate 320). Most of their ice decoy production was in the early to mid years of this period.

The fish-spearing decoys ranged in size from 4" to 11½" long with most being 6" to 7" long (Plate 321). Species included emerald shiners, dace, sunfish, perch, suckers, pike, trout, and cisco (Plate 322). The cedar wood bodies had integral relief-carved double gill plates, a detailed mouth with lips, and raised eyes. The side, dorsal, and adipose fins were hand cut from sheet metal using a template. The tail had a small hole drilled in it. This hole could be used for hanging the decoy during the painting and paint drying opera-

tions or for adding colored cloth or yarn as an attractor. The side, dorsal, anal, adipose fins, and tail were pressed into slits in the body, and only the tail was then nail attached. Ballast was lead poured into a rectangular hole in the frontal belly area.

Spray-painted finishes came in a variety of two or three solid colors. Others were of a realistic perch scale paint pattern or a realistic green scale herring paint pattern. More examples of the green herring decoy have been found than any of the others. The eyes were two-color flat white and black hand-painted. The line tie utilized the Stump Dodger lure's screw-attached hook hanger hardware (Plate 320). These Winnie decoys were some of the earliest commercial fish-spearing decoys made. Their survival rate is a testament to the quality of their material and paint as well as the high quality of the workmanship. For 80 years after their manufacture, they are still being used under the winter ice by ardent ice spear fishermen.

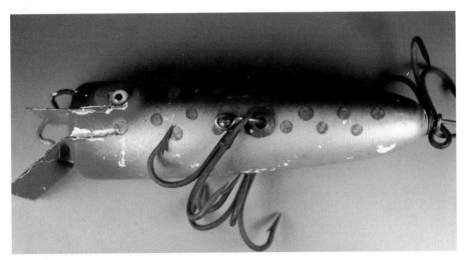

Plate 320. Bert Winnie's popular selling Michigan Stump Dodger lure. Note the side hook hanger hardware also used as a line tie on Bert Winnie's ice fish-spearing decoy.

Plate 321. Two examples of Bert Winnie's fish-spearing decoy. Top: His largest decoy, the 11½" long herring. Bottom: Smaller 7" long herring decoy with added red yarn attractor.

Plate 322. Three more examples of Bert Winnie's fish-spearing decoys. Top: Scarce cisco decoy. Second from top right: Rare panfish decoy. Third from top right: Herring.

By Joe Fossey

With a lifelong interest in sport fishing and boat building, I was fortunate to be employed during the booming 1960s and 1970s by a major international marine motor manufacturer. This allowed me the unprecedented opportunity to visit hundreds of marine dealers and marinas across the great expanse of Canada, from Atlantic Newfoundland to the Queen Charlotte Islands in British Columbia.

As an active member of the Canadian Antique and Classic Boat Society for 20 years, I had the opportunity to study the marine history in this area, an invaluable experience. With my retirement, a new interest in researching the lore of Canadian spear fishing and carving of antique-style fish decoys has led to practicing many new skills. It has also resulted in countless hours of detective work researching the history of this age-old folk art craft in Canada.

The Boating Industry Association states that approximately 50% of the recreational marine products and related sporting items were sold within a 200-mile radius of Canada's largest city of Toronto, Ontario. This is quite believable because of the huge concentration of population, now approximately 3 million, and hundreds of lakes in the Precambrian Shield of surrounding cottage country, plus being centered in the "Golden Horseshoe" of three Great Lakes, Ontario, Erie, and Huron. Not to say that commercial wooden ice fishing decoys were never manufactured and marketed elsewhere in Canada, but I have simply not uncovered any factual evidence to support this at this time.

Like the great city of Detroit lying in the shadow of Lake St. Clair with its very rich history of market fishing and hunting, the city of Toronto, although located on the shores of Lake Ontario, is similarly located a short distance south of Lake Simcoe. This lake has historically played a large role in sport and commercial fishing in that area.

Fig. 323. Artist's illustration of a native North American ice spear fishing in the early 1800s.

Canada's native and Arctic populations relied heavily on using decoys to fish in winter from the beginning of recorded time. My research to date, however, only leads to cold trails at native research centers throughout the country. It is strange but true, that most present day archivists and curators of museums or cultural centers have never even heard of fish decoys. This fact drives my ongoing thirst for historical data.

A local pioneer settler, George Cook, recorded in his diary of 1815 that, when arriving on frozen Lake Simcoe for the first time, he observed "the use of an artificial fish 8" to 9" long of white wood, with leaden eyes, tin fins and weighted bodies.... The Native fisherman after chopping holes in the thick ice completely enveloped himself in a large buffalo skin, with a short spear ready to transfix any fish attracted to his bait" (Plates 323 and 324).

As time went on, the early settlers cleared the

land surrounding Lake Simcoe for farming. It was natural that other forms of commerce supporting agriculture developed around the lake, such as timbering and commercial fish harvesting. Because of its great natural beauty and proximity, this area also became a very early recreation destination for people from the Toronto area. Before the invention of the motorcar, railroads ran to almost every town and hamlet along the shores of Lake Simcoe.

To supply fish for food and to supplement their meager farming incomes, many settlers turned to commercial winter spear fishing. They built shanties of light cedar wood that could be easily moved to follow fish movements. Local blacksmiths turned out hundreds of forged spears for the fishermen, and winter ice fishing shanty rentals were introduced to the public.

Because Lake Simcoe is almost 50 miles long, many fishermen with little or no means of transportation had problems marketing their fish. Commercial buyers made daily rounds of the lake, collecting and buying the frozen fish with horse teams or early Ford model T trucks. They then transported the fish to railway towns for train shipment to Toronto and other large centers in Ontario, as well as for export to major cities in the United States. Lake trout and whitefish were most common species taken (Plates 325 and Plate 326).

Spearing fish was a very controversial means of taking fish then just as now. Conservationists howled in protest as various governments allowed or disallowed spear fishing depending on their legislative rulings. Ontario finally ended spear fishing in 1940 (Plate 327).

Commercial fish decoy carving was practiced by the many fish shanty rental operators and boat yard operators around the lake. It was commercial in the sense that these people made decoys for their own use and for renters of their shanties and occasionally sold them for a dollar or less to their regular customers.

In many cases, special identifying decoy designs were made by various fish shanty operators to prevent loss by theft. They also made their own gaff hooks and tip-ups with special curves or details to make the hut owner's identification visual and easy.

For this reason alone, there are a lot of local fish decoy design differences in this area, rather than many thousands of similar fish decoys churned out by large fishing tackle factories. It is clear that many, if not most, decoy makers could only be classified as "cottage industries."

A few exceptions to this rule do exist. The now-defunct Rolland Boats of Orillia, Ontario; Busty Baits of Parry Sound, Ontario, on Georgian Bay; The Dominion Tackle Company of Oro, Ontario; and Decoy Manufacturing Company of Brantford, Ontario, can be classified as commercial manufacturers. Capsule histories of these little-known Canadian commercial fish decoy manufacturers begin on page 175.

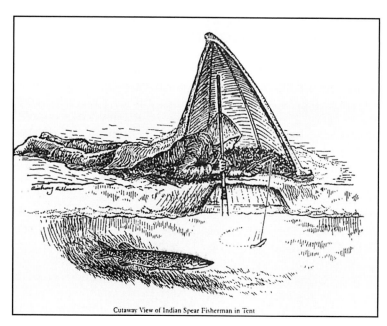

Cutaway View of Indian Spear Fisherman in Tent

Plate 324. Artist's illustration of a native North American ice spear fishing in the early 1800s. Courtesy of Anthony Hillman.

Plate 325. Jack Mitchell of Beaverton, Ontario is shown holding a speared white-fish next to his spearing hut, circa 1935.

Plate 326. Jack Mitchell's catch of large lake trout stacked frozen. The dark spot on the ice is fish blood where Jack shook the speared trout off his spear, circa 1935.

For Darrell
Love Mum   *This was your grandfathers*
in the Ontario later

Form F 5
200 Nov., 1939
P 3280

GAME and FISHERIES DEPARTMENT

No. S. 35

Fee $3.00

ORIGINAL

ONTARIO

IDENTIFICATION

Age ___ 38 ___

Height ___ 5' 7" ___

Weight ___ 150 ___

Color of Hair ___ Brown ___

Color of Eyes ___ Grey ___

Special Spearing License

LAKE SIMCOE

Issued under the Game and Fisheries Act and Dominion Special
Fishery Regulations for the Province of Ontario

1940

The herein named _____ Harmon Fountain _____ Resident

of _____ Beaverton _____ on payment of the sum of Three Dollars

is licensed to fish with ONE SPEAR in the public waters of Lake Simcoe

_____ Fronting Georgina Township _____

during the months of January, February and March, 1940, for the taking of whitefish, herring,
lake trout and coarse fish.

This license is not transferable and the holder thereof must conform strictly to the Fishery
Laws and Regulations, and to all lawful directions of fishery officers, and must produce same
when required to do so by any officer of the Game and Fisheries Department.

This spear must have a tag with the name of the owner and number of license marked
thereon.

Not valid unless countersigned by authorized Issuer.

Dated at _____ Toronto _____ January 29 _____ 1940

Countersigned

_____

_____
Deputy Minister of Game and Fisheries

Plate 327. *Special spearing license issued to non-native Americans, 1940. This was the last year these special
spearing licenses were issued.*

Rolland Boats of Orillia, Ontario

Enterprising and ambitious men like the Rolland family of Orillia were in the boat building and outboard motor business for two generations. They earned excellent money making fish decoys in slow winter months without tying up any money in inventory or expensive raw materials. During the 1940s and 1950s they used their grandfather's early fish decoys as a pattern. In a production line scheme using shop equipment, they milled out blanks of local lumber, band sawed them to rough shape, routered out the lead cavity, sanded them, and then inserted the fins. The decoys were never painted or preserved in any way. John Rolland said they could easily finish 100 pieces per day. He would then jump in the truck and sell them all for $1.00 each to fishermen in shanties on Lake Simcoe or their many O.M.C. companion dealers (Plate 328).

Plate 328. A typical 5" long Rolland Boats fish-spearing decoy, circa 1940.

Busty's Baits of Parry Sound, Ontario, Canada

William Stanley ("Busty") Flesher was a pioneer of the Parry Sound area. He was born in Parry Sound in 1890 and died there August 19, 1967, spending his entire life in that Georgian Bay area. How, why or where Busty got his unusual nickname, which followed him everywhere throughout his life, even to the company name of his patented fishing lures, is not known.

Busty Flesher married Evelyn Hoburn (1905 – 1996) of Parry Sound. Their marriage produced two sons and two daughters. Throughout his life Busty was an active bushman/sportsman hunter, and he also held a commercial fishing license for many years. It is thought that his commercial fishing experiences led to the creation and development of the "Busty Bait" around 1935, which was always associated with very successful winter ice fishing in the Parry Sound area. Instructions packaged in the box also included the multi-usage instructions for trolling in open waters. This bait in fish decoy history is known as a "cheater" because of the hooks (Plates 329 and 330).

To protect himself from design theft and any possible reproduction of his successful baits, Busty went to the trouble of having his design patented. He was very guarded about his design, and his brother-in-law Bun Hoburn stated that Busty turned down a firm offer of $10,000 cash plus royalties from a major USA bait manufacturer. Busty is remembered as a stickler for fine detail and thought that mass production might possibly take away bait quality, so he decided to stay small and independent.

Busty manufactured his 4" – 7" baits in the basement workshop of his home. With a minimum of machinery, he produced hundreds of baits. The baits were made from clear local white cedar, and the hook holders and front trolling eye were drilled through and anchored firmly into the lead ballast. He hand painted all of them using many colors, but his favorite was shades of green or else a white body with red head and many red spots. Today, any Busty Bait that fishermen own or fortunately find at a sale is much appreciated.

Busty could turn his hand to many handcrafted skills and was also considered an excellent boatman. He was a guide with his own boat, and for many years he repaired local wooden fishing boats of all sizes in the off seasons by replacing ribs, planking, keels, etc.

Like many of the lure and bait makers of the day, when the duck hunting season came along, Busty would have long since carved a ready supply of duck decoys for himself and hunting friends.

In his later years, Busty sought out steadier employment as a watchman for the local Department of Transport marine facility, while continuing to make and invent new fishing lures in his home basement workshop. He was always inventive and constantly

had a new and different project on the back burner. His nephew Ken Brown remembers that one of Busty's last experiments was trying to perfect a "Winter Bobber," an automatic line-recoiling device that reeled in the fish after it had taken the bait.

Although Busty was considered a little gruff at times in his public manners, he was said to have had a heart of gold and he helped many people out in difficult times. Money was never as important to this

fiercely independent man as the joys of hunting and fishing in beautiful Georgian Bay.

Evidence of Busty's great pride in his baits can be immediately recognized in the very detailed usage instructions that were neatly packed into every box sent to dealers or customers. We thank Parry Sound historian and author Dave Thomas and Busty's nephew Ken Brown for their assistance in providing information for this brief profile of Busty Flesher.

INSTRUCTIONS FOR USING BUSTY'S BAITS

To get the best results for still fishing through the ice or from a boat, use a fine strong line, also an 18" wire leader with a small swivel and snap, a swivel must be used to keep line from twisting, do not use any weights or sinkers. Fasten the snap in the front top staple as shown in diagram below, use a short wooden pole with bracket for winding line on about 14" long. First let the bait down in 3 or 4 feet of water, hold the pole in hand pointing slightly downward, then give it a short snappy jerk upward from 4 to 6 inches, immediately drop it down to starting position, pause from 5 to 10 seconds, then repeat the movement. This allows you to see the movement of the bait and get the best action; then you can use it as deep as you want to fish without seeing it.

For fishing pickerel and pike, let the bait down to the bottom, then lift it up from 18" to 5 feet and the bait will be about the right distance from the bottom for good fishing. Always keep the bait above the fish that you want to catch. If you get a strike and miss the fish, lift the bait and replace the hooks on the pins if any are off, the pins just hold the hooks in place until the fish bites. The hooks must be kept on the pins a all times.

FASTEN HERE FOR STILL FISHING

BUSTY'S BAITS

CASTING & TROLLING

For fishing trout through the ice, if a small fish house is used, keep it dark inside so as the fish cannot see any movement of the pole or hand. When fishing outside, cover the top of the water with loose snow. Along the shore line or at a point where the water is 20 feet deep or more, this bait gives good results used from 12 to 25 feet below the ice surface.

For casting and trolling, these baits can be used with or without a spinner. If a spinner is used it should be spaced from 4" to 6" ahead of the bait, move the rod forward and backward for greater attraction. These baits are made in different sizes and colours and your tackle box is not complete without several of them in it. They are one of the best lures money can buy, if not the best. These baits have become very popular with fishermen for winter fishing especially.

Made by W. S. FLESHER,
Inventor and Patentee,
Parry Sound, Ontario, Can.

Plate 329. A copy of the brochure included with each Busty Bait sold, circa 1940.

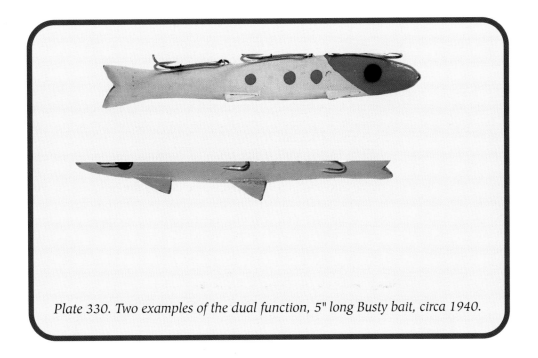

Plate 330. Two examples of the dual function, 5" long Busty bait, circa 1940.

Dizzy Decoy Company of Brantford, Ontario

The "Dizzy Decoy" was the brainchild of Charles R. Dailey, who moved from the United States to Brantford, Ontario, Canada, around 1950. He moved to Brantford located in southwestern Ontario with the specific purpose of starting a new machine shop business, which he named Bridgewater Machine.

Besides being a well-trained machinist with an inventive flair, Dailey also had a keen knack for marketing strategy, which served him well. Charles, Charlie to friends, was an ardent fisherman and soon found many new places to fish in Ontario.

Pleased with the Canadian winter ice fishing available, he was drawn to Lake Simcoe, where he enjoyed excellent results using a wooden fish decoy made by a local native Indian guide. The friendly guide gave Charlie one of his decoys as a gift.

Back home in Brantford, Charlie studied the rather crude homemade decoy, and his inventive thoughts soon turned to ways to make a better one. He wanted his decoy to look a lot better and still have effective fish-catching capabilities. He began a series of home workshop experiments to make a new and successful decoy.

The "Dizzy Decoy" name was given to the decoy by Charlie because of the very erratic movements in water of his redesigned decoy. Convinced his new decoy was a real winner, he began to make small quantities for retail sales as a hobby business in his home workshop at 10 Edgewood Avenue in Brantford. Originally the company was known as The Decoy Mfg. Company, but later literature and logo show DAI-LURE "Hand Crafted Lures" at the same address.

With his son Gordon at his side, Charlie made many weekend combination leisure and business trips to Lake Simcoe and Lake Nipissing. His productive catches of fish soon had other fishermen asking for the new decoy. The Dizzy Decoy business began to expand quite rapidly and unknown hundreds were made and sold in the 1950s and 1960s (Plate 331).

Charlie never stopped improving on the finish and durability of the decoy. He was a real stickler for quality workmanship because of his machinist background. This led to the use of more durable paint and the use of stainless steel for the die-punched bottom located side fin base plate, with a down-standing steerable rear fin. The name and address of Decoy Mfg. Co. were proudly stamped into the design, with a notation of "Patent Pending." The decoys were sold in individual clear plastic hinged-lid boxes.

Gordon Dailey is certain that his father was successful in trademarking the "Dizzy Decoy" name and patenting the unusual top wing design. Family and legal files are currently being searched to locate the confirming documentation.

After all, Charlie was in a hobby business to have some pleasure fishing as well as to make some profit.

Gordon remembers his dad's upbeat approach to any weekend fishing trips that did not produce a lot of fish and good sales — "Well, Gord, we didn't make much money today, but we sure had a lot of fun."

Continuing to improve his product, Charlie started making Dizzy Decoys in several sizes from 4" to 7" and in many color variations. He lathe-turned every one himself from selected imported American woods. Lead ballast was placed in the nose, making the decoy sink fast in the water, and its erratic swimming action was determined by the fisherman's skill in jigging the decoy.

Some baits were experimentally made into casting and trolling models by installing a front-mounted screw eye instead of the top-mounted jigging line tie. Although moderately successful, best results were obtained from the original design.

Many of Charlie's later lathe-turned wooden bodies were reinforced with carefully machined and fitted brass bands at both the head and tail. This eliminated possible splitting of the wood by large fish action, a feature thought necessary to accommodate the larger Coho salmon that had been introduced to Lake Ontario waters by that time.

Little is known of the first 35 years of Charlie's life in the United States before he came to Canada. In a thumbnail historical sketch of the Decoy Mfg. Company, we can only follow the known Canadian path. Charles R. Daily died in 1970 at age 70. Gordon did not wish to continue his father's fishing tackle business on his own because of other personal commitments, so he closed the business down permanently.

The author thanks Gordon Daily and boating friend Garnet Shaver for their advice and information in preparing this brief Dizzy Decoy history.

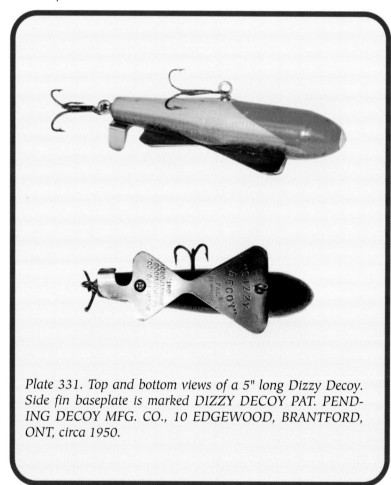

Plate 331. Top and bottom views of a 5" long Dizzy Decoy. Side fin baseplate is marked DIZZY DECOY PAT. PENDING DECOY MFG. CO., 10 EDGEWOOD, BRANTFORD, ONT, circa 1950.

Dominion Fishing Tackle Company of Toronto

The Dominion Fishing Tackle Company began business around 1925 in a very small way and was located at 2107 Danforth Avenue in Toronto's East End. The proprietor of the original storefront fishing tackle business was Owen A. Jones. He is reported in original company literature as a well-known Toronto fisherman.

To survive in the fishing tackle manufacturing business during the 1930s depression required a great deal of skill. It meant combining good salesmanship to market what might be then thought of as a "nonessential product" and considerable mechanical aptitude to invent, manufacture, and run competitive lure-making machinery.

Until 1937, Dominion Fishing Tackle Company literature was limited to the simple economic lithograph or Gestetner machine "flyer type" advertising. The first trade catalog was printed in 1937 with a multicolored front page. Inside, 31 pages of extremely ornate hand-drawn artwork beautifully illustrated and described each bait. The cover boasts of the company being known "From Coast to Coast" and displayed their registered trademark, a curved "Leaping Largemouth Bass" and "Dominion Brand Metal Baits of Quality For Every Fishing Purpose."

The catalog, with several mail order forms enclosed, lists over 50 different metal spoon design baits. Each was available in several sizes and several different finishes, for example polished nickel, polished brass, polished copper or painted. As well, they invited customer enquiries to supply tubular fishing rods, solid or tubular, fly or level wind reels, fly or bait casting lines, plugs, landing nets, gaff hooks, tackle boxes, sinkers and all kinds of hooks. Obviously this was a very complete supply house for the angling enthusiast.

The effect that the severe metal shortages during World War II had the operation or success of the Dominion Tackle Company business is not known at this time, nor the speed of the postwar return to regular sport fishing activities and increased sales. As our research continues, we hope to report more on this.

In 1955, however, the Dominion Tackle Company with all of its machinery and business was purchased by Lester (Les) Bedford (1902 – 1989) of Toronto. The entire operation was moved to Oro Station, Ontario, on the west side of Lake Simcoe, north of Barrie. Les Bedford enlisted the services of his son Douglas, at that time employed in the mining industry of northern Ontario, to help him get the tackle-making equipment business up and running again.

As Doug now recalls with a smile this "temporary" assignment lasted for 33 years, from 1955 until 1988, when the company was sold for the last time.

Les Bedford was a graduate mechanical engineer with much industrial experience. He was clever at innovative machine changes and ideas to make the complex wire-forming and stamping machinery work better. The small plant began to expand to meet dealers' orders across the country in the buoyant 1960s and 1970s.

The quality tackle products made were (and still are) very labor intensive to manufacture. Although smooth-running punch presses and custom-made assembly jigs of all kinds were used, it was still a "hand-made" product, reflecting much hand assembly and careful packaging to ensure a good quality bait safely reaching the discerning dealers and fishermen.

A lot of personal skills were involved in the production of the metal lures. Some tasks were assigned only to key or special talent employees, because they were the only people who could successfully operate special wire-forming fixtures.

During Dominion Tackle seasonal production peaks, there were up to 18 full-time employees and 6 part-time workers. In several instances, women on the staff with special wire-forming or assembly skills were allowed to make parts or assemble lures in their own homes and were paid on a piecework basis.

It was necessary to set up a new plating and polishing line to guarantee not only the brightest but also the long-lasting appearance of the Dominion Tackle products. As with all fishing tackle products, the appearance and appeal of the lure to the fisherman buyer are the first steps to successful sales.

Of special interest to this writer was the company's new and quite different style of metal ice fishing lure. This Dominion ice fishing lure was developed out of a stretched elliptical willow leaf in brass stamping, folded lengthwise in the center to form an approximate 90° angle. Four slots were also stamped evenly into the sides, dividing the lure into five sections. The second and fourth sections were then folded on each side about 45° to give the impression of fins or wings.

The lure had a two-position formed wire pick-up on the top, approximately one-third of the way aft. A preformed lead weight was soldered into the nose section for proper balancing. After plating, the bait was very impressive looking. It was dressed with treble hooks held by split rings through holes at each end. Made in two sizes of 4½" and 6" in length, the lure was a popular seller in its day.

However, when I interviewed a few old ice fishermen who had owned and tried this lure, for some reason they were less than impressed with its productivity. It was truly a great new idea to mass produce a high-quality and very durable ice fishing lure, and this lure has since been copied again by a com-

petitor tackle company in a modified form. For those ice fishermen who still have one in their box, this Dominion Fishing Tackle lure is a great little piece of tackle history to own (Plate 332).

In 1988, after 33 continuous years of business in the same location at Oro Station, Doug Bedford decided to sell the company to an anxious purchaser. An agreement was made, and the new owner moved the business to Thessalon, Ontario. As a temporary help and convenience to the new owner, Doug Bedford continued to do some contractual plating work at the old plant location.

Despite ambitious plans by the owner to substantially expand the company's production and marketing activities, a sudden and unforeseen economic downturn in 1990 resulted in much lower than expected sales. This in turn left large inventories of unsold products, a classic textbook recipe for a looming company disaster.

The company was forced to suspend operations. As a result, the major bank involved in financing the new company seized all assets and machinery to protect their investment. When another suitable purchaser could not be found, the trustees sold the machinery and tooling to a former competitor, the Lucky Strike Bait Company of Peterborough, Ontario. With this purchase, the Lucky Strike Bait Company effectively removed any future competition from their long-standing 70-year rival, the Dominion Fishing Tackle Company.

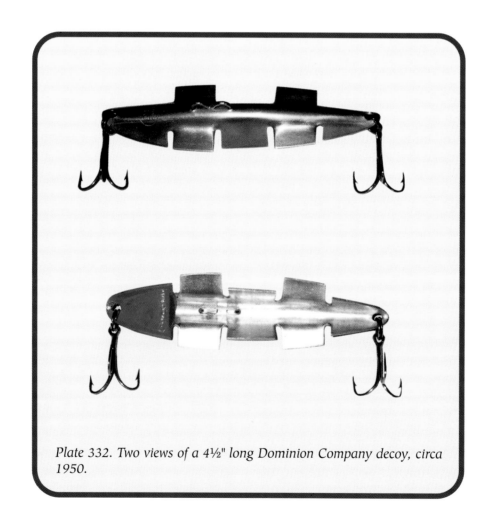

Plate 332. Two views of a 4½" long Dominion Company decoy, circa 1950.

A Lost Lake Simcoe "Treasure" Fish Decoy Found Alive
U.S. Patent No. 1,391,030 (1921)!

This is the strange but true story of the most complex ice fishing decoy that we think was ever invented in Canada. The inventor was George Washington Wheeler from the tiny village of Lefroy, Ontario, located on the east side of Cooks Bay at the south end of Lake Simcoe. He applied for a United States patent on October 10, 1919, which was granted on September 20, 1921 (Plate 333). I am sure that the inventor eventually realized that the high cost of tooling and the close assembly tolerances required made the manufacturing of this mechanical fish decoy prohibitive, for there was only small potential market at this time.

The passage of 75 years and the absence of heirs (George was a bachelor) have eroded most of the critical data of George W. Wheeler's past. His only known relative was Sherman Wheeler, a brother who also lived in the village of Lefroy.

After receiving a copy of the patent granted to George Wheeler in 1921, to save a little research time I decided to call on a marine industry friend of 30 years, Wilson Forbes, who also lived in the Lefroy area most of his life. As a young lad growing up there, Wilson actually knew George Wheeler and his brother Sherman. Wilson gave me a profile of George, but suggested that I call his brother Bill, also of Lefroy, who was interested in fishing tackle and had a few baits hanging on his workshop wall.

When I phoned and introduced myself to Bill, I cut directly to the patented fish decoy with a brief description. There was silence on the other end and Bill said, "You know, Joe, I just might have what you are looking for right here!" When Sherman Wheeler's grand-niece and her husband cleaned out the attic of Sherman's old house over 20 years ago, they found a large, strange-looking fishing lure. With no interest at all in fishing, they gave it to their friend Bill, who had randomly collected a few baits over the years.

Could this really be true! Was I going to find the proverbial "needle in the haystack?" I lost no time driving to Lefroy and Bill Forbes' shop. There Bill brought out the mechanical lure given him by Sherman Wheeler's grand-niece, which exactly matched the detailed patent drawings, with the exception of missing hooks. We were delighted to find it in such a well-preserved state. As Bill is interested in local history, it was only natural that after keeping this artifact for 20 years, he was not inclined in any way to part with it. He graciously allowed me to bring it home to take detailed photographs.

Basically, this is a 7" wooden fish decoy with four plain brass fins and a nickel-plated brass tail. The hand-painted body was green on top and silver on the bottom. The decoy has no eyes, and the bottom of the

decoy was carved out to contain the complex hidden 4-spring hook release mechanism. Two shaped nickel-plated brass plates attached with brass screws concealed four release springs, four hooks, and a pressure-sensitive release bar.

To quote in part from the very elaborate and eloquent patent description, "When the unsuspecting fish took the bait into its mouth from either side, the bottom release bar mechanism was triggered, which in turn spring-released the four concealed hooks to impale the fish onto the bait." There is also the possibility, that with hooks easy to remove, the decoy could then be used as a normal spear fishing attractor type decoy if desired.

We have been able to assemble only a very small profile of patentee George W. Wheeler from verbal reminiscences of the Forbes family. Wheeler was a fisherman, hunter, and trapper who lived at Lefroy and supported himself with these activities. His family background, schooling, and other trades or occupation are not known. In winter, he always snowshoed up local Wilson Creek to service his productive traplines. When not trapping, he spent the rest of his time ice fishing on Lake Simcoe.

He lived a very simple life as a bachelor, residing most of the year in a tiny old settler's log cabin at the mouth of Wilson Creek. In open water season, he set fishing lines on Lake Simcoe and always paddled a beat-up old canoe, never in a power craft. During very severe winter conditions, he would temporarily stay with his brother Sherman, who had a small home in Lefroy. Local lore indicated they occasionally sold off some family land for income.

Both George and Sherman are remembered as very quiet men who stuck pretty much to themselves. It is also an important fact that both men were truly quite small physically, in real terms, neither one was over five feet in height. How did the Wheeler brothers come by such historical American given names? Were they from Loyalist or patriot stock?

How George Washington Wheeler was able to devise and patent such a complex fishing decoy is a mystery that will never be solved. Was it a marketing success or an obscure inventor's dream? Large amounts of time, money, and, for sure, good connections to pursue this project would have been needed.

This surviving United States decoy patented No. 1,391,030 may be the only one. But there is absolutely no question that it was made by experienced hands. The quality of workmanship of all the parts, including the chrome-plated brass, speaks for itself. Whether dies and jigs or formal production lines were ever established is not known. It certainly wasn't just

"hacked out" by some person in a backyard or basement workshop. I will continue to pursue further details concerning this unique decoy.

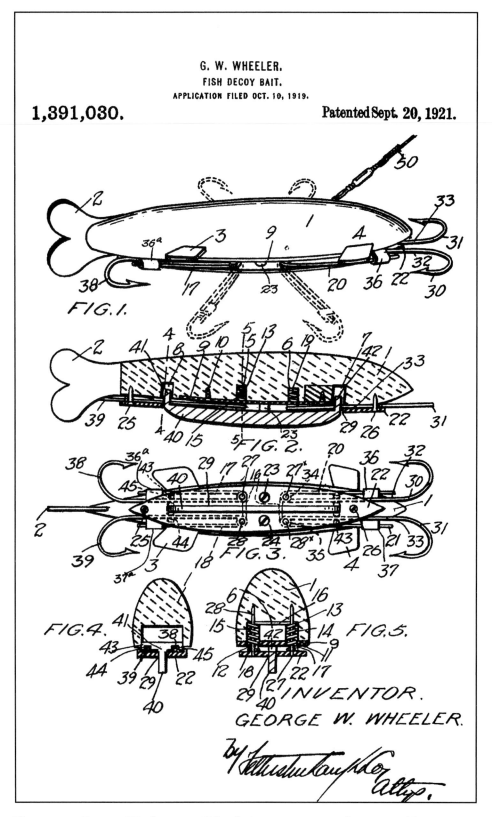

Plate 333. George Washington Wheeler's 1921 patent drawing of his unique mechanical casting, trolling, and fish-spearing lure.

Plate 334. Side view of George Wheeler's mechanical lure, minus hooks, 7" long, circa 1921.

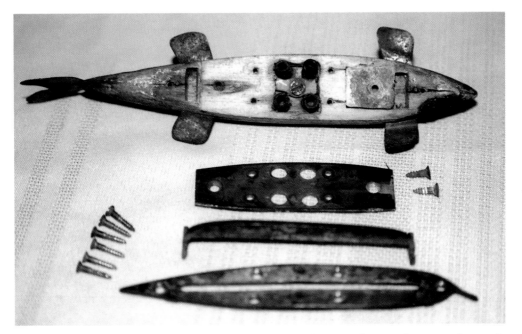

Plate 335. Bottom view of George Wheeler's dual-function lure with its mechanical components, minus hooks.

Other Canadian Commercial Decoys Maker(s)
Known and Unknown

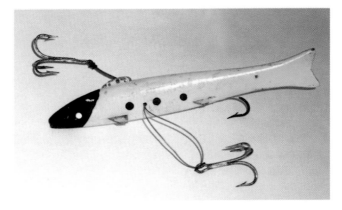

Plate 336. Fish decoy, 5" long, by an unknown Lake Simcoe area maker, circa 1960.

Plate 337. Fish decoy, 6" long, by William Baker, Cookstown, Ontario. Possibly cottage factory, circa 1950.

Plate 338. Cottage factory fish decoy, 6" long, by Bruce Rolling, Mount Albert, Ontario. Unique two-piece, single-pin mounted tail design, allows tail to be fanned out vertically to suit decoy's desired swimming mode, circa 1950.

Plate 339. Recent cottage factory fish decoy, 5" long, by unknown Lake Simcoe area maker, circa 1980.

AUTHOR'S NOTE: I hope you enjoyed reading about these unique Canadian fishing decoy manufacturers. As my research continues, particularly in western Canada, I hope to obtain more information about other commercial Canadian fish decoy makers and tackle companies to add to international fishing history records. I invite readers to contact me anytime with any history or spear fishing related items to continue my ongoing research of Canadian spear fishing.

Joe Fossey
305 Duckworth St.
Barrie, Ontario, Canada L4M3X5

Chapter Five

Commercial Decoys From Unknown Makers

A small number of quality, sophisticated, commercially made fish decoys whose makers are not known and fish decoy patents with no found examples found are showcased in this chapter. With the amount of money expended for designing, prototyping, testing, tooling, checking fixtures, and marketing, it is somewhat difficult to believe that the makers of some of these quality decoys still remain anonymous. But by the same rationale, it is easy to understand why most of the patented decoys with no examples found were never marketed. Ice spear fishing was highly popular before and during the Great Depression when fishermen fished for food rather than sport. Because money to buy a commercially made fish decoy was scarce, most fishermen made their own. By the same reasoning, manufacturing was not practical with such a weak commercial market for somewhat expensive decoys during that time. Most of the patents shown are for decoys with many components with high tolerances for fit and finish required. Therefore, the prototypes were handmade and production examples were never made because of the large expenditures that would be needed for tooling and labor.

The fact that the provenance of these beautiful commercially made decoys is not known does not detract from their collectibility, for with their beauty in both form and paint they speak for themselves to the collector. In fact, the mystique of their origin and scarcity only serves to make them more desirable to many collectors.

If readers of this book can identify one of these decoys whose maker is not known or has an example of a decoy made according to the patent specifications shown here, especially where no previous examples have been found, they are encouraged to contact me.

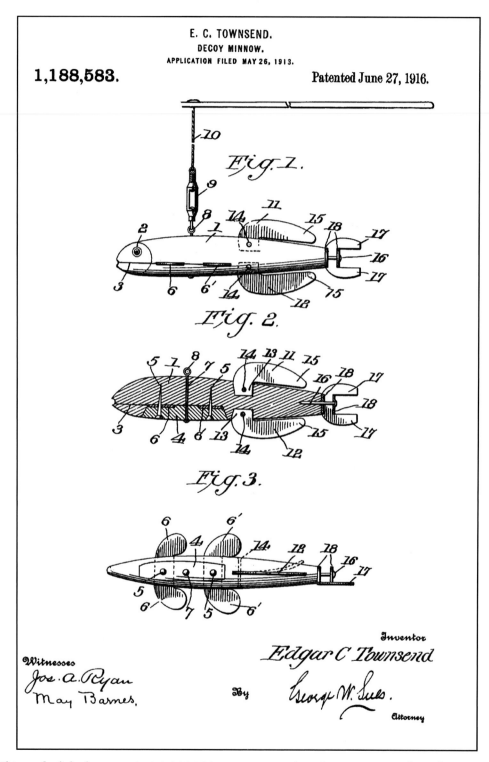

Plate 340. This early fish decoy, patent 1,188,583, was patented on June 27, 1916, by Edgar C. Townsend of Rutledge, Minnesota. Some of the unique quality features of this decoy are the dynamic rotating tail fin design and the rudder-type top and bottom fins, which are designed to be adjustable transversely to make the decoy swim in a desired size circle. The line-tie component is attached through the cast metal ballast for added strength. No example of this decoy has been found.

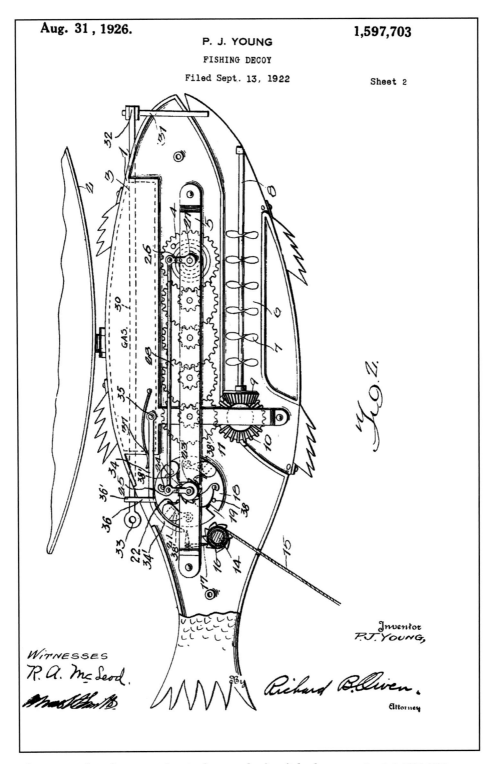

Aug. 31, 1926.

P. J. YOUNG

FISHING DECOY

Filed Sept. 13, 1922

1,597,703

Sheet 2

Inventor
P.J. YOUNG,

WITNESSES
R. A. McLeod.

By Richard B. Given.

Attorney

Plate 341. *This somewhat later mechanical marvel of a fish decoy, patent 1,597,703, was patented on August 31, 1926, by Porus J. Young of Clendenin, West Virginia. One of the most intricately designed fish decoys imaginable, it was basically designed to be dynamic by having water pass through a chamber housing six propellers that were enclosed in two metal fish-shaped stampings. The decoy was designed to open like a woman's purse or compact for adjusting or repairing. The many high-tolerance components surely made it too expensive to market economically.*

Commercial Fish Decoy and Chummer

This vintage item with no provenance or patent found is showcased here to show the ingenuity of an early commercially made quality fish decoy used by fishermen to pursue their quarry.

This 6" long commercially made item by an unknown manufacturer is a unique combination fish decoy and fish chummer (Plate 342). The fish form along with the chum made this fish decoy a great dual function attractor. Chum is chopped fish or the material used to attract fish. All fish, both fresh and salt water species, have a keen sense of smell. Used by both commercial and sport fishermen, this clever fish attractor could be used year round. The body is a fine casting with the side fins and tail solder attached. A die-cast trap-like wire-hinged door at the belly allowed chum to be put in the decoy. The entire decoy is painted in a gold finish. I have been unable to find any reference of origin for this unique decoy at this time. Production date is in the 1900s.

Plate 342. The unknown maker's chummer decoy shown in its suspended position ready to attract fish.

Quality Decoys Made by Unknown Makers

This second group of 17 commercial fish decoys that are without provenance at this time are showcased in order to describe some features that may lead to identification.

EXAMPLE A

The decoys shown in Plates 343 and 344 are of the finest quality in design, materials, and workmanship of any commercially made fish decoys of unknown origin that I have encountered so far. The earliest examples are solid colors with hand-painted gill marks. All of the examples found are 9" to 15" in length (Plate 343). Later examples are spray painted in a scale finish and have been found in 9" and 11" lengths only (Plate 344). All examples found have die-cut galvanized painted metal fins and tails. The side fins are all of an angel wing shape, proportional in size to the decoy's length, making for great slow swimming attractors. Side fins are attached by a down-standing flange and two slotted wood screws. Tail, dorsal, and anal fins are inserted into the wood body. Ballast is lead poured into a series of drilled round holes in the frontal area of the belly. The number, location, and size of holes depend on the size of the decoy. Eyes are of quality glass, and the clear coated quality scale paint patterns indicate the work of a major lure company. Who made these quality fish decoys? Most examples have been found in Michigan, especially in the Kalamazoo area.

Plate 343. Early solid yellow 15" decoy, with hand-painted gill marks.

Plate 344. Top: 11" yellow perch scale model. Bottom: 9" red perch scale model.

EXAMPLE B

These examples of another quality-made commercial fish decoy whose maker has not been identified are reminiscent of a fishing lure. Like many known documented commercially made fish decoys, the body of this decoy may have evolved from a casting or trolling fishing lure. These decoys are 5" long and have been found with both flat nail painted eyes and quality glass fishing lure-type eyes (Plate 345). Ballast is lead poured into three round holes at the center of the belly area. Fins and tail are made of die-cut light-gauge stainless steel. They are unpainted and are inserted into the wooden body. Paint is spray painted with clear coat. Examples like these have been found in both northern and southern Michigan.

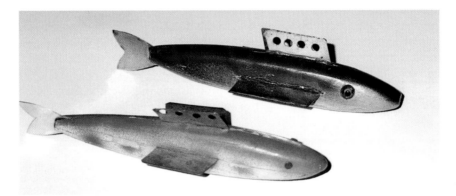

Plate 345. Top: Example has glass eyes. Bottom: An earlier example has flat nail painted eyes.

EXAMPLE C

This commercially made fish decoy by an unknown maker has only been found in this 7" length. All examples found so far have been painted gold with red accent dots and gill marks that are hand painted. The decoy has either large, high-quality bulbous glass fishing lure-type eyes or smaller high-quality glass fishing lure-type eyes that have been set in a concave metal washer (Plate 346). Fins and tail are die cut of light-gauge metal. The painted dorsal fin and side fins are nail attached. The tail is inserted into the body and then also attached by nails. The unusual cast lead ballast is shaped to the lower frontal area of the decoy's body and is screw attached. Line ties have been found with both eye screw and wire form types. Most examples have been found in northern Michigan.

Plate 346. Top: Notice the combination metal washer and glass eyes with an eye screw line tie. Bottom: This example has large bulbous glass eyes with a wire form line tie.

EXAMPLE D

These commercially made decoys have been attributed elsewhere to both Herter's Inc. of Waseca, Minnesota, and the Isle Royale Bait Company of Jackson, Michigan. I have been unable to substantiate their origin by advertisements, brochures, or packaging documentation. The history of Herter's Inc. is included in Chapter 3.

These beautiful commercially made decoys have been found throughout the Midwest. The panfish-shaped example is 5" in length, and the generic fish-shaped decoy is 7" long (Plate 347). Both have triangular die-cut metal fins and the tail-pressed into the wooden body. Ballast is lead poured into an oval hole at the frontal area of the belly. The line tie is a simple eye screw. The body is always spray painted in a scale pattern and finished with a clear coat. All fins and tail are spray painted in a solid color finish and also clear coated. Eyes are always in flat paint.

Plate 347. Top: Panfish example. Bottom: a generic fish form.

EXAMPLE E

This beautiful high-quality fish-spearing decoy is 6⅜" long and is only the second example that I have seen of this type (Plate 348). The four side fins and the dorsal fin are die-cut light-gauge metal and are inserted into its wooden body and painted. The dorsal fin was painted white and the side fins were painted red on this example, but side fin paint has flaked away. The body is unique in that it is covered with a thin layer of gold-colored foil. The eyes are flat painted with two colors, and the gills and tail area are accented with red paint. The tail area has a series of fine gold dots randomly painted on the red accent paint. The entire decoy has been clear coated. The line tie is a simple eye screw. Ballast is lead poured into an oval-shaped cavity at the frontal belly area. This example was found in Michigan.

Plate 348. This beautiful, sleek gold-foiled decoy refracts light and was surely a great attractor.

EXAMPLE F

These panfish or bass decoys by an unidentified maker (Plate 349) have been found in three different lengths from 6" to 8" long. Metal side fins are hand cut to a template and are unpainted and inserted into the wooden body. The animated metal tail is unpainted and is also hand cut to a template and inserted into the body, and then fastened by a single lateral pin. The single round hole in the tail served multiple functions. It could be used for hanging the decoy in the paint drying operation during manufacturing, for hanging the decoy in the fish shanty when not in use, or for tying on an accent, such as red yarn, to attract prey. Eyes are large size convex-shaped thumb tacks, sometimes painted and sometimes not. The line tie is a simple eye screw or wire form. Ballast is lead poured into an oval hole at the front of the belly. All examples found are always red and white with a clear coat with different paint patterns.

Plate 349. Each of these red and white decoys has a different paint pattern. Notice the realistic tail design.

EXAMPLE G

This one-of-a-kind — so far! — decoy was discovered in the tackle box of a retired executive of the William Shakespeare Company of Kalamazoo, Michigan (Plate 350). Possibly it was a prototype for a fish decoy that was never made. The four hand-cut metal side fins and the hand-cut metal dorsal fins are unpainted but appear to have remnants of body color paint near where they are inserted into the wooden body. The hand-cut metal tail is inserted into the rear of the body and nail attached. It also has remnants of body color paint. Gill marks are hand painted. The eyes are finishing nails set in convex washers. The line tie is four drilled or punched holes in the dorsal fin. The hole in the tail was probably used for hanging the decoy in a dark house or jigging the decoy in a cripple swimming mode. Ballast is lead poured into a rectangular hole in this narrow ¼" thick body. The body is spray painted with two colors, a khaki colored back blending to a silver belly. The mystique of this decoy is the possibility that it was a Shakespeare Company prototype that was never manufactured, marketed, or catalogued.

Plate 350. This narrowest of all wooden decoys has the best swimming quality capability.

EXAMPLE H

These beautiful, realistic solid molded rubber fish decoys have no maker's marks to help identify them. They are in sucker form and are 8½" (top) or 5¼" (bottom) long (Plate 351). They have molded rubber integral fins and tail. Pigment was mixed in with the rubber to produce the natural sucker color of the body. No ballast was required, for the density of the rubber allows the decoy to sink or swim nicely. A light-gauge braided wire with a loop at center of the back was functional for a line tie, and a loop at the belly from the same wire assembly held a split ring that was functional for adding more ballast or a cheater hook, as shown. Examples have been found in Michigan, Minnesota, and Wisconsin.

Plate 351. These molded rubber decoys with incredible realism had to be the ultimate fish fooler.

EXAMPLE I

Another example of a Midwestern decoy by an unknown maker is this small metal minnow. It has been found in lengths of 3⅛" and 3⅝" (Plate 352). The body and side fins are die cut from light-gauge sheet metal. A hole simulating an eye and a smaller line tie hole were either punched or drilled into the body. The one-piece side fins are formed into a T-shape and then clipped onto the body and solder attached. The oval ballast is cast lead molded onto the frontal belly area of the sheet metal body. All examples found so far have been painted solid gold. The red paint on the ballast of the lower example seems to have been added by a spear fisherman later. These decoys have been found in both Michigan and Ohio.

Plate 352. These little minnow-like decoys were lively swimming attractors.

EXAMPLE J

Another different type of decoy by an unknown maker is this 5" long metal decoy that was die cut from 0.040 thick sheet metal (Plate 353). Three holes of different sizes were punched or drilled in the body. The front hole simulated an eye, the center hole was for a line tie, and the rear hole toward the tail functioned to attach a cheater hook when desired. Most examples found have a similar split ring and cheater hook, indicating they were factory installed. The angel wing side fins were die cut from the same gauge metal as the body and were then soldered to the body. The ballast is oval-shaped lead molded to the frontal belly area of the sheet metal body. Examples have been found with at least four different red and white paint patterns. This decoy has been misidentified in other writings as being manufactured and marketed by the James Heddon & Sons Bait Company of Dowagiac, Michigan, but none of their catalogs, brochures, or magazine advertisements substantiated this. Examples of this metal decoy have been found throughout the Midwest.

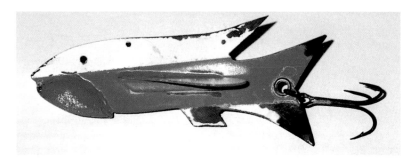

Plate 353. This colorful red and white metal decoy surely was a great attractor.

EXAMPLE K

Plate 354 shows top and bottom views of a sleek 6⅜" long decoy that is the only one of its type that I have ever seen. The four side fins are hand-cut metal from a template, each with a down-standing flange with two drilled holes for screw attachments to the body. The eight attaching screws are of a slotted flat head type. The tail is also hand-cut metal from a template and is pin attached after being inserted into the slit at the rear of the body. The tail has a small round hole drilled approximately in its center. This hole has several functions: for drying the decoy after painting, for housing a cheater hook, or for adding an accent attractor, such as red yarn or cloth.

The uniquely designed ballast is cast lead, shaped to the decoy's lower frontal area and then screw attached. The decoy has a beautiful spray-painted gold back. The color shifts gradually to copper-colored sides and blending to a silver belly. There are four small hand-painted gill marks. The eyes are yellow and black glass, of a quality fish lure type. The line tie is a simple eye screw. The fins are unpainted and were attached after the decoy was painted. As the final operation, the decoy was dipped into a clear varnish that waterproofed the decoy. This example was found in Pennsylvania, a state where almost no ice spear fishing has been documented.

Plate 354. A top and bottom view of a sleek, quality-made commercial fish-spearing decoy by an unknown maker.

EXAMPLE L

Although not documented, it is believed that this unused 9¾" long solid metal fish spearing decoy was made at the Minneapolis, Minnesota, Moline farm tractor plant in the 1950s (Plate 355). It is die-cast solid aluminum, with integral dorsal and anal fins, and tail, but no side fins. A detailed gill plate and mouth are cast in the head area. The eyes have large, faceted costume jewelry beads set into molded cavities, and then the soft aluminum metal around the periphery of the bead eyes was punched to permanently set them. A drilled or cast hole in the dorsal fin was available for a line tie. The hole at the lower center of the belly could be used for a cheater hook or for colored yarn for added attraction. I have not seen any painted examples of this decoy, but they surely exist. Most examples have been found in Minnesota.

Plate 355. This large, dynamic metal straight-tail attractor is made of cast aluminum and has faceted glass bead eyes.

EXAMPLE M

This little 3½" long die-cut fish form metal combination jigging lure and fish-spearing decoy was found in Minnesota (Plate 356). The base plate was die cut from the same gauge metal as the body and then attached to the body by peening two integral metal tabs from the front of body, which are assembled through two small rectangles in the base plate. The body has three holes that were either drilled or punched. The front hole is functional for a jigging line tie, the center hole can be used to swim this lure as a fish decoy, and the rear hole is available to attach a cheater hook or colored yarn as an added attractor. The body has been spray painted with enamel, and the eyes are flat painted in black and white.

Plate 356. This versatile little combination jigging lure and fish spearing decoy has year-round fishing potential.

EXAMPLE N

These three beautiful, animated, colorful wooden fish decoys have been found in lengths of 9½", 9", and 6½" (Plate 357). The body form is symmetrical and proportional to the different size lengths. The side fins and large rudder type anal fin are hand cut from a template. The smallest 6½" long example has no anal fin. For ballast, lead was poured into the belly area, covered by wood filler, and then shaped and sanded to the convex belly shape. Paint is sprayed enamel and clear coated. Eyes are both flat painted and painted dome tack in black and white. The line tie is a simple eye screw. All these examples were found in Michigan.

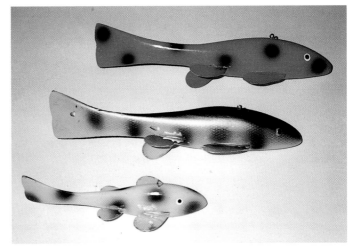

Plate 357. Three great beautiful, colorful, dynamic animated attractors.

EXAMPLE O

The three beautiful, sleek, 8½" long fish spearing decoys shown in Plate 358 are by an unknown maker from the Staples, Minnesota, area. The metal side fins and large metal tail are hand cut to templates. Ballast is lead poured into a rectangular-shaped cavity in the frontal area of the belly. Paint is sprayed enamel with a clear coat. Paint patterns are two or three complementary colors in exotic patterns. Eyes are two-color black and white painted convex thumb tacks. Line ties are a simple eye screw. It is difficult to believe that the origin of these beautiful decoys cannot be pinpointed by local collectors.

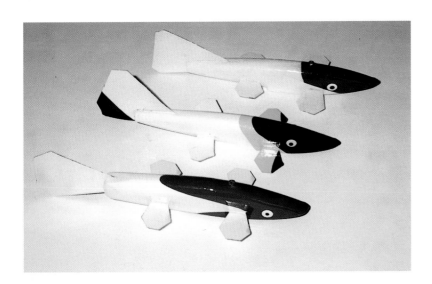

Plate 358. With this sleek pike-like form and art deco style paint, these are some of my favorite decoys from an unknown manufacturer.

EXAMPLE P

This 3¾" long realistically scaled minnow was a dual-function lure (Plate 359). The two line ties indicate that it could be cast, or trolled, swum or jigged under the winter ice by the ice fisherman. It is finely detailed die cast of solid metal, probably aluminum. The rear eye screw and split ring assembly allowed the rear treble hook to be removed when not legal for ice fishing. This versatile lure was marketed with a shiny natural metal finish with red accent paint on the gill areas. This example was found in the midwestern United States.

Plate 359. This year-round versatile bait would be a great addition to any tackle or fish decoy box. Note the fine details molded into the body.

EXAMPLE Q

This large, 10" long lure, commercially made by an unknown manufacturer has dual functions (Plate 360). It can be casted or trolled conventionally, or swum under the winter ice by the ice spear fisherman. The two angel wing side fins were made from aluminum and pressed into the body. Ballast is lead poured into a rectangular slot in the frontal area of the belly, then sanded to the curved belly shape. The finish is beautifully fine scale painted. Eyes are two-color flat-painted black and white. The rear eye screw can have a treble hook attached. This and the single, permanently attached belly hook indicate that this lure was probably a versatile top and underwater casting and trolling bait that was used by ice spear fishermen as a decoy.

Plate 360. This beautiful, quality made lure is not identified in any lure collector books.

MORE DECOYS BY UNKNOWN MAKERS

The following examples (Plates 361 to 367) are candidates to be deemed commercial decoys by unknown makers. However, I have not examined these decoys to judge the quality of workmanship and unusual or typical aspects of them as I have the decoys presented earlier in this chapter. Instead, either the photograph of the decoy was sent to me by people who hoped that I would be able to identify the maker of their decoy or I photographed the decoy myself for my own reference but before I had the concept of creating this book. As a result, the dimensions are estimated and other details are given as accurately as possible from a photograph. Again, if a reader has specific information about one of these decoys by unknown makers, please share the information with me.

Plate 361. Approximately 6" long, this beautiful, symmetric, scale-painted decoy has die-cut metal fins, metal tail, and glass eyes. This decoy was found in northern Michigan.

Plate 362. This large decoy has been found in 3 different sizes, approximately 10", 11", and 12" long. It is symmetrical, with a colorful scale-like finish and large metal die-cut tail and angel wing-shaped side fins. It has large faceted jeweled eyes. All examples have been found in the Kalamazoo, Michigan, area.

Plate 363. Approximately 6" long, this sleek pike form decoy is symmetrical with die-cut flanged screwed-on side and anal fins and die-cut metal tail. Eyes are of a nail-attached bead design. This decoy was found in northern Michigan.

Plate 364. *Approximately 8" long, this beautiful symmetrical, wooden tail, scale-painted rainbow trout decoy appears to have metal die-cut side fins and glass eyes. This example was found in northern Wisconsin.*

Plate 365. *Here is another approximately 8" long decoy found in Wisconsin. This scale-painted decoy has die-cut textured metal side fins, dorsal fins, and tail. The eyes are two-color painted convex thumb tacks.*

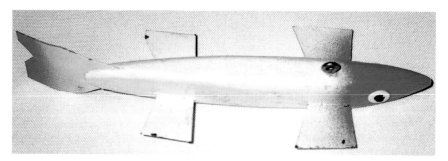

Plate 366. *The almost rectangular side fins and tail of this approximately 7" decoy are metal, hand cut from a template. The body of this neat attractor is spray painted, and the eyes are two-color painted convex-shaped thumb tacks. This example also was found in northern Wisconsin.*

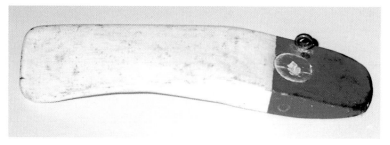

Plate 367. *This plain Jane finless attractor is approximately 6" long and has flat painted eyes. The unique line tie location indicates that this decoy swam with a cripple action. This is another example found in northern Wisconsin.*

Chapter Six

Commercial Items Modified For Spear Fishing

The ingenious creativity of fishermen to modify items, especially the fishing lures that they predominately used in the spring, summer, and fall fishing seasons, to use under the ice in the winter season is to be greatly admired. It was natural for a fisherman to rationalize that if one of his most successful lures worked during the warm months then it would surely produce under the winter ice. As fishermen, we all choose our favorite fishing baits by their success. Color, size, and action are the most important factors when fishermen choose a lure.

Spear fishermen not only modified their favorite casting and trolling lures for use as ice decoys, but they also modified household items to be attractors for spear fishing. The depression era, when almost all fishermen were fishing for food first and sport second because money was in short supply, was the time period when the ice spear fisherman created most of these modified items. In Chapter 2 I documented spear fishermen forgetting their ice decoys and adapting, with success, car keys, shoe horns, and even false teeth as makeshift attractors. The next six pages show some great examples of modified fish lures and household items that I have found among many spear fishing artifacts.

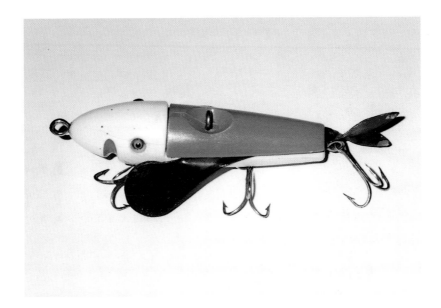

Plate 368. This typical kitchen teaspoon, 5" long, was modified by an unknown Michigan spear fisherman by drilling a small hole at each end of the spoon, then adding a split ring and cheater hook at the heaviest end and a split ring and box swivel at the other end. This became a flashing dynamic attractor when it was jigged.

Plate 369. This 4" long wooden clothespin like my mother and grandmother used was modified by an unknown Michigan spear fisherman, to be used as a spear fishing attractor. The head of the clothespin was painted bright red with white and black painted eyes. The rest of the clothespin was left its natural wood color, then sealed with varnish. Lead solder wire was wrapped around the clothespin at the center of gravity for ballast. An eye screw with a box swivel was added to complete this homemade attractor.

Plate 370. This 3½" long metal shoe horn was adapted to become a fish-spearing attractor by an unknown Michigan spear fisherman. A hole with a split ring and cheater treble hook was added to the wide end of the shoe horn, and a snap swivel was added to an existing hole at the narrow end of the shoe horn, making for an erratic motion attractor when jigged.

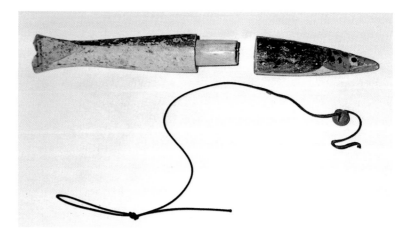

Plate 371. This 4" long wooden fish-spearing decoy started life as a commercially made fish-shaped needle holder. Its hollowed out center, originally designed to hold needles, made a perfect chamber to hold ballast to submerge the decoy. The fisherman placed a number of lead split shot fishing sinkers to nylon fish line, put it into the hollow chamber, and then put the two halves of the needle holder back together. The nylon line became a perfect tether line to swim this former needle holder, now made into a fish decoy.

Metal Decoys Aid in Spearing Fish Through Ice

DECOYS to use in the sport of spearing fish through the ice from a fish house—a sport that is popular in many of the colder sections of the country—can be made as shown from sheet metal or heavy tin. Five-gallon oil cans are a good source of this material, although heavier galvanized stock would probably last longer. The decoys may be from 3″ to 8″ long and patterned after any desired kind of fish.

Cut the metal to shape with tin snips or cold chisel, hammer it flat, cut slots for inserting the fins, and solder the fins in place. Add extra solder under the frontal fins so that the decoy will glide downward when the control string is slack. Drill a few small holes along the top edge for inserting a small hook and swivel.

For running the decoy, a stick about 18″ long with a 6′ or 8′ fishline is used. The hook and swivel are tied to the end of the line. See that the fins of the decoy are horizontal except the back edges of the frontal fins, which are bent up slightly. Bend the body of the decoy to form an arc so that it will travel in a circle of from 12″ to 18″. Insert the hook of the control line in whichever hole permits the decoy to balance properly. The decoy may be left in its natural finish or colored, as preferred. A red head with a white body is a good color combination.

The fisherman usually sits by the edge of the ice hole and gives the control line slow jerks with one hand so the decoy will travel in circles. He holds the spear in the other hand and rests the tines at the edge of the hole until a fish is seen. The spear is ordinarily 4′ or 5′ long.

Decoys of this type can also be used as summer bait by drilling a small hole at the nose and tail. Fasten a gang hook at the tail and a small swivel at the nose. Bend the decoy so it will travel through the water like a crippled minnow.

GIANT HOME WORKSHOP MANUAL

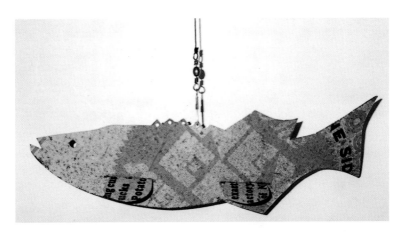

Plate 372. This Popular Science Workshop manual article published in 1941 gives the reader instructions on how to make a fish-spearing decoy from typical used metal containers found around any home, such as oil and anti-freeze containers, food containers, waste paper baskets, or buckets. The working example shown here was made by the author from pieces of a large Nu-Way potato chip container with about one-half hour of work.

This next group of casting and trolling fishing lures, each modified for ice spear fishing by an unknown fisherman, includes some of the most ingenious creations that I have seen.

Plate 373. Modified K & K Animated Minnow, No.1-A by the K & K Manufacturing Company, Toledo, Ohio, 4" long, circa 1907. Lead was added for ballast between the front and rear sections. Metal side fins were screw attached. The metal tail was part of the original lure design. Three staples on back were added for line ties.

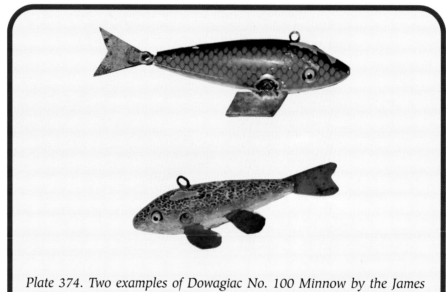

Plate 374. Two examples of Dowagiac No. 100 Minnow by the James Heddon & Sons Company of Dowagiac, Michigan, 2¾" long, circa 1910. On top example, metal side and tail fins were soldered to the existing hook eye screws. On bottom example, metal side and tail fins were inserted into the lure body. An eye screw was added on each back for a line tie. Original lure ballast was used to sink and swim this former casting lure now made into a fish decoy.

Plate 375. Modified Husky Pikie No. 2300 by the Creek Chub Bait Company of Garrett, Indiana, 6" long, circa 1927. Lead was added for ballast at the 3 cup hook cavities, along with an added buck-tail at rear hook cavity. Two eye screws were added on back for line tie.

204

Plate 376. Another modified Creek Chub Bait Company lure, a Pikie Minnow No. 700, 4½" long, circa 1920. Metal side fins were screw attached and tail was inserted into the body. A metal dorsal fin was inserted into the back with drilled holes for line ties. Lead was added to belly for ballast.

Plate 377. Modified Paw Paw Wattafrog by the Paw Paw Bait Company of Paw Paw, Michigan, 3¼" long, circa 1935. A bell sinker was added to the belly hook eye screw and split shots were added to leg hook eye screws for ballast. An eye screw was added to the back for a line tie to create this critter fish decoy.

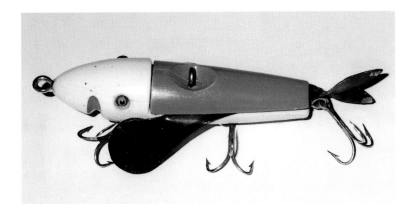

Plate 378. Modified A-B-C Minnow by the Bolton Company of Detroit, Michigan, 4¼" long, circa 1935. A metal plate was added under the removable interchangeable back, creating both side and tail fins, and was also functional as ballast. Hooks were left on for cheaters.

Plate 379. Modification by a fisherman of two, 3" long Dardevle spoons, by drilling a line tie hole and utilizing front and rear existing holes to wire the two spoons together, making a great attractor. These Dardevle spoons were made by the Eppinger Lure Company of Detroit, Michigan, around 1940.

Plate 380. Modified Muskallonge Minnow by the Enterprise Manufacturing Company (Pflueger Company) of Akron, Ohio, 7" long, circa 1895. Modification to an ice decoy was achieved by simply adding an eye screw on the back for a line tie. Original lure's ballast served to sink and swim this former trolling lure now made into a fish decoy. Hooks were left on the bait as cheaters.

Plate 381. Modified Injured Minnow, No. 1500, by the Creek Chub Bait Company of Garrett, Indiana, 3¾" long, circa 1924. Metal side and tail fins were inserted into the body and an eye screw was added to the back for a line tie. Lead was added to belly for ballast.

Plate 382. Modified pair of Baby Sea Witches, No. 6553 by the Shakespeare Bait Company of Kalamazoo, Michigan, 3⅓" long, circa 1928. Lead was added to belly for ballast and an eye screw was added on back for a line tie.

Plate 383. Modified Weedless Minnow No. 902 by the South Bend Bait Company of South Bend, Indiana, 3¼" long, circa 1916. Metal side and tail fins were attached with hook eye screws. Lead was added to belly for ballast and an eye screw was added on the back for a line tie.

Plate 384. Modified Diving Bang-O-B in musky finish by the Bagley Bait Company of Bartow, Florida, 7½" long, circa 1970. Metal side fins were inserted into the body and retained by lead poured into the belly for ballast. Metal tail fin was inserted into the body and retained by a screw. Two eye screws were added on the back for line ties.

Plate 385. This modified Fish-Oreno No. 053 by the South Bend Bait Company of South Bend, Indiana, was a natural for an ice decoy, 4" inches long, circa 1926. A split shot was added to the rear tail hook eye screw for leveling ballast. The lure's original metal head component served to sink this decoy. A brass swivel was added to the lure's casting or line tie for spear fishermen's tether line.

Chapter Seven

Trapping Decoys

Most sportsmen have some knowledge of the function of waterfowl, turkey, dove, owl, and crow decoys which are commonly used when hunting. Most fishermen, especially those fishing in the northern United States and Canada, have some knowledge of the function of the ice spear fishing decoy. Very few sportsmen, unless they have had experience trapping, have any knowledge of trapping decoys. There is a parallel between ice spear fishing decoys and trapping decoys. Like ice spear fishing decoys, trapping decoys are used almost exclusively in or very near bodies of water, ponds, small streams, rivers or lakes. The trappers predominantly use fish, frog, and crawdad critter decoys for their trap baits. Homemade ice spear fishing, fish, and critters decoys are relatively easy to find, but homemade trapping decoys are somewhat rare. Although trappers use both live and dead fish and critters on their trap lines, most often these are commercially made. The fur-bearing animals most often trapped using these decoys are muskrat, otter, beaver, raccoon, and mink. It is not true that most animals are trapped only for their fur, for in most cases the meat is consumed by the trapper, his family, friends, or neighbors.

Commercially manufactured scents are frequently also employed when trapping, but sometimes they are concocted by the trapper himself. These scents are used to enhance the decoys and to mask any human odor on the trap or decoy (Plate 386). Here are some great examples of traps and trapping decoys I have seen (Plates 387 – 394).

Plate 386. An advertisement for scent from a 1927 F.C. Taylor Fur Company trappers supply catalog.

209

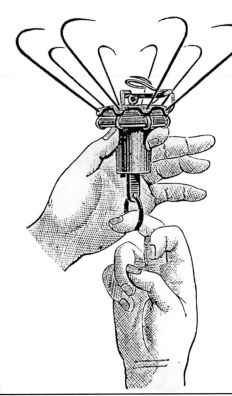

A VICTORIOUS INVENTION.

The Eagle Claw.

An ingenious device for the purpose of catching all kinds of Animals, Fish and Game.

The easy method of setting the Eagle Claw, combined with the simplicity of removing the victim, are among its peculiar advantages.

It is immaterial how to place it when set. It may be buried flat in the ground, suspended from the limb of a tree. or, when occasion requires, covered with grass, leaves or other light material without in any way impairing its certain operation.

It is adapted for bait of any description, and, when set, no Animal, Fish or Bird that touches the bait can possibly escape.

It does not mangle or injure its victims in the slightest degree, nor need they be handled to free them from the trap.

PRICE LIST:

No. 1—For fishing and all kinds of small game and animals sent by mail..35 cents

No. 2—For catching Mink, Muskrats, Raccoons, large Game, Fish. &c...75 cents

No 3, or Rocky Mountain Giant, for catching Bears, Wolves, Pan hers, &c. Can be easily set by a boy, and will stand a strain of several hundred pounds. Weight 10 to 15 lbs. $10

All goods sent charges paid to any address on receipt of price. Adress

Chas, L. Coate,

330 Fulton St., Brooklyn, N. Y.

P. O. Box 214.

AGENTS WANTED.

Plate 387. *Early unique fish and game trap advertisement from May, 1877 Forest & Stream magazine.*

Plate 388. *Another unique fish and game trap advertisement from a 1913 Hunter, Trapper, Trader magazine.*

Taylor Metal Crawfish

A Most Attractive Decoy for Coon, Mink and Other Animals that Travel Along Streams in Search of Food

$0.87 Per Dozen, Postage Extra

These crawfish are made of a carefully selected, chemically treated metal which causes them to take on a natural color after being placed in the water. Coon, Mink and other animals that travel along streams hunting for food prefer crawfish to any other kind. Taylor's Metal Crawfish fit over pan of trap, and when the animal touches the fish with its paw the trap springs and another fur is added to your collection. Trap should be set lightly and placed about two inches under water very close to the shore. Securely fasten trap chain to a log or tree. Many trappers using this set do not cover traps, but to insure best result we recommend that a covering of wet leaves be used, so arranged that only the crawfish can be seen. If carefully taken care of, the fish will last a lifetime.

Price, two sample crawfish, postpaid.....................$0.30
Price, one-half dozen crawfish, postpaid...............55
Price, one dozen crawfish, postpaid.......................95

Tin Fish Water Set

Although most trappers prefer *Taylor's Metal Crawfish* for water sets, there are many who favor the tin fish. The crawfish are by far the best, as they can be used with equal success for Coon, Mink and other animals that travel along the edge of streams in search of food, while the tin fish are most suitable for Coon. The Coon is the most curious of all fur-bearing animals, and when traveling along streams at night, the brightness of these fish will attract them every time.

The tin fish are shaped so as to fit the pan of trap. Trap should be set lightly and placed two or three inches under water near the bank and securely fastened to a log or tree.

Each Fish Has Three Clamps for Attaching to Trap

Not furnished in less than dozen lots

Price, one dozen.........$0.21   Or four dozen, postpaid. $0.85
Postage 4 cents Extra

SEE Page 15 for **Taylor Glow Fish**

Taylor Glow Fish Night Set

Coated with Eradium, a luminous preparation that shines in the dark, Taylor Glow Fish are highly recommended for Coon, Mink and other animals that travel along streams in search of food.

Coon and certain other fur-bearing animals are extremely curious and inquisitive, and any bright object will cause them to stop and investigate. Fasten one of these glow fish to the pan of a trap and you can depend upon the animal to find it.

The fish are shaped so as to fit the pan of trap. Trap should be set lightly and placed along edge of stream. Chain of trap should be securely fastened to a log or tree.

Price of Glow Fish . 79 Cents Per Dozen Postage 6 Cents Extra
Price, Postpaid, Three for $0.25
Or One Dozen Sent Postpaid for 85

Each Fish Has Three Clamps For Attaching To Trap

Plate 389. Two advertisements from a 1927 F.C. Taylor Fur Company trappers supply catalog.

INSTRUCTIONS

Each P & K Trap Bait is equipped with a special clip that will fit all styles of traps. Spread the arms of this clip, place bait on pan of trap before setting, and bend ends of arms back over edge of pan. This will fasten bait securely to trap, and make your catch certain. Bait can be used over and over on same trap, or removed from one trap and placed on another.

Use the P & K Trap Baits for trapping Fox, Skunk, Weasel, Fisher, Marten, Badger, Ringtail, Mink, Civet, Possum and Raccoon. Makes perfect underwater set.

P & K INCORPORATED
3450 Archer Avenue
CHICAGO 8, ILLINOIS

Plate 390. Rubber frog and crawdad decoys with box, box end label, and enclosed instructions from Pachner & Koller, Inc.

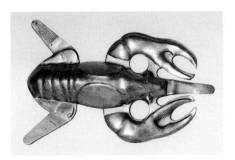

Plate 391. This crawdad trap decoy by an unknown company has three integral bendable tabs to attach to the trap pan.

Plate 392. The crawdad decoy as above on a loaded trap, in the loaded position.

Plate 393. *Fluorescent painted glow-in-the-dark fish trap decoys with original directions, circa 1920s.*

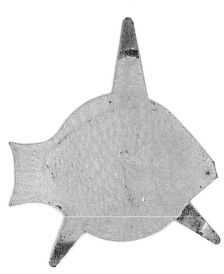

Plate 394. *The Water Wizard trap bait, a wooden rubber-tailed fish, with rod to set underwater near trap.*

Chapter Eight

Potpourri

This final chapter is presented to give the reader a photographic journey through many decades of the history of ice spear fishing in North America. The clothing, hair styles, structures, and various fishing items allow a close estimate of the time periods. In most images the fishermen are unidentified, but the area of the picture's origin is known. Many of these pictures were procured at estate sales where family members no longer knew the names of the people pictured in the photos. In more fortunate cases family members kept great records of old family photographs, and the subjects and time periods are documented.

All of us, whether a fishing artifact collector, historian, or just plain fisherman, will surely enjoy a look at this picture history of North American freshwater ice spear fishing frozen in time.

Plate 395. A Holland, Michigan, ice fisherman with a huge frozen northern pike on an unidentified lake in the area. Clothing shows the Dutch influence of the early settlers of this area, circa 1880.

Plate 396. Two ladies, a male companion, and their pet dog show off the same
fish as in the photo before beside their ice shanty, circa 1880.

Plate 397. Three Muskegon, Michigan, area ice spear fishermen pose by their ice shanty with a
large stringer of perch hanging from the shanty. Notice the pine tree boughs around the base of
the shanty used to keep out the light, circa 1900.

216

Plate 398. The same three spear fishermen as in the photo before, posing off the ice with their stringer of perch and also a nice northern pike, circa 1900.

Plate 399. The Palmer brothers carving ice spear fishing decoys in Michigan's Upper Peninsula, circa 1900. Courtesy of the Les Cheneaux Historical Museum.

Plate 400. Three proud Wisconsin fishermen (left to right,) Julius Steffen, Hank Kaddatz, and Frank Schmidt, posing with fish caught through the ice of Powers Lake in southeastern Wisconsin. Times were hard, and fish and game fed these folks during those tough times. The method used for catching these fish through the ice was primitive. A wood shingle with a small hole through the center was set over the ice hole. A length of line with a hook at one end and a stop knot at the other went through the hole in the shingle. A bait fish of some type was put on the hook and lowered into the water. When a northern pike grabbed the bait, it would run line until the stop knot caught and this jerk would set the hook. Many of these shingles were put out overnight. The snow would blow over them and hide them from sight of the game wardens. The next day the shingles would be checked and the catch removed. The shingles were located by tapping the ice with an ice chisel or spud bar. It was traditional for fishermen to dress in their Sunday best for a brag picture, circa 1915.

Plate 401. Two northern Michigan spear fishermen ready for a day of spear fishing on an unidentified northern Michigan lake, circa 1920.

Plate 402. Spear fisherman Sam Benjamin of the Muskegon, Michigan, area with a trophy-size muskellunge speared in Muskegon Lake, circa 1925.

Plate 403. A 175-pound, 86-inch sturgeon speared by Ward Spray in Mullet Lake in northern Michigan, circa 1950.

Plate 404. Happiness is a trophy-size northern taken by this young lad in a comfortable warm shanty, circa 1950. Courtesy of Hazel Little.

Plate 405. A veteran spear fisherman shows off his great catch of the day on an unidentified Michigan lake, circa 1950. Courtesy of Hazel Little.

Plate 406. Steve Uhouse of Detroit, Michigan, with the largest sturgeon speared in Michigan in 1957. It was 85 pounds and about 6 feet in length. The spear pictured is a throwing spear (note the teardrop shape lead at the base of the handle). This fish was speared at a depth of 25 feet and had to be hit with a second spear at the hole. This fish was speared from inside a shanty using a wooden spearing decoy.

Plate 407. *Revered fish decoy carver and spear fisherman Alton "Chub" Bachman of Mt. Clemens, Michigan (right) with fishing companion Charlie Hart, ready for a day of spear fishing on Lake St. Clair, circa 1970.*

Plate 408. *Spear fisherman and fish decoy carver Mel Aaserude of Cass Lake, Minnesota, in his dark house with a great northern pike, speared on Silver Lake in 1985.*

Plate 409. Left: John Kalash (aka "Michigan's Down-river Outlaw") of Gibraltar, Michigan, with five exceptional speared northern pike and the fish decoy he used. His admiring friend is Jim Foote also of Gibraltar, circa 1992.

Plate 410. Spear fisherman and fish decoy carver Chuck Vogel of McMillan, Michigan, shown with his favorite spear that he used to take a nice northern pike in Manistique Lake in Michigan's western Upper Peninsula, February 1998.

Plate 411. Chuck Vogel's largest northern pike (24½ pounds) also taken in February 1998 on Manistique Lake, shown with his favorite spearing decoy and spear.

Plate 412. A major magazine advertisement, for Maxwell House Coffee depicting an ice fishing scene, circa 1950.

The FOUR ROSES SOCIETY goes fishing

(A great catch!)

They've got the ice and they've got the "Roses." The members have got it made.

Indoors or out, there's no finer combination. It's true—you just can't find another full-bodied whiskey so smooth to the taste as mellow-gold

Four Roses. So warming to body and spirit!

This blended perfection makes every drink an occasion. Ask for Four Roses today at your favorite store or tavern—and you'll agree:

Another great catch is Four Roses!

FOUR ROSES—*Same great quality...new popular price!*

No other full-bodied whiskey is so smooth. 86 proof.

Plate 413. Magazine advertisement for Four Roses Whiskey depicting ice fishing scene, circa 1960.

Plate 414. Goodyear Tires in a magazine advertisement, also depicting an ice fishing scene, circa 1960.

Plate 415. Amusing 12" high folky carving titled "Frog Gone Spearfishing" by folk artisan Grey Eagle of central Ohio, circa 1980.

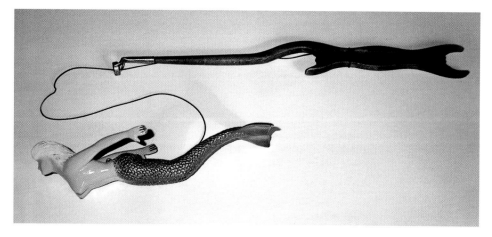

Plate 416. Whimsical 8" long glamorous working mermaid fish-spearing decoy by world class carver Blaine Kimmel of Grand Rapids, Michigan, circa 1990.

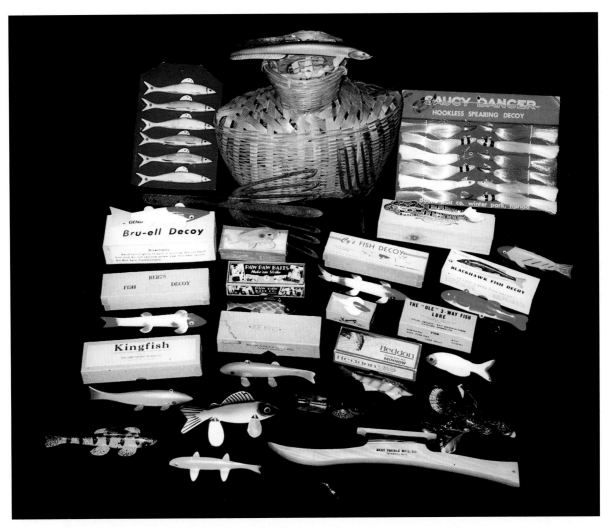

Free appraisal, identification, and buying service by the author. Call 734-427-7758.

Price Guide

I have placed a value range for each decoy pictured. The variables which determine desirability are rarity, age, aesthetics, condition, and whether the decoy is still in its original marketing box. Using the National Fishing Lure Collector's Club lure grading system is recommended for determining price when buying, selling, or trading commercial fish decoys. Why rarity is unimportant to some collectors of these scarce vintage artifacts is puzzling to me as a historian. With this group, popularity seems to be most important. Age is important to most collectors, for older decoys are usually scarcer and more difficult to find in excellent condition. Beauty of the decoy is another important factor, often created by intricate multicolored patterns, especially paint patterns of a particular species. Also special-order colors not catalogued create higher values. The numerical condition

scale with descriptions should be used by all to help determine final value of all decoys, whether rare or common. Boxes and packaging are another important factor, especially picture boxes, that is, a box with an illustration of the decoy within the box. Boxes give the decoy a pedigree, especially when found with a catalogued model number on the box or found with an advertising brochure. As a rule of thumb, boxes and packaging add about 20% to 30% to the value of the decoy. Picture boxes add about 30% to 40% to the decoy's value.

Prices listed in this book reflect the rise in popularity of fish decoys in the late 1990s. The reader is advised that the prices are an estimate for this time period. Prices of collectibles within the market place are highly volatile and fluctuate with the economy.

Scale		Description/Condition
	The NFLCC Standard Lure Grading system, originated by R. L. Streater	
10	New in box (NIB)	Unused with original box
9	Mint (M)	Unused without box
8	Excellent (E)	Very little or no age cracks; very minor defects
7	Very good (VG)	Little age cracks; some minor defects
5 – 6	Good (G)	Some age cracks, starting to chip, small defects
3 – 4	Average (AVE)	Some paint loss and/or chipping
2	Fair (F)	Major paint loss and/or defects much chipping
1	Poor (p)	Parts missing, poor color and/or major chipping
0	Repaint (R)	Original paint covered over in part or all

Conditions may be clarified by the use of (+) or (-) ratings with the regular description, or by using the numerical scale and adding ½ the rating number.

The values indicated in this book are based on a decoy or item in excellent condition and noted rare

color. For particular decoys and items, average condition means some paint loss, and defects may be common while other decoys or items may usually appear in excellent condition. Values are listed by this book's Plate numbers.

Related Ice Spear Fishing Equipment

9. Creepers ....$10 – 15
10. Creepers ....$10 – 15
12. Ice Tester ....$15 – 25

13. Ice Tester ....$15 – 25
14. Ice Awls ....$15 – 20
19. Ice Sled...$25 – 35
21. Ice Chisel ....$25 – 35
22. Ice Saw..$35 – 50

23. Ice Saw (top) ....$25 – 35
23. Ice Saw (bottom) ....$25 – 35
24. Ice Augers ....each $15 – 25
28. Ice Tongs ....$10 – 15
29. Ice Skimmer ....$5 – 10
30. Ice Skimmer ....$3 – 5
32. Ice Shanty ....$35 – 50
34. Ice Shanty tag ....$5 – 10
36. Ice Shanty stoves......................each $20 – 25
38. Jig Fishing lures ....$2 – 5
39. Jig Fishing lures (dual function) ....$10 – 25
40 Jig Fishing/Fish decoy lures (dual
    function)...$35 – 75
42. Decoy box ....$5 – 10
43. Sizing decoy ....$100 – 150
45. Live decoy pins (full card) ....each $25 – 35
47. Ice Shanty reel ....$25 – 35
48. Ice Shanty reel ....$10 – 15
50. Jigging sticks ....each $10 – 15
51. Winter fishing rods ....each $10 – 25
52. Tip-up ....$10 – 15
54. Fish caller ....$10 – 20
55. Minnow trap..$35 – 50
56. Fish charm ....$5 – 10
57. Pflueger spear (top) ....$10 – 20
57. Pflueger spear (bottom)............................$10 – 20
58. Shurkatch spear (top)...............................$10 – 20
58. Shurkatch spear (bottom) ....$5 – 10
59. Ideal Products spear ....$5 – 10
60. Rocket Drop spear ....$75 –100
60. Rocket Drop spear/with box................$100 – 150
61. Randall spears ....each $15 – 25
62. Eel spear (Thistle-shaped) ....$75 – 100
62. Eel spear (Papyrus blossom-shaped).....$75 – 100
62. Eel spear (Rag type) ....$50 – 75
62. Eel spear (Tulip-shaped) ....$100 –150
63. Eel creel..$125 –150
65. Fish gaff ....$5 – 10
66. Fish grabbers ....each $25 – 35
68. Ice Carnival badges ....each $5 – 10
69. NFLCC badges and patches ....each $10 – 15

Commercial Fish Decoys

71. Dick Baker decoys.......................each $35 – 50
72. Bar Lake,Kingfish ....each $100 – 125
73. Bar Lake,Kingfish ....$100 – 125
75. Bear Creek Bait Co.,tip-up ....$10 – 15
76. Bear Creek Bait Co., sailfish plaque.........$50 – 75
77. Bear Creek Bait Co.,shanty reel ....$35 – 50
78. Bear Creek Bait Co., fishing lures....each $15 – 25
79. Bear Creek Bait Co.,Type I(except trout)
    each ....$50 – 75
79. Bear Creek Bait Co., Trout ....$1,000+
80. Bear Creek Bait Co.,Type II ....each $25 – 50
81. Bear Creek Bait Co.,Type III..........each $25 – 35

82. Bear Creek Bait Co.,Type III ....$25 – 35
83. Bear Creek Bait Co.,Type IV...........each $10 – 15
85. Bethel Decoy ....each $25 – 35
87. Bethel Decoy, critters.....................each $35 – 50
89. Blackhawk Enterprises ....each $50 – 75
92. Bob's Fly Tying.............................each $35 – 45
93. Bob's Fly Tying(top) ....$45 – 55
93. Bob's Fly Tying(bottom) ....$35 – 45
96. Bonafide Manufacturing Co., 5 hook ....$1,500+
96. Bonafide Manufacturing Co., 3 hook ....$1,500+
98. Bonafide Manufacturing Co., frog
    spears...each $10 – 15
100. Boone Bait Co. ....$25 – 35
101. Boone Bait Co., dealer marketing card$300 – 350
104. Brown Brothers, lures ....each $25 – 35
105. Brown Brothers, fish decoys ....each $35 – 45
107. Bru-ell Co..................................each $35 – 45
108. Bru-ell Co..$20 – 25
109. Bru-ell Co..$35 – 45
110. Bru-ell Co..$20 – 25
111. Bru-ell Co..$20 – 25
113. Carl Christiansen Co ....each $50 – 75
114. Carl Christiansen Co ....each $25 – 35
115. Carl Christiansen Co ....each $50 – 75
116. Carl Christiansen Co., flower vases.each $150 – 175
117. Carl Christiansen Co., tackle box.......$150 – 175
118. Creek Chub Bait Co ....$1,500+
119. Creek Chub Bait Co., lure ....$125 – 150
120. Creek Chub Bait Co ....$1,500+
122. Creek Chub Bait Co ....$25 – 35
123. Creek Chub Bait Co ....$25 – 35
125. Cy's Decoys ....$25 – 35
126. Cy's Decoys ....$25 – 35
127. Cy's Decoys ....each $50 – 75
128. Cy's Decoys ....$25 – 35
129. Cy's Decoys ....$25 – 35
130. Detroit Bait Co., (top)lure with marketing
    box ....$250 – 300
130. Detroit Bait Co., (bottom) lure ....$100 – 125
132. Detroit Bait Co., (top)fish decoy ....$250 – 300
132. Detroit Bait Co., (bottom) fishing lure....$50 – 75
133. Detroit Bait Co., (top).........................$250 – 300
133. Detroit Bait Co., (bottom) ....$250 – 300
134. Detroit Bait Co. ....$300 – 350
136. Franklin Discher (large) ....$75 – 90
136. Franklin Discher (medium)..................$65 – 80
136. Franklin Discher (small) ....$50 – 60
138. Duey's Decoys (large) ....$20 – 25
138. Duey's Decoys (medium)......................$15 – 20
138. Duey's Decoys (small)..........................$10 – 15
139. Duey's Decoys......................................$35 – 45
142. Edson Fish Lures.................................$25 – 30
143. Edson Fish Lures.................................$25 – 30
145. Enterprise/Pflueger Co ....$500 – 750
146. Enterprise/Pflueger Co ....$500 – 750
148. Enterprise/Pflueger Co...........each $750 – 1,000

231

149. Enterprise/Pflueger Co. (top)..............$500 – 750
149. Enterprise/Pflueger Co. (bottom) ....$750 – 1,000
152. Enterprise/Pflueger Co. ....$1,500+
153. Enterprise/Pflueger Co(top) ....$1,500+
153. Enterprise/Pflueger Co(bottom) ....$600 – 750
154. Enterprise/Pflueger Co(top)................$75 – 125
154. Enterprise/Pflueger Co(bottom) ......$750 – 1,000
155. Fish Bust'R ....each $25 – 35
156. Fish Bust'R ....$30 – 40
157. Fish Bust'R ....$30 – 40
160. James Heddon's Sons Co ....$2,000+
162. James Heddon's Sons Co ....$2,000+
163. James Heddon's Sons Co ....$1,500+
163. James Heddon's Sons Co ....$1,500+
167. James Heddon's Sons Co ....$750 – 1,000
168. James Heddon's Sons Co ....$700 – 850
170. James Heddon's Sons Co..........each $700 – 850
171. James Heddon's Sons Co ....$700 – 850
173. James Heddon's Sons Co., deep diving
     wiggler ....$100 – 150
173. James Heddon's Sons Co., 4 point ice
     decoy....................................$350 – 500
174. James Heddon's Sons Co..........each $350 – 500
175. James Heddon's Sons Co ....$500 – 600
176. James Heddon's Sons Co ....$500 – 600
179. James Heddon's Sons Co ....$300 – 350
180. James Heddon's Sons Co(top)the muskie
     decoy ....$750 – 1,000
180. James Heddon's Sons Co. (bottom) ...$350 – 500
181. James Heddon's Sons Co..........each $350 – 400
184. James Heddon's Sons Co ....$650 – 750+
185. James Heddon's Sons Co ....$350 – 400
187. Herter's Inc(top & middle)..........each $35 – 45
187. Herter's Inc(bottom) ....$75 – 90
193. Hoseney Woodcarvings..................each $75 – 90
194. Hoseney Woodcarvings ....$100 – 125
195. Hoseney Woodcarvings ....$2350 – 400
196. Hoseney Woodcarvings............each $300 – 350
197. Hoseney Woodcarvings..................$300 – 350
198. Hoseney Woodcarvings..................$350 – 400
199. Hoseney Woodcarvings..................$350 – 400
200. Jenkins Decoys ....each $50 – 75
202. Jenkins Decoys ....$50 – 75
204. K & E Tackle Inc...........................each $10 – 15
205. K & E Tackle Inc ....$15 – 20
206. K & E Tackle Inc ....$10 – 15
207. K & E Tackle Inc ....$15 – 20
209. Kohler's Ice Decoys............................$50 – 75
210. Martin Kroph Decoys ....each $50 – 75
213. Kurtis Katch-All Lure..........................$15 – 20
215. Kurtis Katch-All Lure..........................$20 – 25
217. Lakco Tackle(large) ....$10 – 15
217. Lakco Tackle(small)....................each $5 – 10
218. Lakco Tackle ....$10 – 15
219. Lee's Decoys ....$15 – 20
220. Lee's Decoys ....each $25 – 35
222. Macatawa Bait Co.................................$50 – 75

223. Macatawa Bait Co.................................$50 – 75
224. Macatawa Bait Co.................................$90 – 125
226. Marv's Wood Products ....each $25 – 35
227. Marv's Wood Products...................$25 – 35
229. McCormick Decoys ....each $75 – 90
230. McCormick Decoys.............................$75 – 90
233. Minnetonka/Schipper Mfg(top).............$50 – 75
233. Minnetonka/Schipper Mfg(bottom)each $45 – 60
236. Moonlight/Paw Paw Bait Co......each $175 – 200
237. Moonlight/Paw Paw Bait Co. (top) ....$125 – 150
237. Moonlight/Paw Paw Bait Co. (bottom) .$175 – 200
238. Moonlight/Paw Paw Bait Co. (top) ....$125 – 150
238. Moonlight/Paw Paw Bait Co. (middle) (open
     mouth)....................................$150 – 175
238. Moonlight/Paw Paw Bait Co. (bottom) $150 – 175
240. Moonlight/Paw Paw Bait Co ....$125 – 150
241. Moonlight/Paw Paw Bait Co ....$125 – 150
242. Moonlight/Paw Paw Bait Co.......each $75 – 100
243. Moonlight/Paw Paw Bait Co ....$150 – 175
244. Moonlight/Paw Paw Bait Co ....$150 – 175
246. Martin Pestrue Decoys...........................$50 – 75
247. Martin Pestrue Decoys ....each $35 – 45
248. Martin Pestrue Decoys ....each $250 – 300
250. Oscar Quam Co. (fish house minnow)...$50 – 75
250. Oscar Quam Co. (ice fishing stick).........$15 – 25
252. Randall Decoy Co ....$25 – 35
253. Randall Decoy Co ....$25 – 35
254. Randall Decoy Co..........................each $75 – 90
255. Randall Decoy Co..........................each $50 – 75
256. Randall Decoy Co ....$50 – 75
258. Randall Decoy Co. (large) ....$75 – 90
258. Randall Decoy Co. (small) ....$25 – 35
260. Randall Decoy Co ....$25 – 35
261. Randall Decoy Co..........................each $25 – 35
263. Randall Decoy Co ....$30 – 40
264. Reigstad Decoys ....each $35 – 45
265. Reigstad Decoys ....$35 – 45
266. Reigstad Decoys ....$35 – 45
268. J. B. Rhodes Fish Decoy ....$2,000+
271. Ripley's Decoy Minnow ....$45 – 60
272. Ripley's Decoy Minnow.................each $45 – 60
273. D.C. Rivet's Decoys ....each $45 – 60
274. D.C. Rivet's Decoys ....each $75 – 90
275. D.C. Rivet's Decoys ....$125 – 150
276. D.C. Rivet's Decoys ....$125 – 150
277. D.C. Rivet's Decoys ....$45 – 60
279. Sletten Mfg. Co ....each $35 – 45
280. Sletten Mfg. Co ....each $35 – 45
282. Sletten Mfg. Co....................................$40 – 50
284. Sletten Mfg. Co....................................$75 – 90
289. South Bend Bait Co.........................$600 – 750
290. South Bend Bait Co ....$1,000+
291. South Bend Bait Co ....$1,000+
293. Bud Stewart Tackle Co...........................$1,000+
294. Bud Stewart Tackle Co....................$150 – 175
295. Bud Stewart Tackle Co ....each $150 – 175
297. Bud Stewart Tackle Co ....$250 – 350

298. Bud Stewart Tackle Co ....$150 – 175
299. Bud Stewart Tackle Co ....$175 – 225
300. Bud Stewart Tackle Co ....$150 – 200
301. Bud Stewart Tackle Co...............each $75 – 125
302. Bud Stewart Tackle Co ....$150 – 175
304. Art E. Storrs Decoys ....each $35 – 45
305. Art E. Storrs Decoys ....each $75 – 90
307. Art E. Storrs Decoys ....$175 – 200
308. Titloe Heights Bait Mfg........................$35 – 45
309. Titloe Heights Bait Mfg..................each $50 – 75
310. Titloe Heights Bait Mfg..................each $35 – 45
315. Tru-Fish Decoys ....$35 – 50
318. Harry L. Way Decoys ....$50 – 75
319. Harry L. Way Decoys ....each $50 – 75
320. Albert Winnie Decoys (lure) ....$75 – 100
321. Albert Winnie Decoys (top) ....$200 – 250
321. Albert Winnie Decoys (bottom) ....$150 – 175
322. Albert Winnie Decoys ....each $175 – 250

Commercial Fish Decoys of Canada

328. Rolland Boats decoy ....$25 – 35
330. Busty's Baits decoy ....each $75 – 90
331. Dizzy Decoy ....each $75 – 90
332. Dominion Co. decoy ....$25 – 35
334. Wheeler decoy ....$200 – 250
336. Unknown Lake Simcoe decoy...............$25 – 35
337. William Baker decoy............................$25 – 35
338. Bruce Rolling decoy ....$25 – 35
339. Unknown Lake Simcoe decoy...............$25 – 35

Commercial Decoys of Unknown Makers

342. Chummer decoy...............................$125 – 150
343. Example A.......................................$200 – 250
344. Example A(top) ....$200 – 250
344. Example A(bottom)...........................$175 – 225
345. Example B ....each $50 – 75

346. Example C ....each $125 – 150
347. Example D ....$35 – 45
348. Example E ....$75 – 90
349. Example F.....................................each $35 – 50
350. Example G ....$100 – 125
351. Example H ....each $35 – 45
352. Example I ....each $35 – 45
353. Example J ....$35 – 45
354. Example K..$100 – 150
355. Example L ....$50 – 75
356. Example M ....$25 – 35
357. Example N ....each $35 – 45
358. Example O ....each $35 – 50
359. Example P ....$35 – 45
360. Example Q ....$35 – 45

Critiqued Unknown Commercial Decoys

361. Decoy ....$35 – 45
362. Decoy ....$35 – 45
363. Decoy ....$35 – 45
364. Decoy ....$35 – 45
365. Decoy ....$35 – 45
366. Decoy ....$35 – 45
367. Decoy ....$35 – 45

Trapping Decoys

387. The Eagle Claw ....$250 – 350
388. Gabriel Fish Trap.................................$125 – 150
389. Metal Crawfish, Tin fish, & Glow fish.each $25 – 30
390. Crawdad decoy & frog decoy.........each $25 – 35
391. Crawdad decoy ....$25 – 35
392. Fish trap decoys.............................each $25 – 35
394. Water Wizard trap bait ....$25 – 35

SUGGESTED READING

Books

Baron, Frank R. *One Fish, Two Fish, Green Fish, Blue Fish*, Livonia, Baron Inc. 1986.

Baron, Frank R. *Carver, Raymond L. Bud Stewart, Michigan's Legendary Lure Maker*, Hillsdale, Ferguson, 1990.

Borge, Lila J. and Jay A. Leitch. *Winter Darkhouse Spearing in Minnesota: Characteristics of Participants*, Fargo, North Dakota: Tri-College University, Center of Environmental Studies, September 1988.

Carter, Arlan. *19th Century Fishing Lures*, Paducah, Collector Books, 2000.

Harbin, Clyde A. Sr. *James Heddon's Sons Catalogues*, Memphis, CAH Enterprises, 1977.

Irwin, R. Stephen MD. *Sporting Collectibles*, Wayne, Stoeger Publishing Company, 1997.

Kimball, Art, Brad & Scott. *The Fish Decoy: Volume I*, Boulder Junction, Aardvark Publications, Incorporated, 1986.

Kimball, Art, Brad & Scott. *The Fish Decoy: Volume II*, Boulder Junction, Aardvark Publications, Incorporated, 1987.

Kimball, Art, Brad & Scott. *The Fish Decoy: Volume III*, Boulder Junction, Aardvark Publications, Incorporated, 1993.

Leitch, Jay A. *Darkhouse Spearing Across North America*, Fargo, N.D. Tri-College University, Center for Environmental Studies, 1992.

Little, Gene. *Ice Fishing*, Chicago, Henry Regnery Company, 1975.

Lucky, Carl F. *Old Fishing Lures and Tackle*, Fifth Edition, Florence, Books Americana, 1999.

Murphy, Dudley and Rick Edmisten. *Fishing Lure Collectibles*, Paducah, Collector Books, 1995.

Murphy, Dudley and Rick Edmisten. *Fishing Lure Collectibles*, Second Edition, Paducah, Collector Books, 2001.

Petersen, Donald J. *Folk Art Fish Decoys*, Atglen, Schiffer Publishing Ltd., 1996.

Richey, George. *Made in Michigan Fishing Lures*, Grawn, KLR Communications, Inc. 1995.

Salive, Marcel L. *Ice Fishing Spears*. Potomac, MarJac Publications, 1993.

Slade, Robert A. *The History & Collectible Fishing Tackle of Wisconsin*, Muskego, Bob & Tess Slade, 1999.

Smith, Harold E. M.D. *Collector's Guide to Creek Chub Lures & Collectibles*, Paducah, Collector Books, 1997.

Streater, R.L. *The Fishing Lure Collector's Bible*, Paducah, Collector Books, 1999.

Tonelli, Donna. *Top of the Line Fishing Collectibles*, Atglen, Schiffer Publishing Ltd., 1997.

White, Karl T. *Fishing Tackle Antiques and Collectibles*, Luther, Holli Enterprises, 1991.

Wong, Terry. *Identification and Value Guide to South Bend Fishing Lures*, Phoenix, Terry Wong, 2000

Magazines

Babe, Phil, "Franklin Discher Decoys", *N.F.L.C.C Gazette*, June, 1992.

Baron, Frank R. "The Fish Decoy," *The Decoy Hunter*, March/April 1985.

Baron, Frank R. "Bud Stewart, Michigan's Master Lure and Ice Decoy Carver," *Lure Collector*, Spring, 1986.

Baron, Frank R. "Bear Creek Baits," *N.F.L.C.C. Gazette*, June, 1988,

Baron, Frank R. "The Kurtis Katch-All Lure," *N.F.L.C.C. Gazette*, September, 1997.

Brewer, Keith, "South Bend's Ice Decoy," *Lure Collector*, Spring, 1986.

Brewer, Keith, "Don Hoseney, Contemporary Fish Decoy Carver Series," *Lure Collector*, Spring, 1987.

Dewhurst, C. Kurt and Marsha MacDowell, "Fine Fooler of Fish," *Michigan*, September/October 1987.

Frank, Kent, "A Decoy Carving Dynasty: The Bethels of Park Rapids, MN," *N.F.L.C.C. Gazette*, December, 1994.

Kimball, Art and Scott, "The Jay Rhodes Fish Decoy," *N.F.L.C.C. Gazette*, June 1991.

Kimball, Art and Scott, "Behold the Mighty Minnow," *Decoy Magazine*, July/August, 1997.

Linder, Paul T., "The Kaleva Sailfish," *N.F.L.C.C. Gazette*, March, 1999.

McGrath, Brian J., "Brown's Fisheretto Folk Art at its Finest," *Lure Collector*, Fall, 1986.

Miller, Gary L., "Fish Decoys Hottest New Sporting Collectible," *Lure Collector*, Fall, 1986.

Richey, George, "Stump Dodgers are Super," *N.F.L.C.C. Gazette*, December, 1991.

Richey, George, "The Bar Lake Ice Spearing Decoy," *N.F.L.C.C. Gazette*, June,1995.

Richey, George, "Edson's Fish Fooler," *N.F.L.C.C. Gazette*, December, 1995.

Stemberg, Carter, "Oscar Quam, The Professor of Duckology," *Decoy Magazine*, March/April, 1998.

Tonelli, Donna, "Bethel Decoys: Continuing a Family Tradition," *Decoy Magazine*, Jan./Feb. 1992.

Tonelli, Donna, "Heddon & Sons Inc., Breaking the Ice with Spearfishing Decoys," *Decoy Magazine*, Jan./Feb., 1994.

Tonelli, Donna, "Tackle Companies Market Decoys to Hardy Spear Fishermen," *Decoy Magazine*, May/June, 1994.

Tonelli, Donna, "George Herter, The P.T. Barnum of Decoys," *Decoy Magazine*, May/June, 1999.

About the Author

Born in Detroit, Michigan, in 1931 and a graduate of the Henry Ford Trade School in Dearborn, Michigan, the author grew up fishing with his dad and uncles in this area of great year-round sport fishing. He has always been intrigued by winter ice fishing, its methods, and the related tools of the trade, and early on began his collecting hobby and the research that ultimately led to the creation of this book.

Baron is chairman of the Fish Decoy Division of the National Fishing Lure Collectors Club and co-founder, along with world-renowned wildlife artist Jim Foote, of the Great Lakes Fish Decoy Collectors and Carvers Association. Frank is recognized as an authority on both old and new fish-spearing decoys and their related items and is often asked to appraise estates and collections.

Frank is a retired automotive engineer. He and his wife Patricia, their children, and grandchildren all love nature, with fishing an important part of their life in this world, God's beautiful creation.

Author with his grandsons Alex, Ian, and Ryan on some of their first fishing ventures.

Index